ABEL GANCE

NORMAN KING

ABEL GANCE
A politics of spectacle

BFI Publishing

First published in 1984 by the British Film Institute
127 Charing Cross Road
London WC2H OEA

British Library Cataloguing in Publication Data

King, Norman
    Abel Gance.
    1. Gance, Abel   2. Moving-picture producers
    and directors—France—Biography
    I. Title
    791.43'0233'0924   PN1998.A3G/

ISBN 0 85170 135 3
ISBN 0 85170 136 1 Pbk

Cover design: John Gibbs

Typeset and printed by W. S. Cowell Ltd, London and Ipswich

Contents

1. INTRODUCTION: POLITICS AND CRITICISM
   Napoleon resurrected   I
   Gance becomes an *auteur*   3
   The author in contest   6
   Strategies   9

2. GANCE AND HIS CRITICS
   The romantic: Georges Buraud and Jean Arroy   12
   The poetic avant-garde: René Clair, Germaine Dulac and Jean Epstein   21
   The political and the aesthetic: Léon Moussinac and Emile Vuillermoz   30
   The surrealist: Philippe Soupault   49

3. GANCE ON THEORY
   Gance as theorist   55
   The producer   58
   The cinema of tomorrow   61
   Departure towards polyvision   79

4. GANCE AS AUTHOR–DIRECTOR
   The screenplays   82
   La roue   83
   Napoleon   87
   La fin du monde   105
   Gance and his producers   117

5. NARRATIVE AND HISTORY
   Refocusing the debates   123
   Melodrama and the epic   125
   Divided heroes   131

6. POLITICS AND THE AESTHETIC
   Politics and populism   140
   Napoleon the exemplary   146
   Towards a New World   163
   Art for the people   176

7. IMAGE, SPECTACLE, POSITION
   Narrative *mise en scène*   179
   The mediating look   191

Performance and spectacle 197
Politics and the spectator 212

8. CONCLUSION 216

NOTES 219

FILMOGRAPHY 233

BIBLIOGRAPHY 249

INDEX 257

Front cover: Napoleon (Albert Dieudonné)
Back cover: Abel Gance in *La fin du monde*

Acknowledgments

This book could not have been written without the assistance of the institutions and individuals who made film and archive material available to me, often in difficult circumstances.

My special thanks are due to Claude Lafaye of the Centre national de la cinématographie and custodian of the principal Gance archive. In addition to allowing me free access to the archive, he was helpful in a great variety of ways, from arranging interviews to obtaining copies of photographs and responding to urgent calls for intervention. I am also grateful to Marianne de Fleury and her assistants, Omar de Amorin Cedran, Philippe Nedellec and Dominique Brun, and to Jacqueline Vairel for their goodwill and friendly encouragement while I was working through the Gance holdings in the Cinémathèque française archives and the library of the Institut des hautes études cinématographiques.

Print availability is a major problem for the study of Gance's films. For their assistance in helping to resolve this difficulty, I am grateful to André Rieupeyrout, Renée Lichtig and Patricia Fouque of the Cinémathèque française, Freddy Buache and Marcel Jordan of the Cinémathèque suisse, Raymond Borde and the staff of the Cinémathèque de Toulouse, Jim Damour of the Cinémathèque de Paris III, Elaine Burrows and the staff of the National Film Archive viewing service, Ted Heath and Erich Sargeant of BFI Distribution, the British Universities Film Council, the Cultural Services of the French Embassy, the Institut français d'Ecosse and the British Institute in Paris.

My thanks for assistance while I was researching books, periodicals, ephemera and illustrations are due to Emmanuelle Toulet, Catherine Bony, Anita Mengozzi and the unusually helpful *gardiens* at the Bibliothèque de l'Arsenal, Noëlle Giret at the library of the Cinémathèque française, Michelle Snapes of the British Film Institute Stills Department, Sybille de Luze, Catherine Ficat and Jean-Pierre Jolly at the Phototèque of the Cinémathèque française, and especially to Gillian Hartnoll who greatly simplified research in the BFI library, and Roma Gibson who somehow managed to make complex organisational problems appear simple. Frame enlargements were made by Jim Adams of BFI Education, Gerald McKee, and the photographers of the Cinémathèque suisse and the Cinémathèque de Toulouse.

Of the many individuals who were important during the long research stage, I would like to single out Roger Icart, who gave up part of his holiday to go through with me the remarkable tinted and toned print of *La roue* on loan from the Cinémathèque suisse to the Cinémathèque de Toulouse. He allowed me to read through the early chapters of his book on Gance and has been a thoughtful and reliable correspondent. Publication delays have unfortunately made it impossible for me to study the bulk of his text before mine went to press. I would also like to address particular thanks to Jean Collomb and Jean Dréville, who shared their recollections of Gance with me, and to Kevin Brownlow for the promptness and precision of his answers to a barrage of questions, to Guy Dupuigrenet-Desroussilles for searching out articles I could not find elsewhere, Roland Cosandey for sending me cuttings I might otherwise have overlooked, Bambi Ballard for allowing me to read the Gance-t'Serstevens correspondence, Philippe Soupault for finding time to see me, Micheline Laroche for being imperturbable, Ian Christie, Claude Schumacher, Nicole Jaques-Chaquin, Martine Chatelain, Patrick Vieuville, Jacques Deslandes and Claudia Gorbman.

Drafts of my text were scrutinised by John Caughie, a Gentle Reader whose encouraging remarks helped to reassure me, by Diane Macdonell, whose critique resulted in some radical changes, and by Gillian Macdonald, without whose thoroughness this book would have been even fuller of inconsistencies, obscurities and unrelated participles. My editors, Ed Buscombe and David Wilson, have provided a subtle blend of encouragement, prodding and attentiveness to detail. They also should be thanked for turning the text into a less corrupt one.

Acknowledgment is made to the British Academy for a grant in 1983 which enabled me to complete the final stages of research in Paris, to the Society for Education in Film and Television, and to colleagues in film and television studies in the Universities of Glasgow and Strathclyde for the way they have stimulated my interest over the years in the political history of cinema.

Acknowledgments for frame enlargements and production stills are made to the distributors of Gance's films and to Abel Gance, who gave permission to reproduce photographs from his personal collection, Claude Lafaye and the Centre national de la cinématographie, the Cinémathèque de Toulouse, the Cinémathèque française, the Cinémathèque suisse, the Bibliothèque nationale, the Institut des hautes études cinématographiques, the British Film Institute, Kevin Brownlow and Jean Collomb. Authorisation to reproduce archive material and extracts from screenplays were given by Abel Gance in

1981. Philippe Soupault's article on *La fin du monde* is translated with the author's permission. Acknowledgment is made to Editions Gallimard for permission to reprint in translation an extract from: René Clair, *Cinéma d'hier, cinéma d'aujourd'hui*, copyright © Editions Gallimard 1970.

All translations of articles, screenplays and archive material are my own (copyright © Norman King 1984).

NORMAN KING

Abbreviations

In notes and references in the text, the following abbreviations are used to indicate sources of archive material:

CNC: Centre national de la cinématographie, Paris.
CF: Cinémathèque française, Paris.
IDHEC: Institut des hautes études cinématographiques, Paris.

1 Introduction: Politics and Criticism

NAPOLEON RESURRECTED

The name Abel Gance has become indissolubly linked with that of Napoleon Bonaparte. As Jean-Luc Douin asked in an obituary of Gance in November 1981: 'Do we not refer today to the *Napoleon* of Abel Gance in much the same way as to the Venus of Milo?'[1]

Douin's comparison is an apt one. It is not just that Gance has been identified with a single 'masterpiece' to the detriment of the rest of his output. The film itself has, for most of its history, been known only in truncated versions, like a museum piece that no longer exists in its original form. It figured prominently of course in all the major accounts of French cinema, but descriptions based on re-edits, distant recollections or hearsay were often wildly inaccurate. And when, at the age of 82, Gance released his final remake, *Bonaparte et la Révolution*, it seemed as though the silent epic of 1927 had been definitively buried in the verbiage of connective commentaries. Instead of the excitement of the original prologue (the young Napoleon and the snowball fight at Brienne), there was an old man attempting to explain the message of his updated film for the youth of 1971.

All that was changed by Kevin Brownlow's reconstruction of the silent version. Although many important scenes were still missing, it was at last possible to see something that resembled fairly closely what spectators had enthused about and critics done battle over in 1927. The ecstatic response to the reconstructed film at Telluride (1979), London (1980), Rome (1981) and the major American cities is already part of history, a history in process as revivals in London and the belated screenings in Paris in July 1983 demonstrate.

Gance is now widely recognised as one of the most powerful presences in the whole of cinema and as one of the great innovators. But the way the film has been received and especially the way it has been presented have given rise to misgivings. These have rarely been made explicit, usually taking the form of questions like 'Whose *Napoleon* is this?', a thinly disguised attack on the abridgment of the film in the

United States and on its promotion in Europe as an event for social-ites.[2] The problem is in fact the effacement of the historical and political inscription of the film.

Matching the enthusiasm of the spectators, most reviews of the reconstructed *Napoleon* were fulsome, even adulatory. 'A sublime opera of images,' ran the headline of a local newspaper after the French première at Le Havre in November 1982,[3] underlining with unconscious irony the transformation of a popular epic into an elitist spectacle. Reservations were expressed about the film's sentimental-ity, and the 'deification' of the young Bonaparte as romantic vision-ary, but these were considered secondary, regrettable errors of content, which momentarily interrupted the visual impact.

On the few occasions when criticisms were politicised, the director was usually exonerated. 'But was it Abel Gance that the American and Italian audiences admired?' asked one French critic reporting on the screenings at the Rome Colosseum in September 1981. 'Over and above the massive publicity and the festivities of the "Roman Sum-mer", one is tempted to think it is the image of Napoleon that attracts the crowds. In Italy, disgruntled minds immediately saw in the film a nostalgia for fascism, for the providential figure who could put an end to disorder and to "new terrors".'[4] Alain Rémond, a much more irreverent critic, reminds his readers of the importance of authoritarian movements in 1927 and describes the film's aesthetic as pre-fascist, but even he goes on to excuse this aesthetic or 'alchemy of images', arguing that it was *dictated* by the subject matter.[5]

In fact, apart from the substitution of the nostalgic for the prospec-tive, critical terms of reference have changed little since 1927. They have simply been attenuated. While fully recognising the immense importance of the innovatory aspects of the film, the more incisive critics took Gance to task in 1927 for his fascistic representation of Bonaparte as restorer of order in the midst of chaos. Form was set against content but did not excuse it. In the 1980s, it is the innovatory form of a rediscovered masterpiece that has really mattered. What is represented may not always be palatable but it can be overlooked. As 'the cinematic wonder of the age', *Napoleon* has been assumed into the eternal innocence of great Art. In the words of Pauline Kael, one of the critics who protest most about Gance's 'gushing romanticism' and 'hyperbolic symbolism', his film presents 'a Napoleon without politics'.[6]

The principal concern of this book is to reinsert the political into the discussion of the aesthetic. To investigate the problematical area of reactionary innovation, in an analysis based not on *Napoleon* as an isolated masterpiece but on Gance as a committed film-maker working within a complex of historical struggles.

The problem is a delicate one in that even the term 'reactionary innovation' would, in many critical discourses, seem contradictory, challenging both the dominant avant-gardist assumption that all formal innovation is progressive since it acts against established modes of representation, and the common view of reactionary art as tending towards an idealised naturalism or pure spectacle. Like Céline, with whom, in terms of aesthetic position, he has much in common, Gance raises awkward questions, demands new approaches. But whereas Céline has been assimilated into new discourses on literature Gance has been overlooked by film theorists, squeezed out by inadequate polarities of the kind modernism/realism or montage/composition in depth. That is not to say that Gance is the Céline of the cinema, but that the challenge he poses needs to be taken up.

More generally, there is a need for a politics of spectacle which takes account not just of the Eisensteins and the Riefenstahls, but of film-makers who are both anti-marxist and anti-establishment, whose *mise en scène* and concept of the audience is no less dynamic but whose practice cannot easily be analysed in terms of current notions of political progressiveness or reactionary ideology.[7] Gance's films, not just *Napoleon* but his melodramas, epics and unrealised projects, can provide a starting point for the opening out of this debate.

GANCE BECOMES AN AUTEUR

Before he even began work on *Napoleon* in 1923, Gance was already considered within the industry as the most promising of a younger generation of French directors, promoted by Louis Nalpas (head of Le film d'art) and especially by Charles Pathé who both, in their different ways, considered him as a *protégé* and *enfant terrible*. Critical attention was attracted by *La folie du docteur Tube* (1915), a film Nalpas was reluctant to put into distribution because it was too experimental; but it was *Mater dolorosa* (1917), a cheaply made melodrama, that brought commercial success, and *J'accuse* (1919), produced by Pathé, that brought international acclaim. Made while the war was in progress and in collaboration with the Cinematographic Service of the French army, it was seen as a radical intervention, showing the horrors of the trenches and the need for a new society.

It was another melodrama, *La roue*, filmed in 1920–21 and first screened at the end of 1922, that established Gance as the dominant presence in French cinema. Although its critical reception was ambivalent, it quickly became a point of reference for the cinema of the future. To an industry struggling to preserve something of its former

3

prominence in the face of increasing international competition it brought a new optimism. Here was a film that was breaking commercial records in Parisian cinemas[8] as well as introducing radically new techniques.

It was the use of rapid montage that attracted most attention, but camerawork, lighting, locations, acting, masking, tinting and toning were also widely discussed and admired. It was especially the contrasting rhythms of the film that seemed to indicate how cinema might develop. Cinema could at last aspire to be considered on a level with poetry and music. In the often quoted words of Jean Epstein, Gance had become 'notre maître actuel à tous', a founding instance, a cinematic author.

Even though *Napoleon* had initially been financed by an international syndicate under German control, it seemed to confirm that there could be a national cinema which was artistic, innovatory and popular, able to resist the hegemony of Hollywood. Soon it was to be seen, along with *La roue*, as a kind of symbol, illustrating what cinema might have been if it had been allowed to flourish unhampered by commercialism, like a final salute to a capitalist Emperor by an art that was about to die with the arrival of sound.

The disastrous reception of Gance's first talking picture, *La fin du monde* (1931), radically affected his prestige. It was not, as many people claimed at the time, that Gance was too extravagant or that he was too threatening to a cinematic institution which was having to confront the problems of the transition to sound with all the re-equipment of studios and cinemas which that entailed. On the contrary, he quickly abandoned his plans to make the film for triple screen and concentrated instead on the innovatory possibilities of sound. In fact he made the transition more easily than most of his contemporaries since he had already been experimenting with sound during the 'silent' period. The remake of *Mater dolorosa* (1932), the sonorised *Napoleon Bonaparte* (1935) and *Un grand amour de Beethoven* (1936) were all hailed as pioneering works in a new medium. If *La fin du monde* failed so badly, it was especially because commercial and political circumstances had changed. In that sense it is *La fin du monde* rather than *Napoleon* that marks the end of an era.

Between 1919 and 1932 Gance had released only three feature films: *La roue*, *Napoleon* and *La fin du monde*. In each case the lapse of time between conception and release had been considerable and there were numerous financial problems and disagreements between producers and director. The new generation of small producers operating in the 1930s could not raise the funds for such ambitious projects. Besides, Gance found little favour with the new radicals who were

4

more willing to support films that promoted the ideology of the Popular Front.

The 1930s were nevertheless the most prolific period in Gance's career. Though most of the films he directed were adaptations of novels and plays made for commercially oriented independent producers, they constitute an output which, if *La roue* and *Napoleon* did not exist, would be much more esteemed than it habitually is. If they are often dismissed as pot-boilers, it is perhaps because Gance himself later spoke of them disparagingly, as films he made with one eye shut, 'not to earn a living but to avoid dying'.

It was his departure for Spain in 1943 to escape from the Nazis that brought the eclipse, along with the abortive attempts in the late 1940s and early 1950s to raise funds for *La divine tragédie*. Between 1943 and 1954 not a single Gance film was released, and he seemed to have become the archetypal 'neglected genius'.

Then, in 1954, the release of *La Tour de Nesle* triggered a revival of interest. The Cardinet cinema in Paris organised a retrospective of Gance's films and an exhibition. The sonorised *Napoleon* with triptychs ran for several months at the Studio 28 in 1955 and Gance embarked on new polyvision projects, competing with CinemaScope and Cinerama. Nothing much came of these projects, but along with the retrospective and the exhibition they provoked a fundamental change in critical perspective. Gance became an exemplification of auteurism at a time when *la politique des auteurs* was seeking to establish itself. He was taken up as the inventor of the wide screen and as the great master of lyrical cinema. François Truffaut's article 'Sir Abel Gance' (*Arts*, 1 September 1954) was in this respect a consecration. In Britain, Truffaut argues (quoting Jacques Becker), Gance would have a knighthood and unlimited funds for the promotion of national prestige. In France he is dismissed as a has-been because critics have systematically rejected the sound films of directors who made their reputation during the silent period. Not surprisingly, Truffaut bases his article on a defence of the sound films: they show the same Abel Gance with all his virtues and excesses, an argument that would soon be taken up in the *Cahiers du cinéma*.[9]

There have been other revivals since the 1950s, corresponding broadly to the release of *Austerlitz* (1960) and *Cyrano et d'Artagnan* (1963), Gance's work for French television in the mid-1960s, *Bonaparte et la Révolution* (1971), the reconstructed *Napoleon*, and Gance's death in November 1981. The problem is, fundamentally, that the debates and even the terminology have been left much as they were in the 1950s and early 1960s.

5

There are two predominant trends in Gance criticism, the dismissive and the celebratory. For some critics, Gance is merely a naive and overbearing sentimentalist; for others, he is a neglected genius, variously referred to as the Leonardo, the Shakespeare and, more ambivalently, the Victor Hugo of the cinema. On the one hand Roger Boussinot blithely dismisses him as an artist of monstrous insensitivity and his output as incoherent, pretentious, bombastic and prodigiously conformist.[10] On the other, René Jeanne and Charles Ford piously refer to him as the *only* man in the cinematographic universe to whom the term 'genius' could be applied.[11] These may be extremes, but they illustrate clearly the main terms of the debate.

Frequently, and especially in recent criticism, these two apparently opposed positions occur within a single piece of writing. While few can match the crispness of Pauline Kael's description of Gance as 'like an avant-garde De Mille', one often encounters the argument that Gance is a great innovator but his grandiloquence and lack of a sense of proportion prevent him from attaining the rank of genius. Or, more commonly, the same argument turned on its head: Gance may sometimes be naive, pompous and sentimental, but he also demonstrates a unique force of invention and, in any case, genius is by its very nature undisciplined, uncritical, excessive.

My concern here is not to intervene in an ultimately futile debate but to stress that both camps operate within the same discourse, producing a romantic criticism which corresponds to Gance's own romantic conception of the cinema. In fact, the myth of the neglected genius was, to a great extent, constructed by Gance himself, though he was referring less to the unavailability of his early films than to the difficulties he experienced during his later years in raising capital for the ambitious masterpieces he wished to present to the world.

The process of evaluation is also a selective one. Boussinot is perhaps just being perverse when he rejects all the films on which Gance's reputation is commonly based, retaining only *Paradis perdu* (1939), *La Tour de Nesle* and a few scenes from *Un grand amour de Beethoven* and *Cyrano et d'Artagnan*. Most critics construct a corpus consisting of a handful of films for which Gance wrote his own screenplay, rejecting the rest as pot-boilers or unfortunate errors of judgment. Curiously, this kind of auteurism is exactly the opposite of that proclaimed by the *Cahiers du cinéma* team. The thrust of Truffaut's 1954 article is an insistence that because Gance is an *auteur*, all his films merit critical attention. More importantly, this selectivity means that many of the most interesting features of Gance's *mise en*

6

scène are simply overlooked because they occur in the so-called pot-boilers. And when this selectivity is applied as well to individual films, Gance's work can easily be reduced to an anthology of strong moments: the climax of *J'accuse*, the railway and Alpine scenes in *La roue*, the Marseillaise, Convention and triptych sequences in *Napoleon*, the deafness episode in *Beethoven*.

The intention may seem honourable enough: to demonstrate Gance's greatness, praising the most powerful images, conceding that there are others which don't show him at his very best and dismissing the rest as the inevitable darker side of genius. The effect is to position Gance as the innovator who was so far ahead of his time that his genius was not recognised, and who is thus outside history and beyond ideology.

Surprisingly little work has been done which locates itself outside this romantic framework, and very little of what there is confronts directly the problem of political reading.

Roger Icart's book on Gance[12] seems certain to become the standard general study. It is carefully researched, contains much new information drawn from the CNC archive and charts a clear path through the whole of Gance's career, avoiding both the concessive and the over-defensive. It also contextualises the films in terms of Gance's ideas and ambitions, conditions of production and critical reception. Icart has also published articles on *La roue* and on the different versions of *Napoleon*.[13] His analysis of shifts in the representation of Bonaparte is an important contribution to the political study of Gance's films, even though it does reach the unexpected conclusion that Gance is, after all, a progressive.

At the other extreme, articles are beginning to appear in which Gance is summarily dismissed as reactionary. A typical example is Jean-Pierre Jeancolas' article 'Abel Gance entre Napoléon et Philippe Pétain' (*Positif*, June 1982), which consists mostly of a survey of supposedly Pétainist elements in the screenplay of *Jérôme Perreau*, directed by Gance in 1935. At first the approach seems promising since, although set in the 17th century, the film frequently raises the issue of the relation between strong authority and the masses. Unfortunately, as the author has to concede, Gance had absolutely no control over the screenplay of what was, for him, merely a bread-and-butter film. As no attempt is made to analyse the *mise en scène*, Jeancolas can only feebly reproach Gance with having agreed to direct a film which, after all, he did not have to make. Since the rest of the 1930s films have already been disdainfully dismissed, Jeancolas ends by taking Gance to task for the brief dedication to Pétain added to *La Vénus aveugle* for the gala premiere at Vichy in 1941, but makes no attempt to examine what political importance the film may have had.

If this article deserves to be singled out, it is because it illustrates negatively the need for a problematic. Since Gance is one of the most self-conscious *authors* in the history of cinema, by which I mean that few film-makers have had a more resolute and self-assured sense of mission, his screenplays have to be as carefully scrutinised as his *mise en scène*. If, instead of blaming Gance for directing Georges Milton's script, Jeancolas had bothered to look at the footage he added to his *Napoleon* in the sonorised version released in the same year, he would have found more convincing evidence of a political message. The article also demonstrates the need for more thorough empirical research. A study of contemporary reviews would have revealed that Gance made a long speech at the Vichy screening of *Vénus*, addressing to the *Maréchal* much more 'compromising' remarks than those contained in a rather anodyne dedication. Lastly, inference is not only counterproductive, it is unnecessary. Along with many of his contemporaries, Gance did for a time admire Pétain. He also, at other moments, expressed admiration for Mussolini and Franco. Jeancolas' approach is perhaps understandable in view of attempts by French socialists on Gance's death to recuperate him as 'one of us', but its reliance on the insidious merely foregrounds the inadequacy of his analysis.

Peter Pappas' article on *Napoleon* published in *Cineaste* in 1981[14] is a much more incisive attempt to identify right-wing ideology in Gance's work. After an analysis of the politics of genius, Pappas first establishes an aesthetic of fascism (the art of superimposition), sets this against *Napoleon*, and asserts that Gance's film is 'the greatest – and certainly the most profound – fascist film in the history of the cinema'. The argument is forceful and opens up an important line of enquiry. If one has misgivings, it is on account of a monolithic view of fascism and a too easy conflation of superimposition as an attribute of fascism and as characteristic of Gance's film. The proof is in fact based more on an analysis of the film's content than on its images.

It is worth noting the angry reply of Steven Kramer in the following issue of *Cineaste*,[15] in which he claims that Pappas' view of fascism is incoherent, that his decision that *Napoleon* is a fascist work is based on incompetent reasoning and that in any case there is no evidence that Gance ever belonged to or ever expressed approbation for any of the fascist organisations operating in France in the 1930s. Gance, he concludes, was a 'romantic' whose political ideas were incoherent ('and his films reflect that incoherence'). If incoherence there is, it's to be found less in Pappas' reasoning than in Kramer's argument: that *Napoleon* is not a fascist film because Gance was never a member of a fascist organisation.

8

There are, then, the beginnings of a political debate, but most of the participants still seem intent on arguing about whether or not Gance was reactionary, leaving aside almost entirely the issue of innovation. A politics of spectacle has, therefore, to raise new questions. It needs to pursue the kind of analysis conducted by Pappas, but to refine and broaden the approach. Gance's aesthetic can't be defined on the basis of a few scenes taken from a single film. It needs to take account of and extend Icart's work on representation and to analyse Gance's films in relation to specific political and intellectual movements as well as conditions of production and reception.

Essentially, we have to abandon the temptation to treat the image as if it were a discrete entity, somehow separable from its historical 'content' or consigned to its own teleological history (innovation). The image exists only within a strategy of narrative. As such, it has to be examined not just in terms of the technological development of the apparatus or of a particular aesthetic, but ideologically. The positions a film constructs for the spectator are as much a part of history as the invention of portable cameras, rapid montage or the triple screen. It is in this sense that I would argue for a politics of spectacle.

The difficulty is that the historic of the film and of the spectator can never exactly coincide. Modes of representation change but so does their effectivity. It isn't just a question of the difference between a gala presentation of *Napoleon* at the Paris Opera and a screening in some provincial fleapit. *Napoleon* signifies something quite other in 1927, 1935, 1955 and 1984, even if in all these instances the images, strategies and positions constructed for the spectator remain the same. In Gance's case, the situation is further complicated by the fact that the films were not in fact the same, not just because there is no such thing as a 'definitive' version of *Napoleon* but because Gance re-edited his film several times and remade it twice, just as he remade *Mater dolorosa* and *J'accuse* and re-edited these and several other films for release at different moments or in different countries.

STRATEGIES

It is in order to confront this problem that I have, in the early sections of this book, given primacy to history, concentrating in particular on some of the debates within which the politics of innovation took shape before moving on to an analysis of the films.

Section Two begins with a literary portrait of Gance, illustrating how notions of originality have themselves to be seen in context, as part of a 'politics' of genius. This is followed by a selection of critical texts written by avant-garde film-makers showing something of the

9

controversy surrounding Gance's films and especially the beginnings of a form:content divide. Moussinac and Vuillermoz's articles on *Napoleon* show this divide politicised, as the attempt to confront a theoretical difficulty leads them to distinguish between progressive form and reactionary content – a distinction that has been implicitly adopted in most Gance criticism since that time. The issue is resolved, in a way, by the Surrealists, but only by the rejection of both terms in the polarity.

These texts are included as exemplifications of positions within a history, with all the antagonisms and unresolved contradictions which that entails. They show on the one hand what views of cinema Gance's films made possible, and on the other how these films were recuperated into different critical – and political – discourses.

The time-span here is deliberately a limited one, from the first enthusiastic responses to *La roue* in 1922 to the rejection of *La fin du monde* in 1931. This is partly because the critical debates around Gance's films were at their most acute during those years, and partly to provide a more precise historical perspective, mapping their insertion into specific debates – the avant-gardist response to *La roue*, the political and aesthetic issues raised by *Napoleon*, the placing of *La fin du monde* in the transition to new forms of cinema with the arrival of sound.

However much the notion of authorial autonomy has been undermined by discourse theory, to go on from there to dismiss the author as merely a fiction constructed from traces or consistencies within the films is just another way of denying history. The author is not primary source of meaning, but as subject is nevertheless constructed within a particular history as site of specific struggles. Gance exists within a moment of cinema when the whole notion of authorship was of paramount importance in the new medium's fight for recognition. And few film-makers have more forcefully proclaimed a sense of mission, of responsibility both to cinema and to humanity. Account has to be taken, then, of Gance's theoretical writings, partly as responses to the critics, mostly as illustration of the construction of the cinematic author in terms of a material practice and of *authority*. In other words, cinema's attempts to be recognised as an art form and the artist's desire to appropriate cinema as privileged mode of expression fused in a defence of autonomy. This is the principal function of the third section of this book.

Section Four carries this discussion a stage further via the screenplays. These illustrate a cinematic practice and particularly highlight the issue of directiveness or 'intentionality'. In particular, they explode the progressive form:reactionary content debate, imposing a reformulation. Few screenplays demonstrate so clearly that it is all a question of effects. There is a message, a highly authoritarian and prescriptive one, but it can be carried only within an institutional practice. Complex strategies are mapped out not to express an inner truth but to impose that truth, to make it incontrovertible. The artist constructs himself as a force of history.

Section Five is an attempt to reconstrue these debates, broadening the perspective by taking account not just of the 'epics' but also of the melodramas that were commercially the most successful of Gance's films. The main concern here is with narrative structures and their relation to history, a problem that is more fully explored in Section Six through an analysis of the political inscription of Gance's work in the 1930s and early 1940s.

Section Seven is concerned with the spectator the films construct. It attempts to show, through an analysis of spectacle, how the political is subsumed into the aesthetic, ultimately producing reactionary positions.

2 Gance and his Critics

Georges Buraud's portrait of Gance dates from the autumn of 1928, i.e. at a time when Gance was concentrating on the publication of some of his writings. It is preserved in typescript in the Gance archive (CNC and IDHEC). Jean Arroy's essay was written two years earlier, just after *Napoleon* had been completed, and was published as the preface to his book on the making of the film (*En tournant 'Napoléon' avec Abel Gance*, 1927).[1]

As portraitists, Buraud and Arroy were able to study their model closely since they were both employed for several years as part-time personal assistants. (Arroy also worked as a 'trainee' on *Napoleon* and Buraud as literary adviser on *La fin du monde*.) This explains to an extent the reverent tone that is sometimes apparent in the two texts. But their interest lies less in the accuracy or vitality of their portrayal of Gance than in their romantic notion of the artist of genius.

In placing great emphasis on the vastness of his culture, his literary and philosophical gifts, Buraud is not simply promoting Gance's future publications. Cinema's search for respectability had throughout the 1920s frequently taken the form of a comparison with literature in an attempt to prove that the cinematic could be as profound as the literary, and just as suitable a medium for the transmission of profound ideas and feelings.

But if cinema was to be considered as a *great* art, it needed its own men of genius, and this was what made Gance so important. He was both innovator and philosopher, master of techniques but also creative mind, the artist-writer, the equal of the great romantic poets. Hence a tendency here to focus more on the creator than his creations, on the poet's personality, his radiance, spiritual intensity, tenderness and dynamism. Hence also the recourse to romantic symbolism, the artist as angel with wings of light or as Christ suffering for the redemption of man. And the prevalence of metaphors of energy: electricity, personal magnetism, radioactivity.

Buraud and Arroy highlight the continuing prevalence of romanticism in film culture in France during the 1920s. But they are representatives of a tendency rather than members of a school of criticism. We will encounter similar concerns and indeed many of the same metaphors in texts like those of Epstein, Vuillermoz and Moussinac which, given the very different positions from which they were produced, might at first glance seem to have little in common.

Georges Buraud
A literary revelation—with Abel Gance

I am with the man without whom Cinema wouldn't be what it is today, the man to whom it owes at least two-thirds of its rhythm and its techniques. *La roue* gave the new art a soul. This film remains the prototype of the great cinematographic interiorised tragedy. It is a spiritual achievement which has not yet been surpassed in our art. I am with the man who has succeeded in giving the camera a heart and a mind, breathing into it life and movement as imperceptible and mysterious as the silent gestures of love, enveloping the recorded images in a magical atmosphere, making them seem to be carried away to an unknown destination. Gance casts a spell on everything he puts his hand to. These are the secrets of poetry and of suffering.

This striking head, with silvery hair, a courageous and faintly ironic smile, and an expression of noble tenderness, all emitting a radiant light, leans over towards me. It's like an apparition. The mundane fabric of my everyday impressions is rent, I feel a gentle but profound stirring. It's as though behind us, in the invisible, there were great white wings nailed to a cross of light. A smiling face offered up to suffering, keen to know all its facets so that it can pass through them like some romantic archangel flying serenely and ardently through all the storms of life.

Here are the things that bear witness to a culture of the highest order: old books, musical instruments, bibles of all epochs. From Paracelsus to Corneille, from Omar Khayam to Keyserling, from Spinoza to Cendrars, like hives of images and ideas swarming round him, as if he were some great queen bee, overcome by their store of treasures but secretly even more intoxicated by the mystery he carries within himself. And in a massive cupboard, the manuscripts. There aren't just the screenplays of his films, from *La dixième symphonie* to *Napoleon*, but five or six literary works of genius. He points them out to me one by one: philosophy, journal, poems, plays, essays on aesthetics and sociology, a swarm of ideas, forms, images, waiting with folded wings in the cells of the great hive of activity. 'All that is soon going to take to the air,' he says with a laugh. 'During the last few months I've been putting the finishing touches to four or five books of various kinds, which my friends at the *Nouvelle revue française*, that noble and hospitable establishment, have agreed to publish.

'Alongside my creative work in the cinema, in which, as you know, I am trying to establish the elements of a visual alphabet – rapid montage, the triple screen, the mobile camera and other inventions which all seem to me essential to the development of our art, I have been trying since my youth to keep myself in close contact with my destiny, by writing plays, philosophy and essays . . . In fact, since I was twenty-five, I haven't stopped writing and if these works have not yet appeared in print, it's because I wanted to let them live in me in a state of independence, it's because I didn't want to harm the wings of my butterflies by unfolding them too soon, while they were still enclosed in their chrysalis – it's also because reaching a situation like the one I now occupy in the cinema seemed necessary if I was to excite people's curiosity to the full and establish the contacts I dream of between the two worlds. . . .

'So I have patiently and silently constructed several monuments of differing degrees of importance: my play, *La victoire de Samothrace*,[2] which will perhaps prove to be my most important work (even taking the cinema into account) and in which I think I have managed to achieve a lyrical and ideological synthesis that first took shape spontaneously within myself – a whole sociology of cinema, a plan for the worldwide organisation of our art, using the League of Nations as central body. This aesthetic sociology, if I can call it that, is capped by a project for a laboratory for psychological research on a universal scale. Over here, these are my visual poems, *Arcole* and *Sainte-Hélène*,[3] both finished – the latter is being filmed at this very moment in Germany by my friend Lupu Pick.[4] This is a little book on the aesthetics of cinema with technical details and drawings.[5] And that fat manuscript on the table in front of you is my autobiography, *Prisme*, which Gallimard is, I hope, going to publish very soon.[6] Many other characters are stirring within me, just waiting to be born: Cadet Rousselle, about whom I want to write a kind of popular epic, François Villon, Watteau . . .'

'But doesn't this excess of spiritual life and creativity stifle your work for cinema, doesn't it efface the moving pictures from your mind?'

'On the contrary, it helps me to shape them. Let me explain how cinema and literature interact in the world of my thoughts.'

'How do they?'

'They clear the way for each other. In terms just of great art, cinema, in its present state, can only show us selected moments, the

Abel Gance, the young poet

peaks, it can only create works of synthesis. The object of literature –
diaries, plays, essays – is to produce an analytical work from the
murky and treasure-laden depths of the creative mind, a setting out of
its gems, an illumination of their hidden and mysterious facets. By
taking possession of my self in a literary mode of expression, which is
the method I prefer, I can manage to separate out the principal
land-masses of my experience and my memory, on which I will later
build temples dedicated to love or to God. Or, if you like, I pluck from
the flood of sensations, ideas, afflictions and cosmic intuitions which
flow through me incessantly a few ideas, some diamonds that I will
later insert into my cinematic works. Thus introspections, the most
vehement confessions, the upward thrust of my soul, pursued by the
demons of suffering and incomprehension, attempting to escape from
itself and to reach up to the serenity of spiritual necessity – all that is
ultimately only the method used by my unconscious to *clear the way
ahead*. What cinema alone could not achieve (you really couldn't
imagine a film director spending his life writing a diary of his personal
experience or searching for his inner self in the studios), my mind
accomplishes with the means of expression – analysis and literary
poetry – that it has at its disposal and which I think it commands with
as much spontaneity as the language of light in the cinema. Yes, I put
as much of myself into my books as into my films. I put as much of

myself into *Prisme* as into *La roue*. I will go further: those who look deeply will see them in an absolutely different light, developed and matured to a point that is far distant from the stage I had reached before. To quote that wonderful image inherited from the ancients, in *La roue* as in all my visual poems Venus (the Idea) has completely emerged from the waves: her beautiful naked body dried by the sunlight shines out from the summit of the cliff; in *Prisme* she is still covered by the sea; embroiled in the countless elements that sway her, she is at one with the forces that issue from the infinity of the world and from my heart modelling her divine shape. . . .

'For me cinematographic creation is a period of synthesis. A synthesis which is both internal and external. The search for a greater, more elevated and dynamic order – financial and artistic ventures drawing in more people, more values, and also absorbing a whole network of new resistances that are more difficult to overcome, technical innovations that seek to broaden and alter art's field of action. These periods are, of necessity, followed by a different phase: after I have constructed my temple or my humble abode on the highest point of the island, I set out again in my boat to explore the spot on the surface of the unconscious where the sun and the abyss espouse each other – the great internal currents that impel me. It's precisely those years of technical work in the studio which allow me to return periodically to introspection. There is a movement from one to the other which is a basic need of my spiritual nature – something like the act of breathing. In this double movement, you see, cinema and literature collaborate, or rather interpenetrate and fertilise each other. So far people have seen me only as film director. I would now like to unveil that other side of my activity, by presenting to the public those of my writings which seem to me the most emotive and the most successful. That, as you can see, entails a whole new way of posing the problem of the relationship between literature and cinema, a problem which I resolve not abstractly, but in the way I live, by being myself as much as I possibly can, which is how I usually do things.'

Impelled by a passionate curiosity with regard to this miracle of Goethean activity, I turn the pages of the manuscript of *Prisme*, a sum of ideas which encapsulate the whole of life, the origin of things, the cinema, the sufferings of love, the struggle with death, the opening out of new spaces, social ideas, literary judgments. I see a vast river flowing before my eyes, with flashes of lightning illuminating its surface. Reading some of these reflections, I think of Novalis, even of Nietzsche.

On the first page there are these two observations:

'I do not absorb, I refract (A.G.).'

'It is possible, however, that I am mistaken, and that what I take for diamonds are merely bits of glass (Descartes).'

'All in all,' says Gance, 'I am reasonably satisfied. *Prisme* will be published in two volumes, covering a period of fifteen years. The first ends with the onset of the illness that caused the death of a young woman I loved, the sister of my dear wife – she was my first wife. The second comprises the intimate drama surrounding her death and my long exploration of the world in the light of this divine suffering. As I have constructed it, the first volume presents itself, I think, as a jetty across the Ocean. The second is the Ocean itself, the floodtide of grief which, with my heart and my mind, drives the world up to higher ground. As you know, something similar happens in *La roue*, fatality surging up to the peaks. I think the privilege of powerful souls is to take implacable destiny up to the mountain tops, which is, after all, a way of escaping from it. Yes, Nietzsche and death taught me that. What teachers!'

Abel Gance's look becomes more distant and seems to tune into the harmonies of the unknown. 'It's possible,' he adds, 'that I will experience the kind of disappointment that Nietzsche felt with *The Birth of Tragedy*, a book which was not topical enough, because it was "timeless". But I am prepared for that. And to conjure up success and good fortune, there's a "Figaro" element in my character that Nietzsche didn't possess. I think, basically, that my book will, with time, increase in stature. There are a few good fairies watching over my cradle. A dear friend, Elie Faure, for example, has agreed to write a preface.'[7]

While the great animator is speaking, I am irresistibly drawn back to the manuscript lying in front of me. We pass from travels to reflections on history, society, music, literature and cinema, portraits of contemporary personalities, intimate confessions and daring analyses interspersed with the strangest and most powerful of visions. It is an astonishing work, unique in character and style, with intimate revelations and judgments that will fascinate the public. There is 'my heart laid bare', says a voice tinged with a proud melancholy.

The demiurge of *Napoleon*, of the real *Napoleon*, the one that no one or almost no one has seen, smiles at me. I see in superimpression before my eyes the despotic profile of Bonaparte, the wings of the Victory of Samothrace, the Wheel glinting in the clouds. And I see in front of me the Prism in which his soul has chosen to refract its shadows and its light.

'Especially tell people that I am now simply gathering in the fruits of a literary labour begun in my youth and that, far from abandoning the cinema, I plan to devote myself body and soul this winter to my next great film, *L'Annonciation* [. . .],[8] which will be the transposition and projection of the drama of the Passion into the present and the future.'

Getting up to leave Abel Gance, I glance once more at his fascinating face on which the luminous cross evoked by these closing words seems to revolve in a last vision like the Wheel of his past and to shine out like the bright star of his future.

Jean Arroy
Ecce homo, a portrait of Abel Gance[9]

I love Gance for his evangelic gentleness and the sadness of a bewildered child who breathlessly manages to produce a smile through its tears, begging us to forgive it for crying, while remaining desperately sad. I love in him his silent suffering, the meaning and the beauty of his suffering. A melodious melancholy that makes the heart beat stronger for the whole of one's life.

One should not speak of the apostle's face except to compare it to the mask of Beethoven, too vibrant to be the features of a dead man. But where could I find words of fervour, devotion and love while I am still looking for those which will not betray friendship? How can all the beauty of this magnificent soul be conveyed with lucidity and serenity when what is most vibrant in me is still caught up in a passionate maelstrom?

His face has the warm luminosity, the radiant spirituality and the opaque transparency of a stained-glass window. I cast my mind back over all the rosaces I have ever looked at, without being able to remember exactly which one it was that had a similar radiance at its centre. But I know that I will soon see again that consuming flame at the heart of the great rose in the cathedral of light which he is in the process of building, single-handed, in the painful joy of superhuman labours. And I know too that the gothic sun transformed by this wheel with crystal shafts into smiles and tears of light will not inflict more dangerous wounds of love on the soul than the slow-burning fever already induced by a face that still looks twenty in spite of the silvery hair that crowns it.

From this powerfully emotive face, a torch of ardent and consuming passions, a rosace of unappeasable torments and purifying sufferings, of wild illusions, of unattainable hopes and awesome or elating certitudes – from these frenetic eyes, like dischargers in which all the radioactivity of the soul is polarised, in which the devastating electric charge of great spiritual storms flashes from the positive eye to the

Gance as Saint-Just in *Napoleon*

negative eye with fantastic showers of sparks – from that face with
eyes of fire and lightning, there radiates an extraordinary mental
electricity. An irresistible psychic energy emanates from it, elating
and entrancing those who lack the power to resist, unleashing floods
of enthusiasm which the poet does not always know how, or does not
want, to turn to his advantage. Where then is the French Fiume?[10]

One of the Convention scenes in *Napoleon*

I will be understood by those who watched the filming of *Napoleon* in the Billancourt studios[11] where for two years the great soul of the French Revolution once more flourished magnificently, by those who witnessed the scenes at the Cordeliers and the Convention, when 1,200 extras who were there only for the money suddenly lost their grip and felt themselves carried away in a whirlwind of storms, disasters, apotheoses. Those who saw them, as they took hold again in the real world, rise spontaneously to their feet to acclaim endlessly the man who had achieved this miracle, those who heard that long shout of admiration, devotion and love mingled with a spirit of sacrifice – they will understand me when I claim for Gance the adventure into which Byron and D'Annunzio wildly threw themselves. But the heroic laurels of the authors of *Vittoria mutilata* and *Manfred*[12] do not concern the visionary of *Ecce Homo*. To found the *Kingdom of the Earth*,[13] he will conquer the screens of the world at the head of his cohorts of light.

There is in this man a truly extraordinary power of enthusiasm which annihilates all the forces of inertia born from the critical faculties, from prudence or weariness and the laziness of thought; which casts down all the material barriers that imprison the dream, projecting him, the explosive intellectual, beyond the confines of time and space.[. . .]

THE POETIC AVANT-GARDE: RENÉ CLAIR, GERMAINE DULAC AND
JEAN EPSTEIN

In contrast to romantics like Arroy and Buraud, the poetic or 'impressionist' avant-garde admired Gance for only a small part of his output: his work on the sensations constructed by the image. Curiously, even after 1927, they pay little attention to *Napoleon*, preferring instead to quote examples from *La roue*, usually the same ones, illustrating how montage, tracks and inserts create a new form of poetry which is essentially cinematic.

René Clair's article on *La roue*, dating from 1923 but republished in 1951 and, with a commentary, in 1970,[14] is in this respect typical. It also shows the beginnings of a form/content split which, although as yet unpoliticised, informs much of the more perceptive later criticism. But perhaps the most interesting feature of Clair's argument is his attempt to open up a space between the *romantic*, seen not as sign of originality but as an inheritance of the theatrical and the novelistic, and the *lyrical*, the basis for a cinematic poetry of the image that is neither narrative nor literary.

Clair's text is similar in its general terms of reference to an article by Fernand Léger who, as well as designing the poster for *La roue*, was encouraged by Gance to report on the film's 'plastic qualities'. Not surprisingly, Léger concentrates on those sections in which the mechanical plays the major role, in which the machine becomes '*the leading character, the leading actor*'. But he adds: 'the advent of this film is also interesting in that it is going to determine a place in the plastic order for an art that has until now remained almost completely descriptive, sentimental and documentary. [...] With *La roue*, Abel Gance has elevated the art of film to the level of the plastic arts.'[15]

Clair and Léger thus come into conflict with Ricciotto Canudo, whose article published in the same newspaper as Léger's is one of the few which does ¬attempt to politicise the issue of film aesthetics. Praising the modernity of *La roue*, Canudo notes: 'The film's vision of the world corresponds to the most modern of aesthetic imperatives, that which impels a few artists and a few writers to represent the undercurrents of crowd psychology. They want to replace the artistic portrayal of individual passions by the evocation of the formation they are part of and which they construct.'[16]

A great admirer of Gance, Germaine Dulac takes up a position that is similar to René Clair's and focuses on the same segments of the film as he does. She is less extreme, though, on the subject of narrative and of excess. While rejecting the theatrical, she maintains the need for a cinematic form of drama and for psychology. Of all the impressionist

Léger's poster for *La roue*

22

theorists, she explains most clearly what was meant by the poetic and why *La roue* seemed to signal the way ahead. Her text is extracted from an illustrated lecture she gave to *Les amis du cinéma* in December 1924.[17]

Even Jean Epstein, one of Gance's closest friends, dismisses *Napoleon*, referring only to the triple screen as an attempt to bring the image closer to actual vision, a process which would be taken over by the Americans. Otherwise he, too, refers systematically to *La roue* (and, because of Gance's discovery that the camera could be subjective and active, to *La folie du docteur Tube*). His text on *La roue* illustrates the Impressionists' concern with symbolism. It was apparently written in late 1922 and survives in typescript in the Gance archive. Sections of it were later reworked and inserted in a longer piece on Gance published in 1927 (translated in *Afterimage*, 10, 1981). Epstein's syntax is occasionally obscure, but since the same ambiguities recur in the 1927 text, I have as far as possible left them unresolved.

René Clair
La roue

La roue is the perfect example of a film in the romantic spirit. As in a romantic drama, you will find in Abel Gance's film a lack of verisimilitude, a superficial psychology, a relentless search for visual as well as for verbal effects, and you will find passages of an extraordinary lyricism, what one might call an inspired flow of the sublime and the grotesque.

Confronted with a drama which is so evidently 'thought out', so carefully filled with ideas and literary intentions, one is tempted to take the author of these thoughts and intentions to task. That would be a waste of effort. If the screenplay should only be a pretext, it is in this instance all too pervasive a pretext, often irritating and rarely useful, but not worth discussing at length. That Gance as scriptwriter has like most film-makers made an error is not really very interesting even if the error is sometimes a more serious one than those we are used to. If I were asked to judge Gance on the basis of the psychological intentions he displays on the screen and the subtitles he writes, I must admit that my judgment would be unfavourable. But our concern here is with cinema.

For me, the real subject of the film is not its curious plot, but a train, rails, signals, jets of steam, a mountain, snow and clouds. These impressive visual themes dominate the work, and Gance develops

23

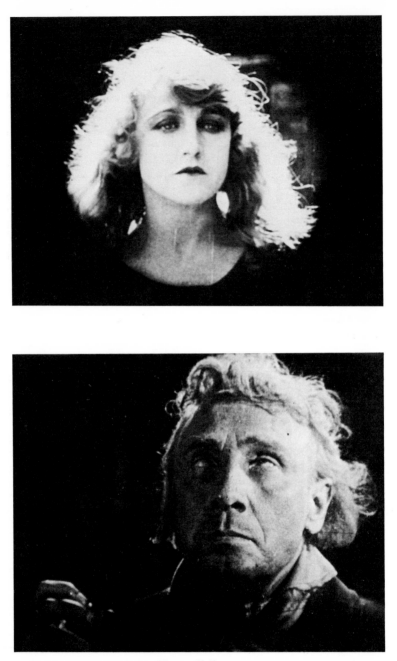

La roue as romantic melodrama: Norma, Sisif ...

. . . Elie and Hersan

them in a masterful way. We had already seen trains rushing along on rails at a speed accelerated by the manipulation of the camera; but we had not before felt ourselves, stalls, dress-circle and everywhere in the theatre, engulfed by the screen.

You may say that is only a sensation. Maybe so. But we did not go there to think. Seeing and feeling are enough. You can talk about the cinema of ideas in fifty years time. That unforgettable passage is not the only one that demonstrates Gance's value. The catastrophe at the beginning of the film, the first accident that Sisif tries to bring about, the funicular climbing up into the mountains, the death of Elie, the bringing down of the corpse, the mountaineers' dance and the impressive ending veiled in clouds, these are high moments whose lyrical composition owes nothing to the other arts. Looking at them, one forgets the quotations from Kipling, Aeschylus and Abel Gance which from one end of the film to the other produce a kind of discouragement. And one begins to be hopeful.

If only Abel Gance would give up making his railway engines say 'yes' and 'no', putting the thoughts of a classical hero into the head of an engine driver and quoting his favourite authors! If only this man, who can bring to life one detail of a machine, a hand, a branch, a puff of smoke, was willing to create a pure documentary! If only he would make this contribution to the creation of the FILM that we can still only imagine!

If he would only renounce literature and have confidence in cinema!

Germaine Dulac
La roue: The song of the rails

[. . .] You can appeal to the emotions without the need for characters, and thus without recourse to the theatrical. Witness the Song of rails and wheels.

A theme but not a drama . . . The railway, a criss-crossed road of straight steel tracks, the railway, all that is distanced from life, a poem whose rhymes are lines that move first singly then in series: I don't think cinema has ever come so close to the peak of its potential as in this short poem by Abel Gance, our master. A play of light, of forms, of perspectives. An intense emotion that is generated simply by the vision of something that is absorbed through our senses. And then wheels, rhythm, speed . . . The mechanical motion of a connecting rod that echoes the beating of a heart. [. . .]

26

La roue

Abel Gance [. . .] is above all a poet. His songs are not in words but in images. What gives his stories their impact is all their spiritual intensity, their philosophical implications.

Do you remember that extraordinary scene in *La roue*? A locomotive driven by a man whose jealousy is so extreme that he can no longer cope with the responsibility for his own life or other people's. He is taking the woman he loves towards a destiny that he cannot accept. Abel Gance expresses the unrestrained ferocity and the grandeur of his passion fragmentarily through movement: speed, rhythm, the blackness of the tunnels, the daylight, the engine whistle, the vibration of the driving wheels, glimpses of passengers' faces expressing contrasted feelings, and suddenly calm restored, the locomotive arriving majestically in the station as if nothing had happened. Man has dominated the aberrations of his brain and the impulses of his heart. Movements of the eye, of wheels, of landscapes, black, white, quavers, semi-quavers, a complex visual orchestration: Cinema! Dramatic, yes, but a drama conceived in a completely new way, completely divorced from the rules that govern theatre and literature. Like a great symphony the film swells into profoundly disturbing harmonies. It soars above the petty little stories that the public is far too inclined to lap up unthinkingly.

Jean Epstein
La roue

With Abel Gance's film the first cinematographic symbol is born.

The wheel. Modern martyrs who believe in our dogma of toughened lies bear it on their brow, a crown of steel, as heavy to bear as an intelligent love. On the predestined rails of Fortune, good and especially bad, it rolls on as long as there is a heart that beats. The cycle of life and death has become so wounding that it had to be forged to prevent it from breaking. Imprisoned hope radiates at its centre. The wheel. A hoop binding the body to the will, desires chase round and round in it like agitated and over-anxious foxes in a cage. From the moment of birth, none of us can hope to escape from it, and as if alone in the world, alone in our wheel, we stay there because no one knows the flagrant word which would melt a breach of sympathy in the barrier. The wheel. Each of us, bonded by it to the heart of another, remains deaf and dumb. While its daily schedule of death and oblivion rolls on, erasing faces from people's hearts, overprinting the seasons and the years, the showcases of memories, something that is never what we are watching out for is maturing. Wheels, roaring wheels of express trains, brushing past stations, shorthand signs and drawn blinds, with rapid farewells, sway along rhythmically in their dreary nocturnal journey. The connecting rods precipitate an irrevocable drama, darker than the whole of Greek tragedy. We are summoned to leave. A cross that turns very quickly takes on the form of a wheel. That is why, Gance, at the top of your hill of Calvary there is a wheel. By hastening towards death, we have made the flower of the cross bloom, the wheel, rosicrucian. More than a symbol, it is a scar, an inflamed mark, as fatal as the one incendiaries bear below their left breast.

Poetry is not to be found only in verse. Abel Gance is one, and an outstanding one, of the four or five lyrical temperaments that exist.

I know people, even quite intelligent ones, who find poetry only in harmony, balance and good taste; in feelings that have been trained to give a paw, moderate disasters, disciplined catastrophes, storms in a teacup and, in short, in a kind of well-mown beauty which seems like perfection only to mediocre hearts.

Poetry is quite other, and it is not without horror. As cruel as it is gentle, excessive sometimes and sometimes inadequate, more often raucous than melodious, immoderate and immodest, loyal and faithful or faked and untruthful, duplicity and triplicity, false at times, honest and dishonest, always entire and alive, poetry is passion. An impoverished art like, for example, the decorative arts – domestic arts

La roue: 'cinematic symbol'

– has to be concerned with the frontiers of taste and the median limits of sensibility. A rich art sets aside that concern with scale, or it falls into decadence. *La roue* overflows. A human heart catches fire in each of its four corners. The blaze spreads from person to person, carried simply by the flashing of their eyes. Which of Nero's sapphires is worth the lens that observes these torches of tears burning? It is when an excess of life destroys the validity of art that poetry erupts like a storm.

However meticulously a film is made, there is one thing that defies all predictions: the conviction that radiates from it. This is a human element, a volatile element that no technique can be certain of stabilising. It comes only from the person who is filtered through the lens. A long time ago, I went into a cinema with a friend, now dead: the film breathed out into our eyes a spiritual atmosphere that has stayed with me. It was the second part of *J'accuse*. I hardly knew Gance's name then. The conviction that emanates from *La roue* is overwhelming.

Like Cocteau, I think there are angels that fly close to the earth. They think a little about those of us who think about them a lot. They know about the unpredictable things that were all mapped out a long time ago, and whose earthly shadow we can just make out, if they keep us awake for long enough. They are nameless and their wings beat in time that moves gently forwards or backwards. They protect aspirations that have become as incurable as the most ferocious diseases and as a love that is as strong as life itself. They promise pleasures and bring us higher sufferings. Sometimes, but only rarely, a transparent soul circulates within a film and we see the film through it. Gance, you have the face of an angel.

THE POLITICAL AND THE AESTHETIC: LÉON MOUSSINAC AND EMILE VUILLERMOZ

A committed Marxist, Léon Moussinac began writing about cinema for Louis Delluc's journal *Le film* in 1919 and was appointed film critic of *L'humanité* by Vaillant-Couturier in 1923. His book *Naissance du cinéma*, published in 1925, was later described by the critic Georges Sadoul as the most important work in film theory that had so far appeared.

Although he was an early supporter of Gance, whose *J'accuse* he adapted for publication as a *ciné-roman*,[18] Moussinac was rarely unequivocal when it came to reviewing his films. His article on *La roue*, for example, consists mostly of an appreciation of the film's visual qualities, its pioneering *mise en scène* and the subtlety of its internal rhythms, but he prefaces what is overall a eulogistic piece with some scathing remarks about the 'insufferable and even obnoxious' elements he is prepared to 'overlook': 'the confusion of symbols, the overbearing emphasis of the images, a literariness that is completely out of place in this brilliant flood of images, an extreme display of bad taste.' [19]

His review of *Napoleon*, which appeared in two parts in *L'humanité* (24 April and 1 May 1927), develops this critique of emphatic symbolism and begins to examine its political implications. Although he later revised the text for inclusion in *Panoramique du cinéma* (1929) and *L'âge ingrat du cinéma* (1946), the original version is translated here, partly on account of its greater abrasiveness, mostly because it highlights the bioptical nature of his approach.

Moussinac was not the only critic of the time to have expressed concern about the film's political dimension, but his analysis is by far the most forceful and the most developed. It particularly highlights the difficulty of political criticism in that the argument is constructed entirely on the polarity of progressive form and reactionary content. But at least the dichotomy is squarely confronted: on the level of content *Napoleon* is in Moussinac's view a pernicious film presenting a crude caricature of the young Bonaparte and the French Revolution, yet in his work on the image Gance has made an important contribution to the development of a popular and revolutionary art form.

A similar concern and a similar methodological difficulty inform the assessment of the other main 'political' critic of the time, Emile Vuillermoz. A musician and a prolific writer, Vuillermoz was perhaps the most influential film critic in France during the 1920s. In addition to a weekly column in *Le temps*, an establishment daily, he wrote for a number of other papers and magazines, notably *Comoedia*, *L'impartial français* and *Cinémagazine*. Along with the art historian Elie Faure, he could be said to belong to an 'aesthetic' school of criticism, arguing consistently for the recognition of cinema as a new art form and against excessive commercialisation, but always aware of cinema's specific hold over its audience and of its social inscription.

Attentive to technological innovations as well as to aesthetic effect, his defence of the new art as 'the music of light' led him to support the experiments of the Impressionists and especially of Gance, whom he considered the most original presence in French cinema. Unlike many of his contemporaries, he never republished his articles in book form, or he would certainly be recognised as one of the major theorists of his time.

Vuillermoz wrote a considerable number of articles on Gance's films, including at least seven on *La roue* and six on *Napoleon*. Like Moussinac, he was rarely unequivocal, reproaching Gance frequently

31

for a too literary or theatrical approach to cinema. Gance indubitably has cinematographic genius but not talent, he wrote in one of his articles on *La roue* (*Cinémagazine*, 23 February 1923), a description that has been bandied about countless times since, often in the most unlikely contexts. But Vuillermoz is much more subtle in his approach than this neat phrase would suggest, and his articles on *Napoleon* are remarkable for their careful blend of enthusiasm and stricture. Two of these are translated below.

The first, published in *Le temps* (9 April 1927), was written immediately after the première at the Opéra. Invited along with other journalists to a day's shooting in the Billancourt studios and to a screening of the final triptych, he had already published laudatory pieces on Gance's powers as director and on the vast expressive possibilities of the triple screen. His first assessment of the complete film is, in comparison, surprisingly critical. Its usefulness in the present context is that it historicises the genius/excess debate, stressing what for the aesthetic school seemed to be Gance's contribution to the development of film art.

The second, a more considered piece, appeared in the November 1927 issue of *Cinémagazine*, when *Napoleon* at last went on general release in the major French cities. Vuillermoz extends his argument here to take account of the political implications of the film in the specific conjunctures of 1927. It needs to be read alongside what he had already written a year and a half earlier after witnessing the performance of the extras during the shooting of the Marseillaise at the Billancourt studios. The concluding paragraphs of this earlier article, published in *L'impartial français* (19 March 1926), are appended after the 1927 texts.

What is remarkable about both Vuillermoz's and Moussinac's critiques of *Napoleon* is not so much their castigation of the film as a proto-fascist apologia of dictatorship as the fact that both thought it necessary to voice this opinion in spite of their declared admiration for Gance and sympathy for his view of cinema and its mission. They were not alone – an anonymous critic writing in *Candide* (14 April 1927) compares the scene of Bonaparte's appearance at the Convention to a workers' institute giving lessons to Mussolini – but they were in a small minority. They were also, in their turn, castigated, by André Gain among others, who in *La petite tribune* of 10 June 1927 condemns their unpatriotic rejection of the film as imperialist, adding that shortly before both had enthused about *Potemkin* and praised its 'social' message. For Gain, *Napoleon*, like *La roue*, was a great work of *French* cinema, and in art, political considerations were as out of place 'as a polar bear on the plains of Abyssinia'.[20]

As a member of the patriotic right, Gain at least made his own position clear. Most critics simply avoided the problem of ideology or simply assumed the film's dominant discourse, praising its sincerity, energy, harmony and emotional impact without questioning political effects. Gance was the poet of the screen, at times excessive or naive, but a producer of powerful and compelling images, which justifiably aroused an enthusiastic response in the spectator.

Otherwise, criticism tended to take the form of an assessment of Gance's historical accuracy. Thus Victor Méric (*Le Soir*, 2 December 1927) saw Gance's Napoleon as a kind of revolutionary paladin, the disciple of Robespierre and Marat, the bringer of freedom to other peoples and the enemy of tyrants, whereas the real Bonaparte was merely a bloodthirsty opportunist, ugly, lacking presence and unable even to ride a horse. Although he echoes some of Vuillermoz's fears, he is mostly concerned that Gance's legendary Napoleon will gain credence as truth. Others also mentioned the Douglas Fairbanks aspect of Gance's representation of the young Bonaparte, but most, like the Napoleonic specialist Emile Le Gallo,[21] were willing to excuse such inaccuracies and romantic affabulations on the grounds that they served to recreate the spirit of the times with a masterful intensity. Julien Luchaire, a historian and internationalist to whom Gance sent his screenplay for comment, wrote back criticising it for its representation of the Revolution as an 'abominable and chaotic bloodbath' after which Bonaparte re-established peace and order, but even he ends merely by pleading for a portrayal of Danton, Robespierre etc. as creators as well as destroyers and of Bonaparte as the figure who continued and corrected what the Revolution had constructed, restoring order to the chaos. He admits that he was at first apprehensive about the insertion of a fictional and sentimental intrigue into an epic subject but then adds '[. . .] You have the art of reflecting great events in these humble souls which not only makes your method acceptable but confers on it great human and poetic value – and in consequence a historical value.'[22]

The critical debate tended, then, to remain inscribed within the parameters of representation: is this an authentic view of Napoleon? is it historically accurate? do Gance's inventions/fictions contain a poetic truth? can inaccuracies be excused by the film's emotional impact?

As in more recent criticism, few apart from Moussinac and Vuillermoz examined the film as *system* of representations, as interpellation of the spectator.

Léon Moussinac
A French film: Napoléon

This is only the first series of cinematographic images devoted by Gance to the story of Napoleon. Its exact title ought really to be 'Bonaparte' since it starts with the escape from Corsica and finishes with the beginning of the Italian campaign at Montenotte. It is one of the most important achievements we have seen in France for a long time, important on account of the personality of the author, the material and financial resources involved (15 million francs have been spoken of) and the extraordinary publicity campaign that the Franco-American distributors have launched on the basis of a title which could hardly be more 'commercial'.

Abel Gance has already made a number of films, several of which are markers in the development of cinema as a new and original means of expression. The most recent of these was *La roue* (1922). Abel Gance is one of the few cinematographers who can exercise power. The abundance and the force of his creativity command respect even within the disorderliness in which he creates. But the value of a film lies first and foremost in what it expresses.

Images of this kind are not presented to the public as laboratory experiments. We cannot, therefore, place technique above expression. A ridiculous distortion. Gance himself would not be pleased, Gance who desires the communion of the masses in the cinema, Gance who believes in cinema as a social art, who has faith in his work.

That permits me to insist with all the necessary vigour that this *Napoleon* is not only false but dangerous, and deserves to be condemned without leave to appeal.

I will try to summarise as best I can this indictment of the content. We shall spare neither the director, guilty of writing the screenplay, nor the backers, producers and distributors of the film who, to a greater or lesser extent, have imposed on it their anti-artistic and purely mercantile conception of the cinema.

That leads us to dwell, yet again, on the evils of a system and the dangers of a set of erroneous principles. *Napoleon* is, as an example, both typical and sensational. Because it also allows us to spell out what benefit we can derive from Gance's work as an initiation to the cinema, on account of its considerable technical innovations and a fundamentally cinematic beauty that far surpasses what is usually found in the best productions anywhere in the world. Innovations and beautiful effects which contribute to the improvement of the original apparatus and prepare its important revolutionary function.

'A Bonaparte for budding fascists'

The film-maker has, in this instance, taken full responsibility for his subject by announcing a *Napoleon* 'seen' by Abel Gance. We must therefore consider him entirely responsible for a screenplay which reconstructs for us a Bonaparte who is a pure figment of the imagination, who emerges from a French Revolution that is historically false and even from a purely bourgeois point of view totally unacceptable. A Bonaparte for budding fascists.

We begin[23] with the 'Marseillaise' sung at the Cordeliers by Rouget de l'Isle, Danton and the Chorus, introducing the orchestra as well as the images. Then we witness Bonaparte's flight from Corsica where he has been condemned to death (a Hollywood-style chase). In a 'frail barque' with the tricolour flag as sail (a sentimentalism derived from serials), the future Emperor of the French battles against the stormy sea while, at the same moment (literary symbolism), the Convention is assailed by a horrific tempest (the fall of the Girondins).

The siege of Toulon. The genius of the artillery lieutenant which triumphs over the incapacity of the Revolutionary leaders and the policies of the Commissars of the Republic (no doubt to demonstrate that the civilian must always give way to the military which always knows best).

The Reign of Terror. We do not yet know anything of the Revolution, of what it has destroyed, what it has constructed, the ideas and forces that it has brought into confrontation, where, on a fundamental level, it is going. On purpose. We merely witness the carefully staged spectacle of popular dictators concerned only with dispatching people to the guillotine. Sadistic, and always thirsting for more blood; all this in a chaos out of which only two names emerge (subtitles) from among the 'thousands of victims': Lavoisier, a scientist, André Chénier, a poet. The whole business peppered with Robespierre's little manias, Marat's haemoptysis, Danton's effrontery and the scent of the rose that Gance–Saint-Just smells each time the blade of the guillotine falls.

Thermidor. Confusion and obscurity with, as interludes, Bonaparte's courtship of La Beauharnais. The only attempt to explain the constructive efforts of the revolutionaries: just a subtitle, a passing reference to Saint-Just's last speech. One subtitle amid so many images which irrevocably condemn the Revolution!

Bonaparte – sacked already – suffers like a caged eagle (as we know!) in a wretched lodging, but he dreams of nothing less than founding an empire! There . . . (Asia) or there . . . (America)! So the young general, serving his own ambition and the dictates of his nature, accepts the last-ditch proposals of Barras (who is looking for a leader) and the favours of Josephine (who is looking for a man).

He goes like a good boy to listen (apologies to Charlemagne!) to the advice supplied by the shades of beheaded revolutionaries which appear before him in the Convention chamber, empty now and of no further use (after vain words, it's action that counts, isn't it!), where he has gone to collect his thoughts before taking command of the Army of Italy, a revolutionary army which, little by little, after a few massacres, he will transform into the instrument of his imperial ambition.

This is obviously not the place to go into details about images which are more or less directly linked to the basic subject matter, and which are irritatingly sentimental – like Violine's love or Fleuri's constancy. It's rather the meaning of series of images that we must insist on. These are presented to us in an amazingly daring way and they are all the more dangerous in that they are expressed with energy and brilliance, even a kind of rhythmic and plastic grandeur.

Napoleon is addressed to the masses. The masses will rush to see it because of the title, because of Abel Gance, because of the publicity. Well, I challenge these masses not to be convinced by this film that the French Revolution, whose watchwords are still the everyday garglings of the democrats in 1927, destroyed everything that had

The shades of the Revolutionaries at the Convention

been accomplished under the *Ancien régime*, that it just killed off poets, scientists and great-hearted innocents, that it was led by lunatics, maniacs and headcases, and that Napoleon Bonaparte happened on the scene at the right moment to re-establish order in the good name of discipline, authority and country – in a word, military dictatorship.

These are the facts, and one can estimate their consequences in terms of the value of the images used to express them.

One detects here an ill-read library, texts that have not been assimilated, details inflated out of all proportion for purely literary purposes, a lack of scientific method in the preparation and organisation of the work, a subject which is never under control.

A kind of synthesis was the only real possibility, based on a careful choice of elements and materials provided by history, without sinking into the romantic and sentimental lyricism of more or less hidden 'correspondences' and anecdotal gossip. Then the meaning would have emerged unequivocally. Then a unity of expression that is totally lacking in *Napoleon* would have been achieved.

In a second article, we will examine – over and above a subject matter which invites challenge and requires us to condemn it utterly – what lessons can be drawn from the film from a cinematographic point of view: why all is not lost of this enormous effort, of the frequently admirable skill with which it has been made, of the experimentation and technical refinement which are apparent in the form, if not of the film, at least of the images that have been selected from it and strung together, for those 'commercial' reasons which determine everything, even patriotic propaganda.

If, as we concluded last week, Gance's film is indefensible on the level of content, it is remarkable for its technical qualities and on those grounds it merits careful examination. Please do not tell me that these new approaches, methods, skills are useless because they are employed in the service of an erroneous and dangerous idea. They are useful because they will *stay*, signalling a new stage in the development of cinematography, because they enrich a new field, because they improve the apparatus. I mean, for example, that if the images of *Battleship Potemkin*, which is for the moment the masterpiece of this kind of cinema, had been filmed using the new techniques that Gance has pioneered in *Napoleon*, the power and impact of Eisenstein's film would have been ten times greater. The force of expression of an animated picture is increased enormously when its plastic volume is realised with the greatest degree of perfection possible, when it is animated by, or held within, a rhythm sustained by skilled technique.

If *Napoleon*, at least the *Napoleon* which was presented to us, is not a film – that is, an ordered sequence of images conforming to a rhythm and achieving the unity of conception and realisation which is the hallmark of any true work of art – if it is simply a series of fragmented images held together by the very weak link of a subtitle, and, at its best, a kind of anthology, the fault isn't entirely Gance's but rather his distributors'. The film-maker conceived and made a film estimated to be 12,000 to 15,000 metres long. The absurdity of present methods of exhibition has obliged Gance to reduce that, for the Opéra screenings for example, to a selection of about 5,000 metres, that is to say, a sequence of images that can be seen in a single evening.[24]

We must remember that images fixed on celluloid are *definitive*, that the details have been determined in relation to the whole. As a result, to reduce a 12,000-metre film by more than half is as absurd as obliging someone to read a 500-page literary narrative by skipping every other page. If the intention was to exploit *Napoleon* by the kilometre, then Gance should have been told to make several films of different lengths on the same subject. But here we are confronting the open sore from which, fortunately, the cinema of Euro-American shopkeepers and backstreet bars will die – for the greater good of cinema itself.

There is, first of all, an innovation in *Napoleon* that we should dwell on for a moment: the triple screen.

The idea was to an extent already in the air, that is to say that many film-makers were anxious to widen the field of projection. I have already published in this newspaper, well before Gance revealed his system, letters from comrades who showed me how concerned they were about the constraints imposed on the cinematographic image by the conventions of the rectangular screen and who submitted to me various ideas for making the shape of the screen correspond more closely to the human field of vision. An anxiety was evidently there and it was formulated in this precise need to explode the frame.

Gance has not broken the frame but he has increased its size. The three juxtaposed screens in fact make it possible both (in the language of painting) to extend the proportions of the canvas to those of the fresco and to project simultaneously three images which can express an emotion, a feeling, an idea in a new dynamic way, multiplying, first by three then by the variable number of superimpressions, the expressive meaning of the image. Gance has used this invention twice in *Napoleon* with varying degrees of success. The first time merging, in the sentimental ebb and flow of a storm, the seas unleashed against Bonaparte's skiff as he flees Corsica and, in the Convention, the circumstances that lead to the fall of the Girondins; the second, suddenly revealing to us the Army of Italy which Bonaparte has come to take command of and showing us, in a way that is quite wonderful and the high point in Gance's work, the soldiers singing as they march, in images whose rhythm exactly matches that of 'Auprès de ma blonde . . .'. There is, in the simultaneous play on three screens of central images flanked by images shown in symmetry (apart from a few gross errors), an instant power, an energy and a movement that completely win over our emotions. As soon as symbolism reappears, as soon as literature regains the upper hand, as soon as we are no longer looking solely at the cinematographic representation of an army on the march, it all becomes rather vague and we are left simply admiring a technical *tour de force*.

The triple screen process is obviously what is most exciting in Abel Gance's film. But there are other virtues. If you need to have a certain experience of film viewing to be able to discover them, that is no doubt because the meaning of the film itself puts many spectators into such an ill-disposed frame of mind that, quite correctly unless they are professionals, they are not able to take an interest in the techniques being used. Particularly because the most remarkable scenes in plastic terms are perhaps those which serve to convey what is most unacceptable in *Napoleon*, for example Violine's love. The marriage of

Above: Perhaps the only surviving fragment of the Double Tempest sequence. *Below:* Images in symmetry: the final triptychs in *Napoleon.*

this strange heroine is one of the most astonishingly successful uses of white on white yet seen in the cinema, and the moment when we see the character move away towards a magical background of vaporous grey is quite unforgettable. This technique used to express something really human would have a prodigious effect. Also worthy of note are the skies in the storm sequence whose romanticism has never been equalled.

The plastic quality of some of the images superimposed in opposing movements to give some of the paroxysmic passages of the film an emotive cadence creates a truly cinematic rhythm. If Gance does indeed have many talents in addition to those of film-maker, I suppose it is those of the musician that predominate.

The perfection of some of the lenses specially designed for this film must also be mentioned. The result is a very large number of images of exceptionally high quality in which the values of the different planes are respected even in the narrowest and deepest fields (the pursuit in Corsica, the view from the bow of the ship as it reaches France, the panoramic views at the end, for example). Many special effects and innovations that professionals can study with profit. One can affirm that there is not a single passage in *Napoleon* that does not display technical originality.

On the actors' performances there is nothing to say. One would have to say too much. They are bristling with errors. As for the music that Honegger has 'composed' (there are very few original pieces), one can affirm that it is the opposite of what one would have wished. It suffers from the lack of cohesion of the film itself, from the excessively disparate elements that make it a disjointed work. A real scramble. I should say: a lot of noise about nothing. A mishmash of the 'Marseillaise', 'La Carmagnole' and 'Ça ira', etc. The drums have a field day. The 'heart of the townsfolk' has really deserved that.

To sum up.

In social terms, *Napoleon* is a pernicious work. I condemn it.

In cinematographic terms, *Napoleon*, a bad film because it is only a succession of images, has given Abel Gance the opportunity to make use of his unquestionably original talents and these have brought about an enrichment of the domain of photogenics, a significant improvement of the apparatus, in short a major step forward for cinematography. It is an important moment in the history of the technical development of a mode of expression which will be the art of the future.

Emile Vuillermoz
Napoleon

It is characteristic of the epic, whether it is poetic, pictural, musical, theatrical or cinematographic, to sweep along on its stormy waves all kinds of contradictory elements and to throw together in its violent rhythm the good, the mediocre and the worst. In making his *Napoleon*, Abel Gance has not escaped from the law of the genre. His film has splendid qualities and strident defects, it is by turns dazzling and intensely irritating. If one examines this work in strictly critical terms, one cannot possibly approve of it. But it is self-evident that where the critical faculties dominate, there can be no more epics ...

The fundamental limitation of this gigantic composition is that it is not essentially cinematic. Without being aware of it, Abel Gance has gradually distanced himself from the seventh art and made an unexpected return to literature, to the ode, to historical drama, official painting, state sculpture and lyrical theatre. I am not speaking simply of the perfectly legitimate interventions of the chorus, of the drums, of Koubitsky present on the stage, singing the 'Marseillaise' while he was miming it on the screen, or even of the actor who lent his voice to Bonaparte to harangue the Army of Italy; it is rather in the whole conception of the work that I see a tendency which represents a very unfortunate step backwards in the history of the silent art. A reproach that is all the more serious in that Abel Gance is a film-maker who has a real cinematic genius. And it is towards the cinematic, and only towards it, that he should have directed his exceptional gifts. By seeking to imitate verbally and scenically Edmond Rostand and Georges d'Esparbès,[25] this Ingres of the screen has, alas, merely played the violin.[26]

This film is in fact made in an extremely disparate style. Sometimes, as in the first and the third parts, it nobly fulfils its technical mission; sometimes, as in the second, it is merely reduced to the rank of schoolbook illustration. Everywhere there is an abuse of visual and verbal repetitions, of effects that are over-extended. Too often the image is only a camouflaged 'tirade' leading artificially into a dramatic subtitle, which from a cinematic point of view is a crime of high treason. You can too easily sense a desire to go for cheap effects and to make the actor, in the theatrical sense of the word, far too important. As in old Italian operas, there are in all this too many cavatinas, ariosos and bravura arias sung in front of the prompter's box and not enough orchestral and harmonic atmosphere. But, by an effect of immanent justice, it is not this flattery of the masses and the concessions to the dramaturgy of the old Porte Saint-Martin[27] that will bring this formidable work the success Gance has been counting on.

He will in fact owe his success to the few moments in which he searches resolutely and wholeheartedly for the purely cinematic. That is when we find the real Gance, with all his qualities, his technical virtuosity, his insight and visionary mastery. I personally would give up the whole of the second part just for the few metres of that prodigious ride around Corsica in which a translucent horseman, literally a 'journeying soul', passes through landscapes whose contours blend and intertwine with a smoothness of rhythm that is unforgettably beautiful. Every time Gance has sincerely looked for a means of expression within the resources of the moving image, he has triumphed. True cinematic eloquence is indeed to be found not in printed speeches thrown to the crowds like bones to a dog, but in the beautiful visual synthesis, the striking combination, the powerful or really appropriate image conveying feeling or thought, the arrow of light that strikes us in the heart or the reflection that almost penetrates our unconscious. Abel Gance is more expert in this sublime language than anyone else, and he proved that many times in the course of yesterday evening's performance. His triple screen, whose wealth of possibilities I was the first to describe in an earlier issue of this paper,[28] has allowed him to reach effortlessly the highest peaks of the lyricism of the image. The titanic counterpoint of the double storm of the sea and the Convention shows what could be expected from so crucial a technical innovation. When the curtains are drawn back, opening out in the wall of the theatre that immense breach of light, the effect produced is one of an astonishing power.

In the present state of French cinematography, Abel Gance has a liberating mission to fulfil. He is capable of it. Only he is currently in a position to resist the commercial cartels that want to maintain cinema as a slave to a profitable and demagogic Taylorism. He showed us yesterday that we were right to place our trust in him. And that is why I will always offer as a homage to this prophet my most vehement and impassioned curses whenever he forgets to preach his noble gospel.

Abel Gance and Napoleon seen by Emile Vuillermoz

This tremendous work has already been subjected to the same fate as the map of Europe, cut up and pieced back together by the lank-haired Corsican. We have seen it stretched and shrunk like the wild ass's skin . . . that is, like a fragile Empire set up by an over-ambitious soldier. This grandiose and heterogeneous film has at last been reduced to normal dimensions for commercial exploitation. But in this shortened form, it is no less significant a composition. The abridged version merely underlines the essential characteristics of its author's psychology.

In this respect, we must not forget the explicit indication contained in its rather unexpected title. We are not being offered a biography of Napoleon or a page of French history. What we are invited to look at is Napoleon 'seen by Abel Gance', that is to say the heroic encounters of the young Bonaparte and the 'Little Corporal' of French cinema. In fact there is as much in this adventure story, and perhaps more, of Abel Gance as there is of Napoleon.

That is not a reproach. I actually have more sympathy for the former than for the latter. I have frequently had occasion to exalt the exceptional qualities of a dynamic presence who has brought to the screen the advantages of his visionary gifts, his poetic intuition and his pictorial virtuosity. We owe to him all kinds of conquests in the untilled land of animated vision. I feel myself particularly well placed, then, to address to this conqueror – in the sense of the ancient tradition of the march to the Capitol – remarks which are intended to remind him that he is a man and that he must be mistrustful of apotheoses which lead to the paralytic state of demigod.

Abel Gance was born to make films. That is nature's express desire. Light and shade obey him and at every moment he discovers in the vocabulary of luminous vibrations turns of phrase and expressions which are strikingly new and original. He is, then, a man of 1927, perfectly capable of understanding his own times, which is, as you know, an exceptional privilege and something of a rarity in an effete society nurtured on an outdated 'literary' culture.

But by a strange irony of fate, this man of today is afflicted with a handicap that he must at all costs overcome if he is to exert an effective influence on the young generation of creators who will present us with the aesthetic of our century. He is a romantic. Romantic in the most outmoded, anachronistic and 'anti-modern' way. This master of the mechanical eye and of the luminous ray, this virtuoso of the electric brain conceives of lyricism in about as artificial a way as Alexandre Dumas père, Sardou, Edmond Rostand and d'Esparbès.[29] A cruel, almost tragic anomaly: d'Artagnan as factory manager, Cyrano as director of a laboratory. This perfect film-maker will only realise his full potential the day he has cleared his brain and his imagination of an idea of the sublime which is purely literary in essence.

It is in this sense that I have never hesitated to say to this artist, whom I esteem above all others, that his *Napoleon* is at once a fine work and a reprehensible act. On a philosophical level it is impossible to approve of such subject matter especially when Napoleon is seen by Abel Gance, that is to say systematically and tendentiously misrepresented by a man whose lyricism is sincere.

What we have to reproach him with as author of a production whose artistic quality is not at stake is in fact a rather puerile yet dangerous desire to seek at all costs to present more or less fantasised conceptions of the poet as though they were part of history. Just as the director of *King of Kings* hides all the time behind the authority of the Gospels, giving chapter and verse for every single subtitle to prove that it is taken from the New Testament, Gance doesn't give a single line of dialogue or even an exclamation (even something as basic as 'Death to Robespierre!') without certifying in brackets and in italics that the quotations are *authentic*. We should interpret that as meaning that they conform to the literary orthodoxy of a Frederic Masson,[30] which, it has to be admitted, is not a totally convincing argument.

There is something unpleasant in all this. Why does the author not accept responsibility for his inveterate taste for 'panache', that coquettishness so typical of generals and of hearses? He ought to have the courage of his extrapolations and after showing us Bonaparte seizing an enormous tricolour from outside the Ajaccio town hall and using it as a sail during a Shakespearian tempest, he should not insert the subtitle 'Thus Bonaparte left Corsica to go to fight at Toulon'. Of course not: that is obviously not how things really happened! The departure by boat leads into a symbolic and theatrical development which is entirely Gance's own creation. He should assert his paternity here rather than trying to pass off as historical (what, after all, is history?) scenes which, however decorative they may be, should not for loyalty's sake be foisted on to the popular imagination as though they were official truths.

One has no right to let French people, or foreigners for that matter, believe that Napoleon was a kind of Douglas Fairbanks holding out single-handed against a hundred armed opponents, leaping through the window and into the saddle of a fiery charger, galloping across the whole of Corsica like some fantastic cowboy, braving with a smile countless pistol shots at point-blank range and emerging without a scratch. One has no right either to affirm that on arriving at the encampment of the army of Italy, this young upstart had only to throw his sword vigorously on the table, and stare arrogantly at the formidable Masséna, the invincible Augereau and their fierce companions to crush their dignity completely and transform them instantaneously into cowering lackeys, slaves brought to submission by their fear of the master's whip.

All this theatrical romanticism dominates Gance's vision to an unfortunate extent, and that is certainly not the best part of his work. There is, in this over-indulgent apotheosis of dictatorship, a flattery of

45

the basest demagogic instincts of the masses who, as one knows, have never had enough of being kicked in the pants. And it's not very logical on the part of our visionary author to have tried to reconcile the irreconcilable by presenting us with a Bonaparte who is a democrat, the son of the Revolution, of Danton, Marat and Robespierre, placing his sword at the service of an international Republic, whereas the whole of the cinematic portrait clearly denounces the tyrant, the opportunist, the unscrupulous conqueror and the soldier who sowed throughout the whole of Europe the seeds of all the imperialisms of the future. Either Bonaparte was sincere in his love of liberty and, in that case, he should not have been portrayed as conqueror, or he was not and it would have been honest to draw attention to his duplicity.

Since Gance is so partial to historical texts, he will know that his altruistic hero had as his breviary the following dogmas: 'To be a successful conqueror you have to be ferocious . . . Those who haven't learned to make use of circumstances are fools . . . I have an income of a hundred thousand men a year . . . If the aggressors are wrong up in heaven they are right down here . . . Nothing was ever founded except by the sword . . . There are moments of crisis when the public good necessitates the condemnation of an innocent person . . . You can't do anything with a philosopher. A philosopher is a bad citizen, etc.'

Confronted with a social morality of this order, one has to take sides. To go all out, in such conditions, to dress up the figure of a despot in all kinds of romantic frills, to decorate the statue of a tyrant with cinematographic flowers, is to produce a work which is philosophically and historically despicable. That is what Abel Gance will realise in ten years' time, when the evolution of our poor, maimed civilisation has shown him the terrible consequences of warmongering cinematography as it is being organised by the international commercial interests of today, casually throwing into a belligerent crucible the real and the sham, history and fantasy, sacred relics and the trappings of carnival, in order to preserve at all costs those convenient clichés of the masses which leaders of peoples need if they are to be able to mobilise them in the future. Making the strategy of massacre seem noble by romanticising it, making butchery respectable or simply fresh and enjoyable is in effect, my dear Abel Gance, taking on a heavy burden of responsibility in respect of the mothers whose children will be gunned down tomorrow.

These things have to be said to relieve the consciences of many spectators whose dignity as civilised people is beginning to be deeply wounded by Parades great and small.

But, after speaking so bluntly to the author of this portrait of Napoleon, it is only fair to stress the technical values of his achieve-

Bonaparte as Douglas Fairbanks

ment. From the purely professional point of view a film of this kind does the greatest honour to our national cinema. The assurance of its style and the power of its internal rhythm make an irresistible impact. Gance is the most courageous and the most secure of our orchestrators of visual symphonies. He sees everything on a grand scale. The magnificent counterpoint of images that he has created in the duet of the 'double tempest', when the waves of the crowd and those of the sea rise up in synchrony, will continue to be a model of this new form of writing.

At every moment he provides glimpses of new techniques and innovations whose potential cannot yet be measured. One can never praise enough his lightness of touch when the translucent silhouette of the young Bonaparte glides through landscapes of the Enchanted Isle which blend harmoniously into each other with an unforgettable smoothness. One feels that he is the master of all the techniques of shooting images which usually signal the ethnic origins of a film: German etchings, Swedish soft-points, resplendent American chromo-lithos.

Here is a writer of the screen whose dominance of his style is magnificent.

But it is especially his invention of the triple screen which, as one of the great victories of cinematic writing, demands our attention. The use he has made of it in *Napoleon* can only give an idea of its potential, since the cameras were perfected too late to allow him to exploit the

47

process as freely as he would have liked. But we see enough of it in this film to realise that the point has been made. There is an extremely valuable element of polyphony and a plurality of rhythms here which could completely transform our traditional conception of visual harmony. The monody of the optical melody is supplemented by the possibility of a notation of the music of images on three staves. That is truly revolutionary.

We can already see sketched out here what will eventually be the principal applications of so rich a technique. The triple repetition of the same phrase in unison is not the most promising of them. But others are quite remarkable. When the field of vision is stretched to left and right, as if the screen were opening wings of light, the impression that is produced electrifies a crowd. No superimpressions are needed to entrance it then. But, a moment later, the plurality of rhythms comes into play with its infinite resources. The central unit can sing a powerful melody to the double accompaniment of its two neighbours. Sometimes, on the other hand, it is a theme that superimpression – that muted tone of the image – makes it possible to overlay discreetly on the principal orchestration. At yet other times, the same phrase, turned round like a reversible counterpoint, will be played to the right and the left of the principal theme, a moving frieze suddenly as solid and as balanced as a purely decorative composition. Synchronism, delayed rhythms, stylisation, consonance, dissonance, chords, arpeggios and syncopation, all are now available to musicians of the screen who were until now restricted to elementary harmonisation and orchestration.

We must give the warmest possible welcome to this liberation of the screen's vocabulary that we owe to a French film-maker.

Napoleon will go all round the world. It will be acclaimed everywhere. I sincerely hope that spectators of all latitudes will not reserve their enthusiasm for the effects of literary grandiloquence imposed in this tumultuous fresco on the art of silence, and that they will pay homage not to a warrior who left France poorer and weaker than he found it and who stirred up throughout Europe a bitterness and hatred that we are still paying ransom for, but to the creative spirit of a young French artist, whose pacific victories will earn our country a prestige and a glory for which we will not have to pay nearly so high a price. I also hope that Abel Gance will take more carefully into account the heavy sociological responsibilities of tribunes of the screen who have at their disposal a surreptitious but irresistible power to sway audiences. And that he never forgets that by making light of the history of yesterday he is, without realising it, helping to write the history of tomorrow!

48

Emile Vuillermoz
The time machine

[. . .][31] This masterfully handled scene[32] galvanised the people who were acting in it. For someone who knows the mentality of extras, the spectacle offered by this revolutionary gathering was truly a revelation.

These improvised performers had taken their roles terribly seriously. Their costumes had given them a soul and a mentality. The personal charge of Abel Gance, an excellent conductor of men, electrified this mass, transforming it suddenly into a good conductor of emotions. These ordinary men and women instinctively rediscovered their ancestral reactions. They were carried away in a current of enthusiasm that overcame their willpower. The director played on their nerves as an orchestra conductor plays on those of his instrumentalists. This whole screaming and gesticulating mob was his. When he went up for a moment into the pulpit to give them a few simple technical explanations in a soft, husky voice, he was greeted with spontaneous cheers. Tamed and adulating, they were giving themselves body and soul to a leader.

It was an impressive moment because it was both magnificent and terrifying. It was by observing the staging of this little revolution that one understood the mechanisms of the big one.

If, that day, Abel Gance had had at his disposal 10,000 extras who had lost their heads in a blind desire to obey, he could if he had wanted have got them to take any obstacle by storm, made them invade the National Assembly or the Presidential Palace and had himself proclaimed dictator. This reconstruction of history was in fact truly a resurrection of the past. And it was indeed the true nobility of the cinema that we were witnessing because the ambition of its faithful servants must be not to imitate life as it is but to create the life of tomorrow and to recreate the life of yesterday.

THE SURREALIST: PHILIPPE SOUPAULT

While not exactly echoing the formalism of the poetic avant-garde, the Surrealists, in the later 1920s, were much more critical of the mainstream of Gance's work, dismissing it as pretentious and bombastic. Buñuel, supposedly reviewing *Napoleon* in 1927, doesn't even mention the film itself until the end of the penultimate paragraph and then only to reject it out of hand: 'This is not cinema. This turns its back on cinema. Better go and see *The Ingenue*, an American film about the amazon in love, whose finale is a discreet kiss, because it is

49

The Cordeliers sequence in *Napoleon*: production still

at least light, fresh, full of rhythmical images, and made with an intuition that is authentically cinematic.'[33] *L'âge d'or*, it was said at the time, was Buñuel's direct response to Gance's film.

Philippe Soupault, one of the most prominent members of the Surrealist group and film critic for *L'Europe nouvelle* from 1929 to 1931, wrote an equally aggressive review of *La fin du monde*,[34] matched in its hostility only by Denis Marion's in *La revue du cinéma*.[35] The message is, moreover, the same as Buñuel's: this is not cinema, or rather, more extremely, this is what cinema is not.

Marion is in some respects even more disparaging than Soupault, though both are categorical in their rejection of Gance's cinema as naively and ridiculously grandiloquent. *La roue* and *Napoleon* showed promise, *La fin du monde* does not. Clair, L'Herbier and Ruttmann had done it all before, better and less pretentiously (Soupault and Marion quote similar examples).

Gance's formal innovations are thus dismissed partly because the content is unacceptable but largely because the form itself is objectionable. The political has been pushed back into the sidelines and Gance is reproached as lacking precisely those attributes that others saw as the marks of his genius: sensitivity and intuition.

Most critics, though, were of the same persuasion as Soupault and it was left to devotees like André Lang to pick up the pieces. *La fin du*

The Cordeliers sequence: frame enlargement

monde, he writes, is superior to *Metropolis* and *Die Frau im Mond* because while Fritz Lang may be more astute, Gance has a soul. Gance subordinates his art to his mind and heart and employs all his talents as film-maker in the service of humanity.[36] Romanticism to the rescue.

After the critical and commercial disaster of *La fin du monde*, Gance did not suddenly pass over into a Night of the Living Dead. On the contrary, the 1930s were, as we saw, the most prolific stage in his career. But the keenness of the critical debate was blunted. The release of *Un grand amour de Beethoven* and *J'accuse* in 1937–8 stimulated some critics who mostly admired Gance's experiments with image and sound. Others just rejected his melodramatic romanticism. Political circumstances had changed more dramatically than critical terms of reference. Except that, for many, Gance the poet had become a prattler.

By the time Truffaut launched his defence of the sound films in the mid-1950s, the Surrealists had also changed their stance. Along with André Breton, Soupault wrote enthusiastically about Gance's experiments with polyvision.[37] This, at last, was really cinema, a transformation of our modes of perception.

Philippe Soupault
La fin du monde

I am not one of those who poke fun at people who want to produce great things and I gladly applaud the efforts of men who resolutely distance themselves from the vulgar. They are men of courage and this is especially true in the cinema. Grave perils lie in wait for ambitious producers. Abel Gance has just discovered this to his cost. This French film director enjoys a reputation which is completely unjustified if the films of his that I have been able to see over the last five years are anything to go by. He is judged with clemency and his serious misdemeanours are forgiven him because, it is claimed, he has the best of intentions. On the basis of these opinions, Abel Gance is convinced that he is a genius and he makes no bones about it, and because he believes he has genius, he has allowed himself to make a film that *he* considers a masterpiece and that I, a humble critic, find totally devoid of interest. The title of this film is quite simply *La fin du monde*, 'seen, heard and performed' by Abel Gance (that is what the posters announce). The theme is, it seems, by Mme Camille Flammarion.[38] That is unfortunate because, even though I am not very well up in the progress of astronomy, I was very much aware of the scientific improbability of this theme.

But that fades into insignificance if you compare it to the *mise en scène*. This is founded on one single idea which, I admit, is an excellent one. To prevent demonstrations of hostility, Abel Gance has orchestrated such a din that he is the only person you can hear. Apart from this piece of ingenuity, the film is painful to watch and to listen to. It is a mixture of the pretentiously naive and the blatantly unrealistic, of the pompous and the trivial. To quote just one example out of hundreds, I noticed that Gance had given the part of a banker to Samson Fainsilber, a tragedian who dictates his orders to the prime minister in stentorian tones (he orders him to decree a general mobilisation, no less. The prime minister obeys, of course).

On the other hand, to be perfectly fair, it has to be pointed out that Abel Gance has a good memory. He has remembered particularly well Ruttmann's *Melodie der Welt*, Marcel L'Herbier's *L'argent* and René Clair's *Paris qui dort*. The Stock Exchange and the Eiffel Tower figure in this film in a totally unexpected way that can be explained only in terms of these reminiscences.

This production, which is described in the programme as the first big spectacular of the French talking cinema, has pacifist aims that would provoke a favourable response if the way they are expressed did not make them ridiculous. The Estates General of the world seen,

Programme cover for *La fin du monde*

heard and performed by Abel Gance are caricatures of the Assembly of the League of Nations. The number of scenes which simply provoke laughter or make you grind your teeth is uncountable. Assuredly, for Gance nothing is sacred. Not content to be the director, Abel Gance acts an important part in *La fin du monde*. He is the poet-prophet-visionary-new Christ-revolutionary-pacifist and, to express his humanitarian ideas, he finds it necessary to weep and even to become deranged.

The other actors in this 'film' have clearly been influenced by the producer. Even when they are saying the most ordinary things, they roar and gesticulate in a way that you will not see on any stage, not even, any longer, at the Comédie Française.

I will stop there. It is sad to conclude with this last remark: *La fin du monde* cost, it seems, eighteen million francs to make. If this figure is correct, one can only feel regret at the thought that so many young directors are reduced to complete inactivity for lack of funds. I have to admit, however, that the spectators frequenting the cinema at which I saw this film did not seem unduly surprised by this production and that some sections of the audience even seemed to some extent to be enjoying it.

It was one of those evenings when, coming out of the cinema, I was inclined to agree with Georges Duhamel's dismissal of the cinema as 'entertainment for Helots'. Happily, I saw an evening paper which announced the hundredth screening of *Hallelujah* and the success of *The Blue Angel*.[39]

La fin du monde is perhaps, after all, a useful film: it will teach directors of the future that there are certain errors to be avoided.

3 Gance on Theory

Although he published only a tiny proportion of his output, Gance was, throughout his life, a prolific writer and, as Buraud's portrait shows, he considered himself as much a writer as a film-maker. In addition to a vast correspondence, his archives contain early poems, the manuscript of the notorious *Victoire de Samothrace*, so often referred to but still unpublished and unperformed, plus a quantity of unrealised screenplays and a mass of fragmentary notes of the kind published in *Prisme*. If, in comparison, his theoretical writings seem slight, it is because they consist of a series of lectures, articles, interviews and notes which remain fairly inaccessible since there is still no collected edition – and hardly anything has been translated into English. On various occasions during the 1960s and 1970s, Gance planned to weld all this material into a book which would be a kind of last will and testament, a digest of his reflections over the years on the function of cinema. Despite protracted negotiations with various publishers, including an ambitious scheme which would also have included several screenplays, and a new expanded edition of *Prisme*, the project never seems to have got beyond the planning stage.

We are left, then, with a series of occasional pieces, often hastily cobbled together in intervals between filming, lacking the rigorous argument of a consecutive text and frequently written in a turgid romantic prose, but which remain, even so, significant and influential contributions to film theory.

Gance's first piece of theoretical writing was a short article published in 1912 and clearly influenced by his friend Canudo. In it he already proclaims his belief in cinema as a new art: 'A sixth art which, in the same instant, will bring tears to the eyes of the Arab and the Eskimo with an identical suffering, and will give them at the same moment the same lesson of courage or goodness. A sixth art [. . .] which, the day an artist of genius deigns to consider it as more than just a facile source of entertainment, will propagate its faith throughout the world better than the theatre or the book.'[1] But cinema wasn't just a new art form for Gance, it was *the* new art form, the synthesis of all the others. An art which in 1912 was trying to create its own language and by 1971 had still only reached the letter 'c' in its new alphabet.[2] If progress hadn't been more dramatic, it was because of the excessive commercialisation of cinema, the pre-eminence of profitability over originality, creativity, artistic ambition.[3]

Gance is not especially original in this respect. Just as cinema as the sixth or seventh art is a commonplace in early attempts to attain respectability, the invective against the stultifying effect of philistine commercialism informs the discourse of many European writer-directors during the 1920s. Gance is, though, never simply representative. He is receptive to ideas that were 'in the air', but at the same time he is forcefully and polemically distinctive.

Firstly, in his definition of cinema as an art in progress and the art of progress, he always gives prominence not to an idea or an image but to their inseparability in what he calls an 'image-text'. He writes in 1921: 'Their [the images'] literature and their philosophy are contained within themselves and especially in between each one of them – and if I have come to prefer clothing gestures with light to dressing up words, it's because gestures and actions tell fewer psychological lies and preserve a direct significance for people's minds, whereas the grandest words, too often prostituted alas, have lost their potential and their deeper values.'[4] Refining this idea two years later, he adds: 'One has to judge images not on their material quality but also on what they express – the value of cinema is to be found not in the photography *on the surface of* the images, but in the rhythm, *between* the images, and in the idea, *behind* the image [. . .]. What one *sees* is only of secondary importance, it's what one *feels* that counts.'[5] And from there he goes on to develop, notably in his lecture of May 1928, a theory of the meaning of the image based on its context, place within sequence, lighting, depth of composition, softness or sharpness of focus.[6]

The image was, in fact, to present a new way of seeing: 'The most familiar objects have to be seen as if for the first time, producing a transmutation of all our values. This transformation of our way of looking, in an absolutely new domain unfamiliar to our senses, is in my opinion the most wonderful of modern miracles.'[7] This, then, was the poetry of the image, the ordinary made strange by the artistic use of technology, 'the translation of the invisible world by the visible world'.[8]

Gance thus takes up a position which is radically opposed to L'Herbier's declaration in his influential 1917 article 'Hermès et le silence': 'For isn't it clear to everyone that the object of cinema, art of the real, is the exact opposite [of the other arts, arts of unreality], to transcribe as faithfully and as accurately as possible, without trans-position or stylisation and with the exactitude which is specific to it as a medium, a certain phenomenological truth?'[9] For Gance, cinema had to be the fusion of all the arts, even though it might still be in a stable without even the three wise men to pay homage to it and predict its glorious future. The art of rhythm, movement and of passion, producing a visual harmony, a symphony in time and space, an art of mystery, constructing translucent images rather than repro-ducing the opaque surface of reality. It is on this idea of the distinc-tiveness of the cinematic image and its power to show the world of experience in a dramatically new way that he based his theory of montage and superimpression.

Although Gance remains close here to the impressionist theories of Epstein and Dulac, as he does in his insistence on cinema as 'the music of light', he is totally out of sympathy with certain other features of the avant-garde. For all his dynamic interest in formal experimentation, he was primarily committed to the 'democratic' aspect of cinema and in this respect is much closer to L'Herbier and especially to his mentor, Elie Faure. And it is as innovatory prac-titioner that Gance needs to be taken seriously – as someone who advocated and tried to construct a poetics of cinema while systemati-cally arguing for the inseparability of form, technology and social function. His language was unfashionable. Many of his sentiments were, already in the 1920s and 1930s, considered excessively roman-tic. His political position frequently seemed questionable. But his practice found its ultimate justification not in the skills of the techni-cian recording reality, but in the effects a film could produce for the spectator.

In an early text, undated but seemingly written before his involve-ment with cinema, Gance had already tried to formulate his aims: 'To create a new form of art which will make people lift up their eyes, because they look only at the ground where there's gold, coal and coffins, a new art to steel their courage, stimulate their energies, enlarge their prisons and suppress their twilight zones.'[10] Once he had committed himself to cinema he consistently argued for it not just as 'an essentially social and international art'.[11] It must be, above all, a *popular* art form, an art *for* the masses. Its language must in consequence evolve in terms of the spectator. Art ahead of its time has in that sense no place in Gance's theory. Art should, like Delacroix's 'Liberty', be leading the people towards a new and better world.

Cinema must be for everyone: not, as Griffith once said, 'to make folks think a little', but to transform completely their perceptions.

And cinema was a universal instrument of communion. Here, Gance went further than any of his contemporaries in advocating massive cinematic spectacles for thousands of spectators, in proposing schemes for an international cinema under the patronage of the League of Nations, in pioneering the idea of multilingual and multinational productions.[12]

An art, then, not of the people but resolutely for the people, universalist and unifying, supremely élitist in its conception of the artist. Visionary but also elemental in its reconstruction of perception, in the creation of new forms of apprehension. Fundamentally political, in spite of Gance's refusal of party labels, in its universalism, its attempts to transcend class divisions, and its attack on a mercantilist system of representations. High romanticism, but not naively above and beyond the political.

THE PRODUCER

'The Producer' is one of a series of Appendices preserved in typescript in the Gance archive, presumably annexed to the report he wrote in 1917 for the Cinematographic Section of the French Army on 'the organisation and administration of a production which could [...] render absolutely inestimable services to a France which is on its knees'.[13] Although the text is unsigned, it is a clear statement of Gance's conception of the function and essential qualities of the author-director in a popular art cinema. I have preserved Gance's terminology: what he means here by producer is, as he explains, what was already frequently called the director, and by 'editor' he is clearly referring to the producer or production company.

The Producer

However difficult and delicate his task may be, the mission of the director in the theatre is solely to exteriorise the life contained in a literary work which has its own specific value and which consists of situations and dialogues imagined by an author. The role of the Producer-Director of a film is much more complex, for even when he is not himself the author of the basic screenplay, he is essentially a creator, he 'produces' a complete work in a sequence of living images that he alone invents and structures. A cinematic[14] work which has to entertain, to appeal to emotions, to arouse the same emotions, the same pleasure, and more particularly to suggest the same interesting and sometimes profound thoughts as a stage play. We should note that these various states of the spectator's mind can be at one and the

Gance, the young producer

same time more numerous and more varied in the cinema than in the theatre.

In cinematographic art, the 'producer' (i.e. the director) is all. He is the brain that conceives and the hand that executes.

I do not think, and in this respect I disagree with some famous American specialists, that the producer must always be the sole author of the screenplay he is filming; but I do believe that, whatever the number and quality of the ideas that an author brings to a film, it is the producer, and he alone, who can, who must conceive, organise, construct his work on the basis of those ideas, selecting the ones he finds suitable, using technical means of exteriorisation which he has chosen or invented, and being directed by the dictates of his tastes, his particular talents, his personality. (And that is so true that in the work of the virtuosos of this art, an informed public can recognise the author-producer in the opening images of the film, since each of them bears his mark, an imprint that is apparent in the whole of his production.)

Let us, then, examine the multiple aptitudes that the ideal producer must possess.

Independently of the cinematographer's intuitive understanding, he must first of all possess the good novelist's capacity to organise, the broad and true conceptions of the dramatist. We would like him to have the gift of moving people and making them laugh. And although we would also wish him to be ardent and passionate, we must require, even so, that these two qualities are kept under control by two others, each of them precious and rare, *restraint* and *taste*.

In addition, the talented producer must have, as well as an innovative mind and an interest in progress, a certain culture, an ability to assimilate rapidly the documentation he will need if he is to make films set in specific and infinitely varied environments (industry, finance, science, politics, high society, etc. etc.), or if he is going to reconstitute historical settings. So often, when careful research has not to be done and checked, cinema's approximations simply provoke an ironic smile or a shrug of the shoulder!

He must at all costs possess the eye of a painter, of a sculptor, and the skill of a photographer always on the look-out for new effects.

He will need to be particularly ingenious on the technical level, for he will always have to perfect, frequently by improvising, sometimes by inventing, the equipment that is available, whether it is already tried and tested or whether it is just what happens to be at hand.

He must be a skilled actor (adapted to cinematic vision), for he will have to give meticulous guidance to all his cast about the subtleties of their parts.

We must not forget that one of the most precious secrets of cinematographic art is knowing how to make a judicious use of props, which in any synthetic conception of life are so disturbing, so eloquent, and sometimes so vital. Only an artist with a febrile imagination and a deep and subtle sensitivity will be able to produce a virtuoso sound from the delicate instrument of our art.

Even so, all these qualities would be ineffectual without one last one, 'a highly developed sense of organisation'.

60

The ability to organise a programme of work which is always extraordinarily complex, to save time and money, to exploit a given circumstance, to resolve the countless debilitating problems of personnel relations, of equipment and the *elements*, is one of the chief and one of the rarest qualities of the true professional.

That, without question, is what the really gifted producer must be like, the producer, that is, who generates faith in the future of our art.

Can we be surprised that such a complete artist is still a very rare exception and that even in the future he will always be exceptional?

I would assert that all the factors involved in the realisation of a work (screenplay, actors, technicians, equipment) depend for their value on the merits of the producer, whatever the individual merits of these different factors may be.

There is another thing.

The producer is also the only possible director of finance, the only competent accountant for the film he is making (let us not forget that he hires the actors, recruits the technicians, commissions the sets, orders the props, controls the innumerable outgoings, gratuities, etc.). He is the omnipotent financial director whose expenditure cannot be held in check.

For the work to be well executed, he must, moreover, be the only judge of the utility and the opportuneness of all his expenditure.

One can immediately see the risk for the editor in employing a producer who is prodigal, unscrupulous and insufficiently concerned about the financial side of things. Caring little if he massively increases the cost of the film he is making, and interested solely in producing a work which can bring him a great deal of personal publicity, he is, knowingly or unknowingly, quite capable of driving the editor into bankruptcy.

It will be the more easily understood, after what I have just argued about the vitally important role and the essential qualities of the producer, why, by consciously ignoring his role, French cinema has gone into decline.

THE CINEMA OF TOMORROW

Gance's most frequently quoted theoretical text on cinema is a rather rhetorical essay entitled 'Le temps de l'image est venu!', published in 1927.[15] It is, basically, a revised version of a lecture delivered the previous year, 'La beauté à travers le cinéma',[16] which itself incorporated long extracts from earlier writings. The two illustrated lectures he gave in May 1928 and March 1929 at the Université des Annales are less known but in many ways more incisive.

'The Cinema of Tomorrow' (published in *Conférencia*, xxiii, 1929) is the second of these. In it, Gance describes some of his innovations but, more importantly, he locates his practice as film-maker within an overview of the development of cinema as art. This leads to a prospective section on future developments, particularly interesting in that it was written during the transition period from silent to sound. Contrary to what is often thought, and in opposition to some of his French colleagues, Gance clearly recognises the potential of sound, welcoming it in spite of the new constraints it would impose. His concluding remarks are a radical statement on the function of cinema, illustrating particularly well his views on art in relation to politics.

The Cinema of Tomorrow

[. . .][17] Nineteen years ago – in 1910 – I wrote in one of my notebooks:

The language of silence. We will have to search for and find the language of silence, for as Schiller says: 'It is a pity that thought has first of all to be divided up into lifeless words, that the soul has to be incarnated in sounds in order to be apparent to the soul.' Spoken and written language becomes each day more outmoded and more useless. It needs something to take its place. The arts have claimed to be able to express states of mind more spontaneously and more profoundly. Music has even done this to a certain extent, but it is still inferior to the new art that we have to discover in the mystery of silence. The problem is an enormous and difficult one. As in the other arts, some foreign matter will no doubt come into play, as a kind of photographic plate that is sensitive to states of mind, but how difficult it will be for people to dissimulate and how easily they will be able to recognise their true value in their own lifetime! Words tell too many lies.

I offer you these prophecies which at the time I didn't communicate to anyone, to show you, as it were, the emergent spirit of cinema casting its light across the darkness, across the unknown. Nineteen years ago, artistic cinema hardly existed and I was totally ignorant of it. But I carried it within me, like many men of my generation, and if I'm going to talk about myself, about the discoveries I've been able to make in an immense world that is still largely unexplored, it is in an objective and entirely impersonal way, as a casual witness describing the totally unexpected horizons which sprang into view wherever you looked, at every crossroads on a fantastic journey.

At the beginning, with the first attempts to film little dramas, little comedies, or short documentaries, cinema was called 'animated photography'; scientifically, that's still what it is. But not artistically. There is art only when there is a transposition of reality. A painting, a sonata, a statue are transpositions of this feeling, of that landscape or memory. Photography, on the other hand, is not a transposition, even if it's animated: it is purely and simply reality. That's why the earliest films were not art and why those who watched them were not able to recognise what cinema was contributing to the plastic and the poetic. But wait a moment! There is another equally important reason for this inability to see: some, carried away by their enthusiasm, were already aspiring to create an 'art' cinema, but it was by copying, reproducing the processes, the gestures, the décors of the most conventional of all the arts: theatre. This is very apparent when you look at very old films: it's as though they've been made by pointing the camera at a comedy or a melodrama performed by bad actors in some small provincial theatre. And yet, in live theatre, we didn't think it was at all ridiculous or false. That's precisely because theatre has its own conventions and its own devices which we have always accepted and which make it an art. But when it comes to photographing life (at least in its banal and superficial aspects), the reproduction will never seem to have the unexpectedness, the charm, the mystery that a dramatic or operatic scene can offer.

The same was true, of course, of the first documentary films. Whether it was 'The train arriving at La Garenne-Bezons station' or 'Post office workers leaving the factory',[18] we in fact refused to see anything more in them than an amusing spectacle, or at most a curious one. Even when technique came to the aid of nature, discovering how to set, arrange and display all these precious stones – landscapes, faces, curious customs – with the help of inventions that I will tell you about later, and cinematic documentary became a captivating spectacle, it still needed something before it could accede to the dignity and the grace of the true work of art. It needed that minimal transposition effected by the eye of the poet. A documentary is only interesting to the extent that the cameraman or the director has understood and felt what is beautiful in the scene he is looking at. He translates it in his own style. And that style constitutes for the moment the whole basis of cinema's value. The event in itself counts for nothing. The way it's observed is all that matters. And hasn't that always been the case in all the arts? That is what some authors of documentaries have understood – spontaneously, because they were poets – with, at their head, Flaherty, the director of the amazing *Nanook*, which you're all familiar with, and of *Moana*, along with the

63

authors of *Chang*.[19] We are witnessing at the moment the blossoming of a new artistic genre: the lyrical documentary.

So I will draw from what I have just said some conclusions that can be formulated as follows:

> *Cinema exists only when things are interpreted without being reproduced.*
> *To the extent that all things are seen by an eye which is not human, there is interpretation and thus cinema.*

Everything else, perfection of photography, dramatic sense, plastic sense, is secondary and dependent on this first principle.

But, you may say, if cinema fundamentally consists of seeing things with an eye that isn't human, how can it be poetic? Is poetry not the world seen through our hearts? Are you not going to be led on to making us see life in a way that may well be extraordinary but which is incomprehensible?

Don't worry, I am using the word human here in its narrowest sense and I am saying that your visual faculty can escape from the monotonous circle within which it is usually confined, and can enlarge it, letting in a flood of spectacles, harmonies and forms that will completely renew the world. But how can a way of seeing go beyond the organ on which it depends?

How, as our old friend Montaigne asked, can the arm's-length be longer than the arm and the handful larger than the hand?

It is here that the 'unhuman' eye intervenes, the lens of the motion picture camera. This lens allows us to see, projected on to the screen, a scene that corresponds to the normal laws of vision, but, at the same time, it sees this scene in its own way and, if you will allow an expression that is only a slight exaggeration, it sees things the way it wants to. It is on this very curious phenomenon that the whole art of cinema depends. It's for this reason that cinema can make discoveries, that it can grasp movements, unexpected relationships between things, and that, thanks to it (if we respect it absolutely) the banality of ordinary, everyday spectacles disappears. That is why this face looks like a flame, a landscape, an apparition, a song, why the walls of that house become transparent, and the hearts of those who live within them become transparent too, and the secret images and thoughts of those hearts become visible, as visible and real as our wives and children. Cinematography demands a constant transposition of our ways of seeing into a space that is absolutely new and unknown to our senses. You have to have mastered the technicalities

64

of the camera and know what it can do before you can go any further because from that moment on, an object, without losing its own identity, is not only what it is but becomes an image of the world. Everything can be seen from a better angle, and is cinema not above all the art of discovering for each specific thing the angle that enriches it, shifting it away from the known world of human appearances, transposing it into a lyrical sphere, letting it offer up to our view a new and unsuspected world? You will notice that I speak of cinematic vision as if it were just an effect of the camera and also a conscious effort on the part of the director. Both are true, and cinema owes and always will owe its originality to the close collaboration between the artist and his camera.

In cinema, truth, even if it is captured by the microscopes and antennas of our cameras' visual intuition, is indeed not enough – even the most eloquent tableau, the most pitiful and unexpected expression, the most horrific catastrophe – if there is not art alongside the spectacle. There has to be as much originality in the recording as in what is being recorded, and it is this matching that happens so rarely. Around the steel brain of the camera, a whole ultra-sensitive life must circulate, transforming photography into art. That is the miracle. I will define cinema, then, as: a spontaneous and immediate poetry, taken from nature by the motion picture camera and absorbed, reflected, transformed by the human heart.

This poetry of images and light is like that of sounds: music was discovered through the ages by the Christopher Columbuses of harmony, and these new harmonies, which they drew straight from nature, were used to express the secret dramas of their hearts.

The screen is, in essence, only a mirror in which we can show the best image of ourselves. And this image is multiplied, transformed, transported into worlds of movement that spring up at every moment within our own world with as great a variety as the patterns in a kaleidoscope, and infinitely.

As I already said to you, I think, on an earlier occasion, we have atavistically inherited centuries of education of the ear for music, centuries of education of the eye for painting, and for cinema we have twenty-five years of astonishment. At this moment we are asking far more of sight than it can give us. The eyes of most people are not yet ready for cinema, and it is ignorance of this fact that accounts for all the present inadequacies of our art. The men of genius who will emerge in this art will have as their mission to give cinema to people's eyes, just cinema, but cinema in its entirety, and to imprint it on them using that magical force of persuasion that will be their secret.

La roue: the mirror as indiscretion

It is thanks, then, to some haphazard discoveries, to certain tricks of the camera, that the first film-makers were able to discern in the spectacle of ordinary life things which painters may have been dimly aware of in the past but which most of us have absolutely no knowledge of. [. . .] Cinema allows us to see or at least to glimpse [. . .] aspects of the great and immortal enchantment that is the real life of nature. And the various techniques that film-makers use and that you will all have at least vaguely heard of – artificial or mixed lighting, superimpressions, slow and fast motion, modes of editing, mobile cameras, etc. – are merely ways of imitating, or sometimes simply of recording, the most mysterious and intimate phenomena of nature. That is why a human drama unfolded with the aid of these techniques, in an absolutely new space, fascinates and disturbs us at the same time: it's precisely this double impact that the earliest works of cinematographic art had on their spectators. They were deliberately turning their backs on theatre, on sentimental conventions, on novelistic stereotypes, which does not mean that a true film mustn't be human; on the contrary, for our sufferings, our loves, our hopes are thus multiplied, transposed, magnified, cast out beyond the tiny prison of our existence towards unknown worlds.

What, then, did we film-makers need, to liberate ourselves from a theatrical or purely pictural view of life so that we could create

66

cinema? In theory, very little: some movements imprinted on the diaphragm of our cameras or on the cameras themselves, a series of shots from the same scene or different scenes juxtaposed on a single image. The effect of all that is completely to disrupt the way we represent life. Compare a painting of a train rushing through the night and the passage on the screen of the same train, with its thousands of images giving views of the outside, the engine, the vertiginous motion of the wheels, the carriages, and of the inside, the compartments, the faces of travellers and what they are doing, the dreams of those who are sleeping and the thoughts of those who are awake, all that in rapid succession, juxtaposed, intercut, an incessant flood of images interspersed with flashes of light, smoke, glimpses of the landscape, speeded up by rapid montage and transformed by novel camera angles – and tell me which contains the maximum of reality and life. Well, to produce such effects, to impress such visions on the eye, we have invented techniques or, if you prefer, we have made discoveries which I will enumerate for you simply, leaving the screen to comment on them itself, to demonstrate what will seem self-evident but which mere words could never describe. The enumeration of these discoveries constitutes a very abridged history of the progress of the art of cinema. Close-ups, simultaneity, etc. . . .

You all know the close-up, the astonishing appearance on the screen of the brow, the lips, the eyes of a character who seems to want to go beyond its limits, to lean out of the canvas. The first time a director dared to use the close-up systematically throughout a whole film, it was a real revolution in cinema: a new means of psychological expression, with an extraordinary resonance and an amazingly vibrant subtlety, had been created. Nowadays we don't pay much attention to it. These hallucinations seem quite normal. That's because we are already in the domain of the real enchantment I asked you to cultivate in yourselves. The close-up in cinema is the equivalent of the mask in Greek tragedy.

Then the close-up was directed not just towards the human face but towards objects, and the way the camera was placed in relation to these objects brought them alive, made them as expressive and mysterious as faces.

And then cinema began to explore the depths of mystery, what my friend Maurice Maeterlinck calls in a wonderful book he published recently, the life of space.[20] That was the discovery of *reimpression* or *superimpression*: you remember those images that you see one through the other, like shadows through which other transparent and fluid images appear, transfiguring the harsh, dull and almost empty space

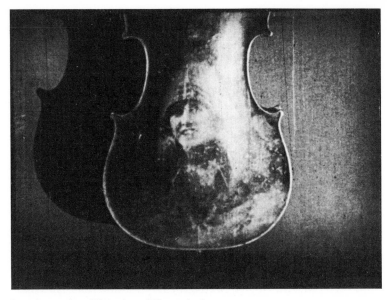

Superimpression: Elie's view of Norma in *La roue*

in which we live, turning it into a new, musical, rich and yet real environment, like the premonitory and visionary space of our dreams. Even when it's combined with simultaneous shots – that is, the extremely rapid succession of scenes taking place in quite different places – superimpression can itself evoke the secret and magical life of the immense space in which our bodies and our souls evolve and put a new face on the drama of human life.

So here we are, carried away like bold navigators into the living heart of space, that is, into movement. And is movement not, in fact, drama? Movement, in art, is rhythm. The possibility of inventing new rhythms, of encapsulating the rhythms of life, of intensifying them and varying them infinitely, becomes, at a given moment, the essential problem for cinematographic techniques. I think I resolved this by inventing what has since been called rapid montage. It was in *La roue* that I think we saw on the screen for the first time those images of a runaway train, of anger, of passion, of hatred that follow one another with increasing rapidity, one image generating another in an unpredictable rhythm and order, an eruption of visions which, at the time, people thought of as apocalyptic and which are now as common in our cinematographic syntax as enumeration or exclamation in literary syntax. [...]

Superimpression: the Double Tempest and Toulon sequences in *Napoleon*

Above: the camera on horseback. *Below*: Superimpression: the snowball fight in *Napoleon*

That wasn't enough. We had to go still further in the transposition of movement. The camera, the only thing that remained motionless, simply recording all the incredible events that were taking place around it, had to take its place in the dance. We made it move, and I think I am one of the people who impelled it most forcefully into the centre of life's spectacle; I put it on a trolley, I rolled it along the ground like a football, I harnessed it to the neck, to the back of galloping horses, I suspended it from a wire like a pendulum and made it turn on its axis in space; I made it go up and come down, I propelled it into the air like a cannonball, thrust it towards a breast like a sabre, threw it into the sea, strapped it to a man and made it walk, run, turn its head, raise its lenses heavenwards; I made it into a living person, a brain, and most of all, I tried to turn it into a heart.

A heart. That reminds me of the prediction of a mystic: 'When the machine has become a mind, the world will be saved.' At least, when the time has come, our art will fly with its own wide-open wings.

I am going to show you the snowball fight from *Napoleon*, a sequence that cinema managers thought it necessary to excise from the film. I would be pleased if you could overcome the visual exhaustion engendered by fifteen hundred juxtaposed shots and understand that the camera was not a witness but an actor in the drama, that it took part in the battle, that it smiled, that it was victorious alongside the young Napoleon, like an inquisitive archangel with a memory of fire. [. . .]

Do you now understand why the world in which we ordinarily live is so poor? It's because we cannot escape from ourselves; we perceive it only through our eyes, those high windows of our prison. Around us there are a thousand, a hundred thousand wonderful worlds that live in the brains of other people, but we can't have access to them. Let us suppose that it's possible, at least in fragments, in flashes, and that we can install ourselves instantaneously beneath the brow of this person, or that one, or the one over there, while still being able to return to our own point of view: what magic, what an extraordinary sequence of visions! That is what cinema can achieve with its mobile cameras, filming from ten different positions, juxtaposing and overlapping shots. You can see what is unique in this art. That is why we must not be afraid of forging ahead.

I have often in my films used more advanced and more daring techniques than my comrades. Essentially these techniques consist in bringing the fundamental laws of rhythm into the foreground. As you saw, this tendency is manifested in *La roue* through accelerated montage. In *Napoleon* it is apparent in the mobility and increasing independence of the camera and in a special use of superimpressions which reveals, overlaid on the characters and their faces, the translucent image of their passions and their thoughts, as if, as Nietzsche so admirably put it, the soul was indeed enveloping the body.

Here, the image of the soul takes precedence over bodies, it's the link between them, it runs and leaps from one to the other like a flame and it's the great hearth in which these beings take shape that I would like to evoke through drama. In the sequence of the snowball fight for example, pure rhythm tends to overlay the anecdotal; the incessant creation of plastic and musical forces envelops the visual narrative, multiplying it, pushing it towards infinity so that the narrative serves only as a pretext for the dazzling arabesques to which it gives rise and for the magical bursts of light which ultimately efface it.

Violating most of our usual ways of seeing, I have at such moments speculated, then, on the rapid and simultaneous perception of the images by my audience, not just in a second but sometimes in a quarter or even an eighth of a second. The eyes of this generation can hardly bear the strain of these moments of paroxysm, but we have to construct this visual counterpoint which our children will consider elementary and which can to a great extent be apprehended even now if we are attentive enough.

I mention visual counterpoints because cinema is increasingly tending to equate itself with music. A great film has to be conceived like a symphony, like a symphony in time and a symphony in space. An orchestra is made up of a hundred instruments, of sections that play different parts together. Cinema has to become a visual orchestra, as rich, complex and monumental as those that play in concerts. Well, through superimpression, of which you have just seen some examples, it has tried to compete with music, juxtaposing shapes, like instruments in space, transparent visions that are contrasted or confronted, that merge, that die and are resurrected in a living harmony. But that was not enough, since these visual harmonies had always to be overlaid on the same confined and uniform surface.

That is when I invented the triple screen. And visual harmony became symphonic. I could project three separate but synchronised images on three screens arranged like a triptych and thus broaden considerably the field of our spiritual vision. Note that I say spiritual and not pictorial because it isn't the dimensions of the field of action that count but the creation of visual harmonies, the transporting of the spectator's imagination into a new and sublime world. By combining superimpression and triptych vision, I was actually able in the double tempest sequence of my *Napoleon* to compose an apocalyptic fresco, a mobile symphony in which, with eight superimpressions per

72

frame, there were sometimes twenty-four interconnected visions.

[. . .] The characters in a truly cinematic work will increasingly have to give us the same impression as a flower [filmed in accelerated motion], the impression of living forces, of souls, of sensibilities evolving in sinuous lines within a space of wonderment. It is within this space that, through drama, comedy and love, they will find their balance and discover their harmony. But we should never forget that at the centre of all these images there must be a heart that beats. Beauty does not arrive on the screen by accident. It has to have, as it were, an excuse for being there.

This excuse is drama. A dramatic skeleton is needed beneath the beauty of the features, and in cinema even more than in the other arts beauty alone, without the skeleton, is not enough.

It is not the images that make a film but the soul and the mind of the images and that is why some works leave a hidden trace whereas very beautiful visions do not remain in the memory for more than a week. Very beautiful films do not need to have beautiful images. They act through a kind of secret emanation which passes between them: the genie of the heart. Why? It's because an image, even when it's an animated one, can rarely convey emotion on its own. It can produce a great deal of it by drawing on the emotion supplied by the images that precede and follow it. All is movement, rhythm, transience. Everything in cinema is drama.

What then are the future dramas that the new art will reveal to us? They will be dramas of space. I mean that human beings will struggle, love, suffer, grow in stature and die in this wondrous environment, in this theatre of universal enchantment. They will depend entirely on it – they will love, suffer, grow in stature and die through it. Already, if you look closely at the psychology of great works of cinema, you will notice the all-powerful role of milieu, but of a new and extraordinary milieu.

The procedures of the cinematographic drama are the opposite of those of the novel and the theatre. Everything comes from the outside. First of all there are drifting mists, then an atmosphere that grips you, stopping you in your tracks, and from it the drama emerges. The earth is formed, people do not yet exist. Kaleidoscopes are formed; a selection is made between them and a few details are kept, wicked, splendid, soothing or treacherous. They carry within them the seeds and mechanisms of the drama that is about to come into being.

Antitheses are established. A snow-covered landscape will engender a landscape of soot and railway lines. Complementary aspects merge. The drama can then be born in the atmosphere. It is on this crest or in this stream, in this hovel or in this desert, on this boat or in this locomotive. We have only to create the human machines that will live it out. People pass by, mysterious but necessary inhabitants of these chosen environments. They are insubstantial and are so indistinguishable from their surroundings that we do not yet know whether it is they or the things which will speak. They are the same colour as the things that surround them, they are their perfume and their voice. And now attention, poetry, creative suffering condense on them, stop them in their tracks; and now, suddenly, as I look at them, they exist, and they exist all the more vividly since they are the children of the things they will base themselves on. The drama takes shape, psychology takes its place, the human machines are ready, the heart gradually starts to beat: the art of cinema begins.

And just as man is born, struggles and loves in the space whose true conformities I have sketched out, so he will be transformed and die. What else can we do to penetrate deeper into this unknown world and to transfigure it with the rays of our hearts, to raise it to the heights? What will be the technical inventions of the future?

One of them is at this very moment being developed and tested out. I won't say much about this one: it's colour. A very good French process – Keller-Dorian[21] – is beginning to open up new magical horizons, the possibility of animating paintings of Rubens, Rembrandt, Delacroix, of all the giants of yesterday, today and tomorrow.

[. . .] The talking picture, synchronised sound are in the process of modifying completely the prospects of cinema. Commercial prospects first and then its artistic horizons. Don't wave your arms in the air and tell me that films with dialogue will signal the death of silent cinema.

There is one thing that I can predict: over a very protracted period, cinema, with all the resources it has already acquired, will be trying to unite in an effective way universal music and spoken drama. The conditions of the artistic production of films and of their distribution will as a result be radically changed. The magnetic pole of cinema is beginning to oscillate and to shift . . .

But, as is often the case, a new and better order will result from this revolution. There will inevitably be a critical reaction against the excesses of this change (bad taste, or a return to theatrical conventions) but fantastic discoveries will have been made, amazing horizons revealed, and even the enemies of sound cinema will realise that the new approaches it has generated have prepared the ground for the great synthesis of the future.

But what I see happening in the near future is the introduction of three-dimensional images, images that are dense, spherical, which revolve in space like the real bodies around us that we can touch. That will be achieved by the union of cinematography and stereoscopy. I know that the problem is like a tunnel being bored from both ends at once and in darkness by optics and physiology. But I feel, I know that they are working only a few years away from each other now, behind a wall whose thickness is gradually diminishing and that soon the light of truth will shine through the open breach. On that day we will see new wonders.

Images will be projected in space, in colour and three dimensions, and their different planes will be held on a series of transparent screens according to their degrees of intensity.

... Not only will human beings speak but also animals, plants, even inanimate objects will have a voice to express their joy, their suffering, their love.

In the meantime, while we are waiting for these happy times, drama and victory in the cinema are always created alongside what we are searching for. Our art cannot yet breathe because it lacks perspective. I mean in terms of the screen. The day three-dimensional cinema is discovered, cinema will exist, not before. Then, the sense of real enchantment will be a little more developed, we will be able to see a little further into the distance.

Instead of just being aware of that wonderful space I have been referring to, we will live in it. The three-dimensional will in fact, to all intents and purposes, suppress the screen; we will no longer see characters and landscapes glide across a flat surface, across a wall. This wall will no longer exist: the characters and landscapes will really come out towards us and, no longer held back by the wall, they will enter the auditorium, come close to us; horses that rear up will really raise their hooves above our heads, rivers will really flow out over there into the sea.

And all this will remain fluid, transparent, fantastic; superimpressions will create crystal-like beings that will pass through each other, waves will bring looks, eyes, hearts, souls rolling to our feet ... The crowd will respond as one man; the chorus of antiquity will be resurrected. The soul of the spectators will merge with that of characters and objects; all will participate in the drama through the magic of their hallucination and they will have to restrain themselves from crying out and replying to the voices issuing from these beings, from this prodigious nature that is as real as they are.

For a new invention is, as you know, just coming into being: sound cinema. Oh yes, still very crude, very imperfect, as far from the way I imagine it as the experiments of Marey and Lumière from the present masterpieces of our art. But it is the indispensable addition, the crowning feature in the aesthetic synthesis that the cinema of tomorrow will achieve. I make an impassioned call for the great symphony of sound and vision which, recording synchronically the noises, roars and murmurs of natural forces, the clamour or stifled complaints of the crowd, the song of the birds, the melody of springs, the clatter of trains, the sobs, the cries of men or the virgin's solitary refrain, will make them a part of its own substance, increasing its internal radiance and its divine energy, and carrying them off in its eternal stream.

Colour, universal sounds, images in relief, multiple screens, it is in the synthesis of these that I see the shape of the cinema of the twentieth century sketched out. I cannot yet tell you everything that I can see or just sense. I would like to be able to express all the inexpressible things that sometimes vibrate inside me. Alas, my friends, it isn't possible! Let me at least, in concluding, describe to you some of the harmonies I hear and filter a few more rays of light for you.

1. Cinema is an art of the people
In cinema, the crowd must first judge and experience, and it is only later that the minds of the élite will understand. Just as with popular songs like 'Au clair de la lune' and 'Si le Roi m'avait donné'. The intellectual who is present at their birth often disdains them or dismisses them and it's only when they have been consecrated by the crowd through long use that he tries, often in vain, to grasp their essence. With the screen, we too are appealing to deep and powerful currents, to the universal soul, a pure fragment of which shines brightly in every simple soul, whereas its presence is always more or less doubtful in the soul of the critic . . .

2. Cinema is the art of light
Light is the only element that travels from world to world, and through it, through a painstaking observation of it, we can discover many secrets. Cinema is a forge of light, a luminous symphony, at once physical and spiritual. How can you kill light to examine it under a microscope? How can you isolate it? Problems as difficult as this have been resolved in other fields during the last few years. Cinema will resolve them for the art of the future. One day, thanks to it, light will be considered as the only real character in every drama. The creative and transfiguring force in every destiny.

76

Every day, while I was making *Napoleon*, people from all walks of life dropped in at the studio. They came in with a smile on their faces as if this was some kind of music-hall. They left, more often than not, looking serious, thoughtful, not to say meditative, as if some hidden god had suddenly opened a golden door for them. They had seen for themselves how the drama of light and shadow is fabricated, with more trials and tribulations than even reality brings to us in our own homes. They had seen how eyes become rose windows in which souls burn flamboyantly, sudden close-ups, the great organ of emotion, and how, with faith, one can turn a studio into a true cathedral of light.

Explain, comment on that? What would be the use? We are racing along on horses of cloud. Stay on the ground or follow us. The eye of Merlin the magician has been changed into a lens.[22] I beg you, my friends, look around you and inside yourselves. Look closely. How many spectators saw in *La roue* only stories of railway engines and train accidents! How can they not have seen, between these images, catastrophes of the heart, so much more poignant and elevated! A shot in soft focus leads this same public to say 'What a pretty photograph!' Whereas it is often simply a shot blurred by tears. In the cinema, the heart is still too far from the eyes. The artist is a temple: his sufferings enter as women and emerge as goddesses. Our images must attempt to immortalise our impressions, so that they can be fixed indelibly in time.

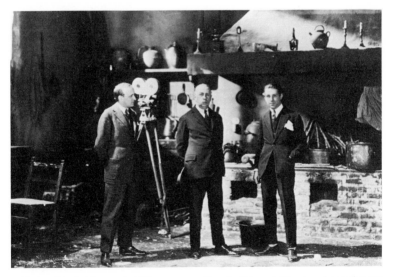

A distinguished visitor at the Billancourt studios: the Prince de Bourbon (centre) poses on the Brienne kitchen set with Albert Dieudonné (left) and Gance (right)

For thirty years, the light of day has been our prisoner and we have been trying to make it repeat its most thrilling songs on our screens, during the night. As Canudo said to me, we have done all the additions of practical and sentimental life. We have married art and science, applying one to the other, to capture and fix the rhythms of light. That is cinema. The seventh art is thus the reconciliation of all the others. We are living the first hour of the new dance of the muses around the new youth of Apollo, a dance of sounds and light around an incomparable hearth: our modern soul.

3. Cinema is an art for the whole of humanity
All legends and all myths, all the founders of religions and indeed all religions, all the great figures of history, all the objective reflections of the imagination of peoples, are awaiting their resurrection to the light, and heroes jostle at the door waiting to enter. The whole life of dream and the dream of life are ready and waiting to rush on to the light-sensitive strip and it isn't just a flippant remark to suggest that Homer would have chosen it for the *Iliad* and the *Odyssey*.

To bring about these great associations of images is to create for the whole of humanity a unique memory, a kind of music of faith, of hope, of recollections. All the visionaries, poets and heroes the world has known must become presences for ever-increasing crowds, must talk to them, come and take them by the hand. Even philosophy is possible in motion pictures: you can show people Plato's Republic, Karl Marx's socialist state or the kingdom of Zarathustra. Conceptions of happiness have to become objective, real. Cinema can explain life like the Bible and the Gospels. And like music, it can and will become an instrument of universal communion. I can't do better, in concluding, than apply to my own art Edouard Herriot's fine words on music:[23]

The obstacle of language, which has done so much to divide people, has disappeared. The cinematographer speaks a language that is accessible to everyone, a language beyond which there is only the play of numbers and the silent oscillation of the spheres. The veil of words has fallen. All the material elements of expression have disappeared. There is nothing here which is not pure idea, pure feeling. On this level, all men can come together.

But beneath the variety of men, there is man himself. He has, after all, so many ways of suffering and weeping. ...

May cinema help us to realise that superior form of human civilisation that is called peace! May it make new and pacific conquests! May it go beyond the élitist spirit and enter into the hearts of all nations and peoples.

The difficult problem will always be how to gauge each people's psychological possibilities of assimilation. Some great films will wait at the frontier of certain countries for many years before being given a passport. Once again genius will pay the same eternal ransom. Its wealth is fortunately sufficient to allow it to be patient.

My next film, *La fin du monde*, will try to respond to the conception that I have sketched out for you. This tragedy of modern times will allow me to use to the full all the wonderful equipment of the cinema of tomorrow. I like to think that, after this new letter which I will be trying to add to our alphabet, sound, colour, human voices and the musical silence of images will interpenetrate even more to create the great symphonies of the future. [. . .][24]

DEPARTURE TOWARDS POLYVISION

Apart from the triptych sequences in *Napoleon*, Gance made only a few short experimental films for the triple screen, based on existing footage and shown in 1928 at the Studio 28, the only cinema permanently equipped to screen them. After that, it was not until the mid-1950s that Gance returned to his invention, with *14 Juillet 1953*, a re-edited version of the final *Napoleon* triptych (1955), and *Magirama* (1956), a programme of short films in polyvision realised in collaboration with Nelly Kaplan.[25] During these years, which seemed to mark a new departure in Gance's career after a long period in the wilderness, he and Nelly Kaplan wrote extensively on the potential of polyvision as the basis of a new kind of cinema, notably the text of a speech published in the *Cahiers du cinéma* (no. 41, December 1954), a short extract from which is reproduced here.

Worth noting is that Gance places less emphasis on the panoramic image at a time when CinemaScope was beginning to invade the European market, than on lateral montage.

Departure towards Polyvision

[. . .] We have seen millions, perhaps even billions of images in their vertical order – and, in the long run, they have reached the point where they begin to devour each other, leaving us only with the formless haze of memories like rose patterns of kaleidoscopes retained in children's eyes. If, then, I no longer believe very much in the impact of an image, I do believe in the flash produced by the collision of two or several images: conferring on us that miraculous power – the gift of ubiquity. This sense of the fourth dimension allows us to suppress the notion 'time/space' and to be everywhere and in every-

thing in the same fraction of a second. This 'tearing out' of our usual
ways of thinking and seeing will cure the illness of our souls. I can
predict for you delirious displays of enthusiasm as fantastic as those
which perhaps the Greek tragedians experienced in their immense
theatres in front of 20,000 breathless spectators. The cinema, whether
we like it or not, is moving towards those great spectacles in which the
spirit of peoples will be forged on the anvil of collective art. The
success of drive-ins in the USA is a foretaste of this.

By introducing this visual music in the form of a counterpoint like
the intervention of the chorus in ancient Greek tragedy, *polyvision* will
suddenly open wide the eyes of modern man who no longer believes in
miracles. You only need to re-read Nietzsche's *Birth of Tragedy* to
understand that the way ahead is the one I am indicating.

The emotional impact of simultaneous horizontal montage can be
equal to the square of that produced by alternating images in the
usual form of montage. If the public is undeniably satiated and, as a
result, is deserting existing cinemas, its hunger is no less keen if the
food on offer is different and richer. I offer its visual appetite the new
language of *polyvision*. Unsuspected territories are going to be opened
up, incredible worlds of poetry are going to be revealed, overturning
worn-out values. The cinema-as-movement, disdained since the
beginning of the talkies, is going to reclaim its extraordinary preroga-
tives, triumphant in its struggle with the spoken word; and although
the latter will not of course disappear, it will once again be subservient. In 1955, cinema is going to play the card of *polyvision* as in the
fourteenth century music played the card of polyphony, and won.

In the little stream of the single-screen narrative, I can open
at will the sluices of all the subsidiaries that simultaneous visual
orchestration places at my disposal. The narrative at first absorbed,
submerged, then rids itself of everything that was holding back
its progress and becomes simply the pearl or the diamond of
foam that resurfaces when it is needed on the crest of the waves: that
is *polyvision*.

True cinema can then reassume its right over the storyteller. Is
painting not also the art of showing things? For centuries the picture
tried to be a frozen narrative. Just look at its development. It doesn't
need narrative any more, or at least it uses only a contracted, synthetic narrative in which colour seeks to predominate. The impotence of
cinema, in my view, was precisely that it was hidebound by narrative.
Imagine a man like McLaren – whom I rank as a genius in our art and
who makes pure cinema using the simplest resources – suddenly able
to use the new range of forces that *polyvision* offers: it would be
overwhelming. What could Cocteau not do with these new instru-

ments of the visual orchestra? And there are a handful of other great film directors and authors that come to mind, although they are still in the limbo of the single image and no doubt a long way from the beam of new hopes that I am directing towards their talent.

I am not pretending that a story, and even a good story, is not necessary in a *polyvisual* film; I am simply saying that cinema must not be sacrificed to narrative and that we must give to narrative the wings of poetry. So far these wings have been for me like a penguin's flippers. [. . .]

Polyvision is a new, more concise, more nuclear and more lyrical way of telling a story. [. . .]

4 Gance as Author-Director

Gance's screenplays provide a wealth of information about his approach to film-making. Although some of the early ones are lost, almost all the scripts for the feature films from 1917 onwards have survived, often in several versions: outline, manuscript first draft, corrected typescript, shooting script with further manuscript amendments. Alongside these there are rough drafts, technical notes, instructions to assistants and a mass of other material relating to the production of the film.

The screenplays themselves are remarkable for their degree of specificity, even in the numerous instances when the film never reached the production stage. The most elaborate of them, the 1948 script of *La divine tragédie*, gives for example details not just of sets, camera placings and movements, but of the exact duration of each shot in seconds or, in rapid montage sequences, in number of frames. Special effects, sound, music, even the measurements of a miniature to be used in an insert, are all meticulously described. Yet apart from some screen tests, nothing was ever filmed.

Perhaps the most striking feature of the scripts, though, is their 'literariness' – not that they are novelistic but that they are verbal equivalents of the image. Many of Gance's observations are clearly there for self-guidance. Others are simply intended to provide the 'professional' reader (producer, advisers, cast, crew) with basic information about what the film will be like. But many, often the majority, are addressed to a more general reader, the reader of an 'image-text' which hasn't yet found its image, which may never find it, but which will survive as a support for an imaginary image. Thus a number of the scripts, including *La divine tragédie* and *Cyrano et d'Artagnan*, are prefaced by an 'Address to the reader'; and most, even the unrealised projects, could be published more or less as they stand.

What all have in common is their directiveness. It is not just that Gance prescribes what kind of shot, angle, gesture, expression or edit is needed; he spells out what *must* be the reaction of the spectator, real or imaginary, specifying a position for him/her with some calculation.

In the selection of extracts, my main concern has been to illustrate this directiveness as the driving force behind different techniques of montage and *mise en scène*. As far as possible I have also tried to provide examples which raise and complicate the political issues involved.

LA ROUE

Although there is no evidence that the original screenplay of *La roue* was destroyed, there is no reference to it in the inventories of Gance's papers drawn up in the 1960s, and only fragments survive in his archive. Copies may well exist in other collections, but none has so far been traced. Before the manuscript disappeared, however, some extracts were published, by Charles Ford (in *On tourne lundi* and the book on Gance he co-authored with René Jeanne[1]) and by Gance himself in the text of his lecture 'Comment on fait un film'.[2] The latter, 'The death of Norma Compound', is translated here.

Interestingly, it is precisely this segment of the film that René Clair singles out for its 'excessive' sentimentality (the locomotive that says yes and no). But it also illustrates Gance's experiments with rapid montage and the literary transposition of images.

Comparing the screenplay of this sequence with the film as re-edited in 1922, Roger Icart suggests it was only after his visit to the United States in 1921 and the encounter with D. W. Griffith that Gance fully developed his theory of montage.[3] This may indeed be the case since, Icart claims, there are almost three times as many shots in the final edit. Even so, the screenplay would seem to indicate that Gance had already decided three years earlier that at key moments in his film he would use rapid cutting and rhythms accelerating to a sequence of shots of only two frames each. In the absence of the manuscript one can't be categorical, but various elements in the published text appear to confirm that this is indeed an extract from the original screenplay written in the autumn of 1919, notably the name of the alcoholic fireman (Buveurdot here, later changed to Machefer) and references to effects Gance would like to achieve but is not sure are possible.

Its principal interest in the present context is a combination of sentiment and excitement, what Clair calls romanticism juxtaposed to the dynamics of rapid montage. The extract illustrates the gradual shift, interspersed with comedy, from a slow, sentimental rhythm through rapid cutting and back to an atmosphere of tranquillity, a feature that will be examined in chapter 7.

La roue (The death of Norma Compound)[4]

Background title: *The Language of Locomotives.*

American shot.[5] Sisif sitting in front of the smoke-box stops eating and talks to his engine.

My eyesight's going, old girl, I can't see more than thirty yards and they're trying to make me leave you.

Close-up of the whistle valve rising. As it whistles, the steam says (if possible a superimpression in black on the smoke):[6]

No, Sisif . . . No, Sisif . . . No, Sisif.

A strident blast of the whistle.

Close-up. Sisif. He listens and understands. He moves up closer to her and after looking round to make sure no one else is listening, he caresses her brass pipes and says feverishly:

Wouldn't you rather die than be handed over to Jacobin?[7]

Continuation of the close-up. He looks to see what the reply is.

Close-up of the chimney. Suddenly there's smoke coming out of it, then a pause, then smoke that seems to be saying:

Oh . . . yes. Oh . . . yes. Oh . . . yes.

Smoke.

Sisif reflects. How might she die? . . .

Close-up. Sisif listening. His look expresses his thanks. He continues to reflect while he is eating.

(Iris out)

THE ROSE OF THE RAIL

Iris in. Elie standing near the embankment as in shot 21 of the prologue. He sees – superimpression – Sisif holding in his arms little Norma wearing her crushed hat. The vision disappears. Elie sighs and looks.

The wild rose with the magnificent flower in the place of the one that Sisif had picked while rescuing the little girl on the night of the accident.[8]

American shot. Elie hesitates, then picks the flower; he looks at it fervently and sits down on the embankment where the father was.

(Iris out)

ACCENTUATE

Background title: *The Death of Norma Compound.*

Dissolve into Buveurdot[9] reading a book, about ten yards away from the engine which is taking on water.

American shot. Sisif. He is looking round: no one can see him; you can tell he's ready to put his plan into effect; he opens the steam valves and pulls the lever to start the engine moving.

84

The engine pulls away. The water-feed carries on pouring into empty space. Buveurdot runs up, scared stiff and waving his arms in the air.

Close-up. Sisif, gritting his teeth, opens the valves even more; the engine speeds up.

The signal box. Buveurdot rushes up in a panic and manages to blurt out:

Sisif's gone mad and driven off on No. 7. How are the points set?

American shot. The signalman turns round, looks at his board and says, phlegmatically:

He's the only one that will get smashed up. He's heading for the sidings, track 17.

Close-up of the control board with details of tracks.

Close-up of Sisif bent forward and peering ahead.

(You can see in the distance the buffers which are indeed getting closer.)

The buffers in the siding, in the distance, get rapidly closer and closer.

Close-up. Panicking, Buveurdot stares at the engine, a black spot in the distance, tugs at his hair and talks to himself.

Close-up. Sisif. He is calm now, standing with his arms crossed, staring at:

The medallion: Norma – London.

The buffers get closer.

Long shot of the approaching engine.

The driving wheels.

The tracks.

The buffer stops get closer and closer.

Shot of Sisif, still calm and with his arms folded.

Close-ups of connecting rods, wheels, smoke, the tracks. Special technique. A rhythmical and accelerating montage going from shots of one second to a tenth of a second.

A terrified peasant walking along the road sees:

The engine crash into the buffers and break up.

Close-up. Sisif. He is leaning his head against the control levers. Fragments of broken machinery fall over him. He takes his hands away from his eyes, blood is streaming from his forehead but he is alive. He gradually comes round and gets out to see if he has really killed Norma.

The engine is groaning with pain like a wounded animal. Sisif walks round it and stops in front of the smoke-box.

The smoke-box door is open; the engine has as it were come to a halt in a field of flowers that reaches the top of the buffers. Every-

La roue: the death of Norma Compound

where, in the smoke-box, on the wheels, there are flowers, carnations, roses, daisies, poppies.

A series of close-ups of Norma's injuries.

Sisif. His distress. He talks to her gently.

Shot of the engine groaning like a sick dog.

Close-up. Sisif up near the chimney which is smoking again.

Shot of the smoke puffed out in long spasms as if they were the last gasps of agony, and saying:

Oh ... Goodbye Sisif ... oh ... Goodbye ... Sisif ...

Heart-rending shot. Sisif talking to her like a father to a dying child: 'Goodbye, old girl ...'

Close-up of the peasant rushing up; he stares at this man with blood on his brow and who is talking to his engine, takes fright and as he runs off drops the spade he was carrying on his shoulder.

Close-up. Sisif. His face is bathed in tears. He is still talking to her in a soft voice as if to soothe her pain.

Shot of the chimney. At first there is still smoke, then nothing. She is dead.

Long shot, revealing the cypress trees that surround the bank Norma crashed into.

The flowers in the smoke box.

Buveurdot arrives on the scene. He stops short, looks around and takes off his cap with a simplicity that will bring tears to the spectator's eyes.

Big close-up of a daisy standing out against the black background of the open smoke-box.

Flowers that seem to embalm the spokes of one of the broken wheels.

Very slow fade moving across to centre on the flowers.

NAPOLEON

When Gance published the screenplay of *Napoleon* at the end of 1927,[10] he omitted a number of episodes on the French Revolution which, for lack of time and money, had been suppressed during the later stages of filming.

One of these, 'The enlistment of 1792', was published in *Cinéa-Ciné pour tous* (15 August 1927), but since the printed version is incomplete I have based the translation on the original preserved in the CNC archive (typescript with very extensive modifications in pencil). It shows a broader view of the Revolution and especially illustrates the extent to which details of montage were already specified in the shooting script. It also highlights two aspects of the film discussed in chapter 6: an élitist populism based on spontaneity and authority, and the importance of the Fleuris as part comic, part sentimental representations of the popular virtues that inspire the young Bonaparte.

A second suppressed sequence, 'The Tenth of August 1792' was subsequently published in *Le rouge et le noir* (July 1928). As well as montage, it illustrates the sophistication of Gance's *mise en scène* and use of multiple exposure – seen once again when effects were still at the planning stage. The view of the French Revolution is at once more subtle and more ambivalent than in the completed film condemned by Moussinac and Vuillermoz. Some sections of this sequence seem to have been filmed[11] but only a few fragments survive in the restored version (Danton breaking the horseshoe, the humiliation of Louis XVI ...). The translation is based on the printed text checked, where appropriate, against manuscript and typescript.

These extracts from the screenplay are preceded by two short texts which Gance wrote to explain his film to his collaborators. The first, according to contemporary newspaper reports, was posted up on the walls of the Billancourt studios during the filming of the Toulon and Marseillaise sequences in 1926, but clearly the text was written much

87

earlier than that since there are references to the complete epic cycle (1792–1815). It was in fact included as a preface to the first screenplay Gance wrote in the summer of 1924, and functions as the equivalent of the 'Address to the reader' in later screenplays.[12] The second text, on the placing of the spectator, is similar in function and follows directly on from it in the screenplay. Both translations are based on type-scripts in the CNC archive.

An appeal to the actors and to everyone who will be working on Napoleon

It is imperative – make sure you fully grasp the deep significance I attach to these words – it is imperative that this film allow us to enter once and for all into the temple of the Arts through the great doorway of History. An inexpressible anguish grips me at the thought that my willpower and even the sacrifice of my life will be to no avail if you do not, each and every one of you, give me your undivided loyalty at every moment.

We are going, thanks to you, to relive the Revolution and the Empire. It is an awe-inspiring prospect.

You will have to rediscover within yourselves the enthusiasm, the madness, the power, mastery and self-sacrifice of the soldiers of Year II. Only personal initiative will matter. I want to feel as I watch you a great surge of strength, powerful enough to sweep away all the dykes of our critical faculties, so that from a distance I can no longer differentiate between your hearts and your red bonnets! ...

Quick on your feet, crazed, unruly, larger than life, rough-edged and good-humoured, Homeric with moments of repose, like prolonged notes that when they stop make silence more arresting: that is what the Revolution, that runaway mare, wants you to be.

And then, a man who looks it straight in the eye, who understands it and wants to use it for the good of France, suddenly leaps on to its back, seizes the reins and gradually calms it down, turning it into the most miraculous instrument of Glory ...

The Revolution and its death rattle, the Empire and its great shadows, the *Grande Armée* in all its splendour: it is your task to resurrect their immortal characters.

My friends, the screens of the whole world await you.

From you all, collaborators at every level, from you all, principals, secondary roles, cameramen, set painters, electricians, technical assistants, from you all – especially you humble extras who are going to have the difficult task of rediscovering the spirit of your ancestors and of recreating through your unity of heart the formidable face of

France between 1792 and 1815 – I expect more, I demand absolute dedication and the setting aside of all petty personal considerations. Only thus will you be able to serve faithfully the already illustrious cause of the great Art of the Future, through the most amazing lesson that History can offer.

Abel Gance

4 June 1924

A note on technical strategies[13]

For the first time in cinema, the audience must not be a *spectator* as it has always been up to now, leaving it the option of holding back and criticising. It must be an *actor*, just as it is in real life, as involved in the drama as the actors on the screen. The essential feature of my technique must be to bring about this psychological transformation: the audience must fight alongside the troops, suffer with the wounded, give orders with the generals, take flight with the vanquished, hate and love. It must be drawn into the visual drama as the Athenians were into the tragedies of Aeschylus, and so completely that through the collective powers of suggestion it will be fused into a single soul, a single heart, a single mind.

Criticism can raise its fences[14] as high as it likes; the horses of collective enthusiasm will knock them over without the slightest difficulty if I can make all my audiences *participate* literally in my dramas.

Abel Gance

Fontainebleau, July 1924[15]

Napoleon: The enlistment of 1792

A Sans-culotte is sticking up a large poster that looks like a flag. It says:

(in big letters) FRENCHMEN!

The whole country is invaded. 300,000 gleaming bayonets are directed against us. 180,000 troops under Coburg's orders have established the frontier at four[16] *leagues from Paris. The Royalists are conspiring against us. The whole of the Vendée has taken up arms. France is being strangled by a foreign war and consumed by the enormous flames of a civil war.*

(in big letters) OUR COUNTRY IS IN DANGER!

To arms, citizens!

The camera closes in rapidly on these last two lines which fill the whole screen, then suddenly the camera takes the place of the poster and looks out at the people reading it.

Indescribable expressions. A heroic excitement. There are ten, twenty, a hundred, a thousand faces, all agitated by the same feelings to the extent that they gradually fuse into a single enormous face, a synthesis of them all, the face of the France of 1792 whose expression goes beyond the bounds of History to become part of the Epic!

Close-up. Bonaparte. His eyes flash, then he becomes impassive. His sister moves up closer to him.

Rapid fade to red.

Keynote of this scene from shots 249 to 350.[17] A lyricism that exceeds the force of Rude's 'La Marseillaise'.[18] Shift down from the general to the individual. Create a wave of enthusiasm flowing through all the different opinions. Allow historical accuracy to be eclipsed when it is too abstract by the images that these abstractions forge in my mind.

Iris in on to the firing of the alarm cannon on the Pont Neuf.[19] The iris opens wide. Thousands of people rush up to the spot where a municipal officer on horseback with a tricolour scarf around his neck is reading out the proclamation of the tragic decree. He cries:

Title: *Our country is in danger.*

Long shot. 3 metres. Drummers marching. 1m.

Cameras on cables, moving alongside the drummers at the same speed as them.[20]

On no account sacrifice the visual lyricism of these scenes.[21]

Buglers marching – 50cm. Close-up.

The Pont Neuf cannon – flash – 20cm.

A street corner. Another municipal officer reading the same proclamation – 1m50.

Drummers marching – 80cm.

Buglers marching – 40cm. Close-up.

Pont Neuf cannon – flash – 20cm.

Another street corner, another official, the same terrible announcement – 1m.

Drummers marching – 60cm.

Buglers marching – 30cm. Close-up.

Pont Neuf cannon – 20cm.

Another street corner, another official – 80cm.

Drummers marching – 40cm.

Buglers marching – 20cm. Close-up.

Pont Neuf cannon – 20cm.

Another corner – 50cm.

Drummers marching – 30cm.

Buglers marching – 20cm. Close-up.

Pont Neuf cannon – 20cm.

Continue this rhythm right down to two frames, accentuating the crowds at each reading of the proclamation and increasing the size of the cannon each time until at the end of the montage it is just an enormous muzzle spewing out hellfire.[22]

Rapid fade to red.

Rapid fade in. The Pont Neuf as before but there has been a change. They are just finishing building an enormous stand for the enlistment of volunteers. Rapid dissolve to the platform draped with tricolours and the table, a plank supported on drums. Everyone is in extraordinarily high spirits. They all want to sign on at the same time.

American shot. An old man of 75 signs. His hand is trembling with age.

The soldiers on guard give a roll on their drums.

A cart converted into an enlistment stand.

American shot. A twelve-year-old child signs. His hand trembles with youth.

The guards give a roll on the drums.

The interior of a church in which the representatives of the people are signing on volunteers.

American shot. A man whose right arm has been amputated signs on with his left hand.

A drum-roll by the guards inside the church.

A rose garden in full flower (it's July). Ignoring the wind, people enlist in the garden.

American shot. A pretty young woman signs on.

Close-up of rose petals falling down on to the register.

Drum-roll.

Long shot [*plan en pied*]. Charlet's flag-bearer looks on as if he were watching all the enlistments at once.

Close-up. His expression doesn't change but two large tears run down over his hollow cheeks.

A crowd sings: 'Aux armes, citoyens!' Crane shot.

Beating of the drums. Crane shot.

In Ramponneau's house. Long shot. The enlistment of volunteers is still going on in front of the fireplace.

Sitting at a table, Marcellin, Violine and Tristan Fleuri. He too is looking at all this, All This. He has a radiant smile on his face. He can't stop blinking, it is as if his eyes were being hit by stardust. Marcellin suddenly runs off.

The enlistment table at Ramponneau's. Marcellin is so small his head barely reaches the top of the trestle table and the recruiting officer can't see him. He looks under the table and bursts out laughing. 'Too short!' They carry him back down, giving him a kiss, but the mortified child scratches them with his nails. Laughter.

A drum roll.

Marcellin in tears. Violine takes him in her arms and brings him back.

Four flashes of the crowd. Faces inebriated by words. They are reeling about in a flood of enthusiasm.

American shot. Standing on a sideboard, lit by the flickering light of the fire that seems to dance across his enormous face, Danton is making a speech; the flames from the hearth a short distance behind him frame him from head to toe, giving the impression that he is actually in the fire. There is a huge bust of Franklin with the name of the famous scientist on it beside him. Danton exclaims:

Title: *What do we need if we are to vanquish the enemies of our country?* ...

Close-up of Danton. He chants, as if it were the flames themselves speaking:

Title: *Audacity, more audacity, still more audacity!*

Continuation of the Danton close-up. The flames surround his face.

American shot. In a corner at Ramponneau's, Bonaparte and Elisa.[23] Bonaparte is propping up his chin on both hands. He is looking on with an open soul and an impenetrable expression. The beginnings of a rush of enthusiasm around them. He looks. He reflects. His eyes plunge into the present, catching in it a glimpse of the whole of the future. His apparent indifference will provide an even greater contrast to Danton's volcanic dynamism.

Fleuri, whose excitement is mounting, is struggling to stop himself rushing up to the enlistment platform.

Close-up. Danton in full flood calls upon the bust of Franklin to confirm what he is saying:

Title: *Isn't that true, Franklin?*

Close-up. The flames in the fireplace light up the physicist's face.

The crowd applauds.

Tristan can no longer resist. He is going to run forward but he holds himself back, looking round at:

Violine who, a little further away, is consoling Marcellin.

And so that he can stay with his beloved children, he ties his foot to the leg of the table and tries to block his ears.

Rapid cut to Danton nearing the end of his speech. Pointing to the enlistment table in a state of delirious elation, he proclaims:

Title: *You don't need ink, citizens! It's with your own blood that you should certify that you will die for the Republic!*

Continuation of the Danton close-up.

Close-up of Fleuri. His eyes are riveted on Danton.

Close-up of Danton. He turns for confirmation:

Title: *Don't you agree, Carnot?*

American shot. Carnot, who is indeed presiding at the enlistment table, signals his agreement.

Thunderous applause in the room.[24]

American shot of a man signing on. He's a kind of amiable giant, with splendid eyes and a childlike smile. He is wearing the breeches, coat and accoutrements of the Constitutional Guards of Louis XVI.

Title: *You're already a soldier!* Spoken by the recruiting officer, instructing him to leave the platform.

Close-up. The giant has sunk his pen into one of the veins of his wrist. He looks up and says:

Title: *Of the King, yes, but not of the Republic!*

Continuation of the American shot. Without batting an eyelid, he asks where he has to sign. The register is pushed across to him.

The last sheet of the register. He writes his name in letters of blood:

Title: *Murat.*

While a few drops of blood from his left wrist fall on to the register.

The crowd sings. Crane shot.

This time Fleuri, a mere drop of water in the ocean of a collective madness, cannot hold himself back. He is going to enlist too and he gets up resolutely. He has completely forgotten that his foot is tied to the table and he falls over taking the table with him while everyone bursts out laughing. His face is covered with spilled ink.

All round him people are guffawing, poking fun and jeering at him.

He retreats shamefacedly.

Exterior. Fleuri's water cart has been converted into an enlistment booth. Madame Sans-Gêne in person is standing on an overturned washtub making such a lyrical speech that even those who have miraculously escaped from Ramponneau's house without signing up are overcome by this final assault of enthusiasm and come up to sign the famous registers. Fleuri, who wanted to rescue his water cart, is once again ensnared in sonorous words, and to cap his misfortune:

Title: *The soldiers of Year II.*

Long shot. The National Guard is leaving for the Northern front, with the same rhythm as in Cogniet's painting (inserts of the painting).[25] Enthusiasm gives way to a kind of collective insanity. People who have never met embrace each other. The most epic soldiers France has ever had are all there.

4 close-ups. Rhythm. Marching.

Even the most resolute Jacobins are caught up in these maelstroms of passion and enlist.

Tristan Fleuri looks on. He can't restrain his tears. His heart is overflowing. He is completely carried away.

Close-up of Fleuri. His legs are beginning to catch the rhythm of the marching soldiers, and he marks time with more and more conviction in the middle of a great puddle of water that splashes up every time he stamps his feet.

Drums.

Close-up of soldiers singing.

A cannon sounding the alarm.

Close-up of Fleuri in ecstasy, caught up again by the demon of war. He sees:

The drummers. Crane shot. The camera moves in towards the drummers who become gigantic. Very rapid.

Marseillaises.[26] Crane shot. The camera moves in towards the faces until they are just enormous mouths. Very rapid.

The cannon. Crane shot. The camera moves in towards the cannon which becomes an abyss of fire. Very rapid.

Drums and bugles – 4, 8, 16, 50, 100, 1000, in five seconds.

Madame Sans-Gêne smiling. Crane shot. The camera moves in towards Madame Sans-Gêne until you can see only her magnificent eyes. Very rapid.

An ineffable smile on Fleuri's face. He has given in. 'A toi, sanguinaire Odin, je m'abandonne!' He rushes up and seems to be leaping over the top of the camera.

The enlistment table. People draw back because Fleuri, radiant, dripping with water, his face black with ink and a handkerchief tied round his ankle, lands in front of the table like a bomb, scattering those who were about to sign, and says to Madame Sans-Gêne: 'I'm going too.'

A glance of her kind eyes is enough for Madame Sans-Gêne to weigh up the lovable soul of this overgrown child and in spite of the water dripping off him, she draws him towards her and gives him a kiss.

Lefèvre, her husband, looks askance at her and grumbles.

Fleuri signs. At the gates of heaven he certainly wouldn't be happier than he is at this moment.

Bonaparte looks out of Ramponneau's window. Outside the soldiers of Year II are passing. He points out to his sister:

In the street, the very young chief of the regiment, on horseback. Everyone seems to be looking at him.

Close-up. Bonaparte saying:

Title: *Marceau!*

Close-up. Mobile camera. It is indeed Marceau, Lieutenant-Colonel in the National Guard at the age of 23! His delicate manner and effeminate features add even more strongly to the effect his youth has on the onlookers. He smiles; he salutes. A sunlit flag flaps behind his untarnished brow.

Close-up. Bonaparte. He is looking at him as the young Caesar looked at the statue of Alexander the Great. Bonaparte's eyes are drawn towards:

The lieutenant-colonel's bands on Marceau's uniform.

Close-up. Bonaparte. His eyes come back to his own uniform. He stares at:

The two thin bands indicating the rank of Captain.

Close-up. Bonaparte. His resolution grows stronger and stronger.

Tristan comes down from the platform like a drunken King. There are no rifles left so they give him an enormous pike and two little lances. Then they take no more notice of him. Besides, his life no longer belongs to him. He has just made delivery of it to France. He stands there staring at the prehistoric weapons he has been given, seeming not to have any idea what to do with them. He sees Marcellin crying on the pavement.

American shot. Tristan taps him on the shoulder and says, as if he was being choked by fifty Legions of Honour:

Title: *It's all right, my lad. I'm going too!*

Shot of their two heads. Marcellin lifts a tearful face towards his father's and, as Tristan speaks, begins to smile.

American shot. Violine rushes up to the group, out of breath, and says joyfully:

Title: *She's not his fiancée, papa, she's his sister!*[27]

And since he doesn't understand, she points to the window.

Bonaparte with Elisa nestling up very close to him.

American shot. Fleuri. That doesn't matter much to him now. What's interesting for him is to understand fully the heart and the soul of this unforgettable day, and sitting on the pavement with his arms round Violine and Marcellin's necks, holding them close to him, he talks of riches and glory and gently he becomes a picture of serenity. Fleeting images pass across these three heads lulled by dreams.

Crane shots. 3 gauzes. Drums, Marseillaises, Madame Sans-Gêne, cannons, bells, Danton, drums, all of this fluid, dissolving in a translucent chain, pitching and tossing and as if flowing from one dream to another.

Close-up. Bonaparte. He moves away from the window. He looks transfigured. A tremendous determination seems suddenly to have taken hold of him. Elisa looks anxiously at him. He says to her, gazing out into the Future:

Title: *I think you can work miracles with a people like that!* [28]

Napoleon: The Tenth of August 1792 [29]

Title: *The sun of the Monarchy rises for the last time.*

Iris in. At the Tuileries palace. The boudoir in which the courtiers allowed to be present at the *petit lever* are waiting. The King enters in his dressing gown with lifeless eyes but smiling. His wig needs curling. He responds mechanically to the greetings addressed to him and looks out of the open window.

The rising sun seen through the Tuileries fountains.

American shot.[30] Louis XVI, smiling, turns to speak to Roederer, the attorney general.

Title: *What a beautiful day it's going to be!*

Roederer and the courtiers bow, indicating their agreement. Only Roederer looks concerned. The others smile, imitating exactly the laughter of their King.

Very rapid fade.

Title: *The Agony of the Monarchy (10 August 1792)* [31]

His Majesty's dressing room. He is being shaved. His chin is covered with soap, and his wig is full of curlers. Three barbers are in attendance. One is doing the shaving, the second is curling the wig and the third passing the instruments. An officer is ushered in. The King beckons him to approach. While the barbers remain at a distance, the officer bends over to whisper in the King's ear:

Title: *Good news, Your Majesty. The Allies are advancing towards Paris by forced marches and the Duke of Brunswick will be here in nine days with a hundred thousand Austrians.*

American shot. Louis XVI looks at him, doesn't reply and, seeming ill-at-ease, calls back the barbers.

A small Boule clock on the mantelpiece. It strikes six.

Continuation of the close-up of the shaving. Louis XVI stops the barber's hand, listening. A silence. He gets up, his chin still covered with soap. He looks worried. The others are all listening too.[32]

4 different close-ups of bells.

Continuation of the barber scene. Louis XVI. The Queen enters in a negligée, looking afraid: the tocsin, THE TOCSIN![33]

4 more shots of bells, closer and very rapid.

The barbers. Louis XVI, still forgetting he has soap all over his chin and his curlers in, hastily sends the barbers away. People are beginning to run about in the adjoining rooms. In the distance they are beginning to panic. But in the King's presence etiquette is respected.[34]

A crowd on the march. Mobile camera.

4 more shots of bells, even more rapid and closer than before.[35]

Iris in with red tint. A blacksmith's forge shot from the outside but with the camera in among the crowd as if there were a thousand people there. Horses in semi-darkness. Sans-culottes everywhere, men and women dangling from the rafters listening to Danton's speech. His face is covered with sweat and grease: Danton has never been more terrifying. Sparks fly all round him.

10 close-ups of faces, visions of the Apocalypse.

Danton takes a horseshoe off the wall.

Close-up of the horseshoe.

Danton shows it to everyone and says:

Title: *The Monarchy!*

Close-up. Danton. He snaps the horseshoe with his bare hands.

The crowd roars.

Danton laughing. The flames of the forge in superimpression on his face.

100 bells in four seconds, blending one into the other.

The Place du Carrousel. Close shot. It is thick with revolutionaries rushing up.

The King's reception room. Panic has set in. Not knowing which course of action to take, Louis XVI hesitates, then, trying to regain control of himself, says to Roederer:

Title: *I'll have the ringleaders killed. Who are they?*

Close-up of Roederer who answers:

Title: *Hunger and poverty, Your Majesty!*

Long shot. The assailants. Mobile camera in a car. They are running up. The camera moves along thirty metres in front of them.

Long shot. The Swiss Guards. Camera in moving car. So that they won't have to do battle with walls and closed doors, they rush down the entrance steps and towards the assailants. The camera moves along thirty metres in front of them.

Continuation of the shot of the assailants. But suddenly the camera pauses for a moment, while they continue to rush ahead, and charges rapidly towards them as if it represented the Swiss Guards.

The same process reversed with the camera moving in towards the Guards.

Mobile camera along the side. A terrific clash (all shots with mobile cameras).

The back view of a young man. His arms are clasped behind him as

97

if he is out for a walk, a casual onlooker. Fixed camera. His hat is removed by a stray bullet. He turns round for a moment. It is Bonaparte, but he doesn't budge.

Title: *Within a space of a hundred square metres, a future Emperor was observing the Agony through the eyes of the Revolution.*

Close-up. Bonaparte looking.

Louis XVI and the Royal family flee through a little door escorted by a few soldiers. They are going to the National Assembly to place themselves under the protection of the Deputies.

Close-up. Bonaparte follows the Royal family with his eyes.

Rout of the Swiss Guards. They are being massacred.

Title: *Bonaparte was interpreting the battle in his own way.*

Close-up. Bonaparte. The camera moves in closer and closer. There are just two enormous eyes that fill the whole screen and in which the following series of rapid images appears.

> *These will be a montage of shots of 2 or 3 frames each, with sometimes 2, 3, 4 or 5 images superimposed one on top of the other, showing the intensity of the young officer's vision and the indescribable turbulence of this horrific event. A paroxysm of cinematographic expression.*
>
> *The images become the veins and the arteries of the Revolution, and the intensity of the turmoil must be such that all possibility of analysing the situation evaporates.*
>
> *This montage, all crane and mobile crane shots, will be intercut with big close-ups of Bonaparte who still hasn't moved.*
>
> *In amongst all this a play on light and shade, action shots of pikes, lances, cannons, guns, arrows, halbards, and of drums, bugles, the tocsin, the Marseillaise, rage, agony, sadism, brief glimpses of the leaders' faces: Danton, Théroigne de Méricourt, Barbaroux, Santerre, Westeman, Fournier l'Américain, the fearsome chief of the pike brigade; Swiss Guards falling through windows, fires starting, all this against a background of raging seas, erupting volcanoes, cataracts, rapidity and vertigo, filmed with hand-cranked camera, Sept camera, camera on crane and mobile crane, camera mounted on car and on horseback, camera on rails and wires, camera in football, camera F: d.p.v. and camera F: p.a.s.l.m.t.r.*[36]

Close-up. Bonaparte, impassive. Blood splashes on to him. He doesn't budge.

American shot. An enormous brute comes up to Bonaparte and asks threateningly:

Title: *Are you for us? ... Against us? ...*

Bonaparte replies:

Title: *Neither for nor against.*

This man says menacingly:

Title: *Then what are you doing here? ...*

Close-up. Bonaparte. He says impassively, and his ability to remain detached will be more emotive than all the unrestrained passion of the people around him:

Title: *I am watching* (in huge letters that fill the screen).

Disconcerted by this unexpected reply and by Bonaparte's flashing eyes, the giant retreats, unable to respond.

The crowd. Seen from inside the Royal Palace. The Revolutionaries have won the day. They rush into all the rooms.

Fade to red.

Sitting by a gatepost and aware neither of the great historical drama that is being played out nor of the thousands of menacing shadows that pass by on the white wall behind him, a child blows big soap bubbles up into the sky through a straw.

Fade to red.

Title: *The Night of the Tenth of August.*

Shoot the following scenes at night at the Military Academy. Iris in with red tint. A battlefield littered with corpses. The Royal Palace. An unforgettable impact. Dead bodies everywhere. The sinister light produced by flames you don't see directly. A panoramic shot takes in Bonaparte standing pensively in the middle of this hecatomb. His compassion is apparent in his expression. He is deeply moved.

Suddenly he is surrounded by a drunken band of Sans-culottes who, thinking he looks suspicious, challenge him. He does not reply. Then a hideous Sans-culotte goes up to him and says, loading his pistol at the same time:

Title: *Shout 'Long live the Nation!'*

American shot. Bonaparte. With a threatening and scornful look on his face, he stares at the man and says:

Title: *Long live France!*

The Sans-culottes look at each other. This shout perplexes them. Is it seditious, counter-revolutionary? They hurl insults at him. He dominates them all, forcing them to submit to his authority, and says:

99

Title: *I am a soldier, a child of the Revolution and a man of the people! I will not be insulted like a King!*

They back down and to show this they hold out a drinking gourd as a sign of fraternity.

American shot. Bonaparte takes the gourd and throws it away. Expressions of anger and astonishment. Bonaparte says:

Title: *All that relies on bloodshed is worth nothing. If no one restores order, the greatest benefits of the Revolution will be lost.*

This time he has gone too far. They look at each other. They are going to execute him. A ferocious-looking Jacobin says: 'Spare yourselves the trouble.' He takes two steps backwards and points his gun at Bonaparte's head. Quick as a flash, a sabre severs the man's hand and he collapses in a horrible fit of convulsions. The person responsible for this sudden intervention, a magnificent individual with long curly hair, Adjutant of the 4th Volunteer Battalion of the Upper Rhine, forces respect on the others and makes them retreat backwards like wild dogs. Bonaparte shakes his hand and asks:

Title: *What's your name, Adjutant, so that I can remember it later?*

Close-up of the Adjutant. He bursts out laughing and replies proudly:

Title: *Kléber.*

American shot. The two men with their hands still clasped. The wild dogs make as if to move forward. Kléber takes one step towards them. This time they are scared stiff and scatter like sheep. In the shadows, the man whose hand was cut off is agonising. The two soldiers separate: Kléber continues on his way. Bonaparte slowly walks off in a different direction.

A box at the National Assembly. The Royal Family is there, Marie-Antoinette haughty and distant, the Dauphin crying in the arms of the King's sister and Louis XVI standing up and talking out loud, still trying to pull the wool over his own eyes. Ten Sans-culottes are guarding him.

An outburst of joy. Then the iris is opened wider: people are dancing round in a ring, illuminated by the flames of a huge bonfire.

Sans-culottes drag the naked corpses of Swiss Guards and aristocrats through the ring of dancers to throw them into the fire.

Close-up. An improvised band: hideous faces swollen with excitement and alcohol; bugles, serpents, cymbals etc. The bugler especially must be indelibly engraved on the eyes of the spectator, like a Goya print; nose eaten away by a cancer, fiery eyes, a face so monstrous that it becomes epic.

Another similar dance further off. Mobile camera. The camera tracks back to reveal a third circle also dancing round a huge bonfire on which corpses are being piled.

On the great staircase of the Tuileries palace, lit by torchlight, people are dancing in pools of wine and blood. People gorging themselves. Jordaens. Bonaparte crosses in the background and goes into one of the rooms.

Louis XVI's dressing room. Two guards at the entrance, Sansculottes. One is completely drunk, the other is asleep. Bonaparte goes in and crosses to another half-open door. He is about to go through it but draws back because he sees:

Louis XVI's office. Everything has been smashed. Ripped-open furniture litters the floor, all the mirrors are broken, the portraits of the Royal Family have daggers plunged into their hearts. In the centre of the office[37] there is an improvised table on trestles. Around the table: Clavière, Monge, Lebrun, Robespierre, Marat and some scribes. Danton is striding up and down. Candles on the table. But the sinister force of the dancing is so strong that great shadows of the dancers stand out on the dark crimson wall. The windows are open. It is as if you can see the screaming and shouting, and the Revolutionary leaders are still in a state of shock.

It's as though they are stupefied and dumbfounded by all the excesses being committed outside.

In a corner, a dead Swiss Guard with a look of horror on his face.

Close-up of singers standing near the band, clapping their hands and shouting at the tops of their inflamed voices:

Title: *Madame Veto avait promis!* ...[38]

A fat woman dances around clutching the corpse of a Swiss Guard: 'Madame Veto avait promis!'

American shot. Danton at the window. He seems very moved by these scenes. He comes back into the room and says:

Title: *The Revolution is a blazing furnace!*

American shot. Robespierre gets up. He goes over and closes the window. The others watch him. He returns to the table and says with a force that suddenly imposes respect:

Title: *A furnace but also a forge! We must shape the Republic now!*

Close-up. Bonaparte at the door, concentrating all his attention on what is about to happen.

Long shot. They all squeeze in round the table. The red gleams disappear from the walls. There is silence. The transfiguration is complete.

Title: *The other face of the Revolution.*

And indeed, the great holy face of the Convention which will remain serene beneath the hideous mask it has to wear – the Terror – this great and profound face will gradually appear before us, its features becoming more pronounced and objectified through contrasts, a face constructing a new social edifice while the past agonises. As if a new dawn was really just beginning, the whole atmosphere changes; the features of these fearsome men, who a few moments before seemed still to have blood in the corners of their mouths, become idealised.

> NOTE – *I know that the enormous achievements of the Convention were not all worked out during the night of 10 August, I know that Saint-Just wasn't there, that Favière was far too unintelligent to make the proposal I attribute to him, but it was necessary to present in a powerful summary some of the main objectives of the Convention in its early days, and psychological truth does, I think, amply justify deliberate historical inaccuracies.*

The glacial Saint-Just, the impassive Robespierre, the sarcastic Couthon and even the hideous Marat will, as they lay the cornerstones of the new social cathedral, take on expressions we did not know they had. And as these powerful souls climb the ladder of idealism, the infernal dancing round of the murderers grows in intensity and Louis XVI gradually sinks down in the little box in the Assembly Chamber that is now his prison.

Bonaparte catches sight of something glinting on the floor behind an upturned armchair. Something that sparkles in the darkness. He bends down and picks up the glittering object. Close-up. It is the royal crown.

Close-up. Bonaparte. His thoughts. Then his attention is drawn to the adjoining room where the Convention is being forged into shape.

Long shot. Louis XVI's office. Robespierre is on his feet and about to speak.

Close-up. Robespierre. He says:

Title: *I propose the creation of a Civil Code.*

A dance round a gigantic bonfire (camera on a pivot, turning on its own axis. Speed 1).

Louis XVI, who had so far maintained a dignified bearing, bows his head.

Bonaparte straightens up. A kind of enthusiasm seems to invest him.

Long shot. Louis XVI's office. Saint-Just gets up.

Close-up. Saint-Just. He says:

Title: *I propose the adoption by the State of orphans and the infirm.*

Napoleon: the agony of Louis XVI

Another infernal dance around the fire (Speed 2).

Louis XVI bows lower.

Bonaparte. Is it an optical illusion? His body seems more luminous.

Long shot. Louis XVI's office. Couthon rises, swaying about in his wheelchair held up by a colossus.[39]

Close-up. Couthon. He says:

Title: *The creation of primary schools.*

Another shot of the dancing (Speed 3).

Louis XVI is more and more prostrate.

Bonaparte increasingly seems to distil light.

Long shot. Louis XVI's office. Danton gets up and says:

Title: *The suppression of all remaining hereditary privileges.*

Another dance (Speed 4).

Louis XVI still more prostrated.

Bonaparte's radioactivity more marked.

Long shot. Louis XVI's office. Monge gets up.

Close-up. Monge. He says:

Title: *The creation of the decimal system.*

Favière gets up and says:

Title: *Of the Museum and the Institute.*

Saint-Just gets up and says:

Title: *A Polytechnic.*

103

Napoleon: the halo effect

The farandole. This time the visual style will once more achieve one of its most impressive effects. The camera will move exactly in time with the people dancing. The two feet of the camera will be two human feet, caught up in the same frenetic madness. If the rhythm is respected, the impact on the nervous system will be considerable. The dancing becomes still more wild (Speed 5).

Louis XVI collapses on to a chair.

Bonaparte, surrounded by an aura of light, lets the crown drop to the floor.

Long shot. Louis XVI's office. Marat gets up.

Close-up. Marat transfigured. He says:

Title: *The creation of state hospitals.*

1, 2, 3, 4, 5 sinister dances, all at the same time. The rhythm accelerates and overspills, tumultuous, crazed, multiple, indescribable. Like a fire spreading rhythmically.

Louis XVI, completely crushed, bent double and head in hands.

Bonaparte surrounded by a halo ...

Long shot. Louis XVI's office. All the Revolutionary leaders are on their feet in a shared enthusiasm for the cause they are defending. A superb moment. A supernatural light increasingly transforms the atmosphere.

The rhythm is reaching its peak of intensity. Are all the giants of the Revolution dancing round in this red light? Is that why it has taken on such fantastic dimensions, as if millions of fireflies were dancing in hope of an eternal night?

Long shot. Louis XVI's office. The apogee.

The dead Swiss Guard in the corner who earlier looked terrified now has an expression of bliss.

Close-up. The broken crown.

Very brief panoramic shot of Bonaparte's ecstatic expression.

The diaphragm plays with light as if it were a violin.

Rapid fade to white.

LA FIN DU MONDE

The extent of Gance's directiveness and sense of mission is best illustrated by the address to his collaborators at the beginning of the screenplay of *La fin du monde*. Dated in the text 15 October 1929, it was written after the screenplay had been completed but before casting and decisions about the technical team.

This is followed by the opening sequence of the film, quoted, like the address, from Gance's own copy (typescript with manuscript amendments and deletions – CNC).[40] Although it also illustrates directiveness, it is included here principally as exemplification of a number of other features discussed later in the book, notably the juxtaposition of epic and melodrama and the way the look is deployed in the construction of spectacle.

The sequence as planned in the screenplay and as it appears in the completed film is basically the same. But we should note that there are a number of important differences between the two. Gance wrote the screenplay between April and October 1929 on the basis of an outline completed in March. As he states in the note appended to his 'address', he was not sure at that stage what sound equipment would be made available by his producer and hence decided to plan the film in terms of 'silent' strategies. In fact he was to exploit sound as much as possible and the film was indeed billed as the first 'all sound and talking' spectacular produced in France. Music and dialogue are thus much more extensively used than the screenplay indicates, especially in the dressing-room scenes. The action was also updated, accentuating the film's relevance and, through their insertion into a contemporary society, the contrast between the unworldly Jean and the materialist Schomburg.

La fin du monde: Preface

This is neither a speech nor a profession of faith, but a humble prayer.

I wrote the great drama, *La fin du monde,* a project that had been taking shape in my mind for ten years, during a kind of crisis of illumination which forces me to value it highly now that I can look at it from the outside. It is in fact the result of a prolonged and constrained suffering that had never been expressed in any art form. Why did I eventually come to believe that images with sound could be the Balm of Galaad[41] that I had vainly searched for in other modes of expression? I don't know, but since I have taken this road, it is trembling with emotion, fear and joy that I want to summon into the life of vision this fruit of my purest intentions.

This film stretches out its arms of images to the world: in the ocean of mankind, it must leave a wake not in people's minds but in their hearts.

Although neither politics nor religion are at stake in it, it seeks out in the human body what God put there above all else: goodness.

Its driving force is love.

Its objective: the brotherhood of mankind.

I know how tired and worn-out through overuse all these grand words like love and brotherhood are; their meaningfulness depends solely on the degree of spiritual elevation of the people who use them, and perhaps I am flattering myself too much in thinking that I can restore to them a part of their virginity.

But I don't want to resort to rhetoric in my words any more than I want my actions to be theatrical: I am concerned with an ardent truth. Let me approach people's hearts, for they will feel its warmth, and the ice of their minds will melt as if by magic.

This film that we are going to make doesn't set out to entertain, it doesn't ask to be liked, it seeks to love, it asks you to let yourselves be loved.

My friends, companions and collaborators, I have already asked you in my preceding films for hard work, loyalty and courage. Today I am asking even more of you: to have faith.

It is essential that you believe in me absolutely, so that people's eyes can in their turn believe in you when you become the living reflection of my love. I will not ask you always to understand what you are doing, but to believe in what you are doing, and in insisting on that distinction I would like you to realise the full importance of the subtle difference in meaning that I have in mind.

I will go about my work with an absolute humility, so that the good seed can take root in the simplest of minds. Follow my example, no pride, no presumption, just enthusiasm, the true and only virtue that wins all the battles on earth and in the heavens. Obey me without question. Anyone around me who complains about problems of time, money or fatigue will not be really worthy of the work I am undertaking and will give me the right to separate the chaff from the wheat.

I am not looking for brains, nor for critics or economists but for hands and hearts for a great task that has to be executed quickly. Where America would give us 10, we have to work with 1. Let's show for once that this 1 is worth 1,000 when it comes from a country like ours where the heart of the world beats even more strongly than anywhere else.

I know that when my back is turned people will say: 'Just another dreamer, a mystic, a madman who believes in the elevation of mankind, in the beauty of morality, in peace, in all that President Wilson stuff that's completely outdated in this age of economic struggle and financial supremacy. He'd do better to draw up a list of the criteria you have to satisfy to get a passport for a 'commercial' film, or to show the Americans that our women's legs can be as exciting as those of Mack Sennett's girls, instead of shooting off in a rocket towards the stars . . .'

I know all that you may be thinking, my friends, and that is perhaps what gives me the most strength, since I have to prove to you that you are mistaken and that my love of people is more powerful and more productive than all the petty feelings of self-interest and greed.

To those who have difficulty in understanding me, yes, I will talk money, but in the opposite way to what you expect. I will say: French cinema is moribund. We have to revive it in the face of vicious competition, of a bad distribution system which doesn't give the producer the rewards he ought to get but instead hands them out to an army of middlemen lying in wait to pounce on our creations.

We have to work almost for a pittance, day and night if necessary, to pull ourselves together, to act in unison, grit our teeth, multiply our determination, make all the financial concessions that are imposed on us, cut back on sets, cut back on extras, cut back on resources but increase the size of our hearts in the same proportions. I do not want to know about your contracts or your salaries but about the moral commitment you are giving me while reading or listening to what I'm saying here. If you agree to give it to the full, I am waiting for you. I am only the conductor of an orchestra. Without you I can do nothing, but let it be said that with the worst-paid musicians in the world he has played the greatest of the symphonies of light.

Where there is constraint, there is no fruit and I beg all those who haven't understood the inner fire of my words or who don't have a scrap of idealism or beauty inside them to move out of my way. I don't want machines but men. I am not looking for pistons but for feelings and I will prove once again that the metal of suffering melted in the crucible of art still gives the finest gold in the world on all the market-places of the universe.[42]

From today, 15 October 1929, I consider that everyone working on *La fin du monde*, whatever their task, from the least to the most important, the humblest extra to the principal actors, must form part of a kind of 'Minor Order' like that of Saint Francis of Assisi, with inflexible rules and artistic discipline.

And it is only on these conditions that *La fin du monde* can become one of the greatest films of all time.

Abel Gance

A VITALLY IMPORTANT NOTE[43]

La fin du monde relies to a considerable extent on the use of sound. I have not rigorously and exactly indicated its role here, since at the moment of writing the screenplay, I am still in the dark about precisely what facilities I will have at my disposal. That is why I have concentrated on the intensity of visual effects, rather as if sound could not produce good results. If I am able to make use of it in its most perfected form, I will obviously be able to cut back considerably on the visual effects in the scenes I have written, by relying on auditory suggestion. I have not done that here because of the state of uncertainty I find myself in.

The whole of the cataclysm sequence, in particular, can be orchestrated, organised in terms of sound, making it possible to achieve some extraordinary effects. But, I repeat, these effects will only be possible if I am given the same facilities as the Americans. Otherwise the risk is too great and we must concentrate on the visual impact.

La fin du monde: The Passion Play

N.S.A.I.

Everything in italics must be emphasised, it is what must remain permanently engraved on the spectator's eye in images of fire. It is the high point of each scene.

1. Start with red tinted stock, 1 metre – A barely visible left hand appears from the side and takes up the whole of the screen. The image becomes sharper: it is a hand nailed to a wooden cross; large drops of blood form, run down or congeal. You can sense the incredible spasm of suffering at its highest degree of intensity.[44]

The camera, on rails, tracks across to the right, along the convulsed arm and gradually reveals the most Magnificent, the most Harrowing, the most Divine of Faces: *that of Christ during his agony.*

Absolute silence.

His expression must be compelling and indelibly imprinted on the memory of every audience. The throes of death along with the heavenly serenity of the crucified Jesus. The light of the soul. The radioactivity of suffering.

Slow dissolve to the tortured body against a hazy view of Golgotha; stardust behind it.

Dissolve to the two thieves.

Dissolve to the complete Passion group. Somewhere between Breughel and Tintoretto.

2. American shot of the mother of Jesus and her sister Mary Magdalene weeping, and the mother of the sons of Zebedee.

Dissolve to a close-up of Mary Magdalene.

3. Roman soldiers sitting down. Laughter and expressions of concern. Mobile camera. Sarcasms and blasphemies of the scribes and senators. Hatred. Its eternal face that we will see often during the film.

Minimise the use of close-ups. Introduce them only when they are essential, like a loud pedal.

4. The insults of one of the thieves.

5. The deep emotion and sublimation of the other.

Beginning of *soundtrack*: the cry and the words *Eli, Eli, lamma, etc.*

6. *Christ, just an enormous head.* His cry rips open the entrails of the future. An earthly moment when he loses his divine hope, when he is only a man who has reached the absolute limit of suffering. He cries: *Eli, Eli, lamma, lamma sabacthani.*

Avoid theatricality. Remain profoundly human and lyrical, concentrate on the sublime. All my actors should be in a trance. An ardent sincerity. I must be moved to tears myself. Beauty here is in itself not enough. I am beginning my film with a scene that is still the main axis of an enormous part of world thought. Preserve its magnificent power and its elevation.

Sound: loud roll of thunder.

None of these scenes must be emphatic. They must be carried off with great subtlety. The intention must not be obvious.

7. Flash. Paroxysm; terror and frozen laughs on the faces of the onlookers.

Variant 6 (7b). His thirst, his delirium, the supplication of his upturned eyes.

8. Taking pity on him, a soldier holds up a sponge soaked in vinegar on the end of a reed.

Variant 6 (8b). Christ offers the world in thanks a martyr's smile. All is accomplished. He gives up the ghost. His head sinks down on to his breast.

9. A flash of lightning cuts across the sky bringing with it a sudden strange darkness. Flash, the fear of the onlookers illuminated by the lightning. The storm music from *Parsifal*.

10. Deleted.

11. The camera pulls back and we realise as the uprights of the stage set come into view to the left and right of the frame that we are watching a religious performance, a Passion play. The camera pulls back as we see the effects of a dust-storm and the flight of the actors in this drama of the centuries. Now we move into the auditorium. Here are all the spectators seen from the back, two rows, five, ten, fifty rows extremely tense – at least half of the audience is on its knees.

12. Close-up. Among the spectators, here is Martial Novalic, with an impassive expression.

13. Sitting near him, de Murcie,[45] an elderly man who can ill conceal his paternal pride. Indeed he leans across towards his neighbour – a sombre and handsome young man with hard, flashing eyes. He says to him: *'Well, Schomburg, what do you think of my daughter?'* The man replies: *'That the real Mary Magdalene was certainly less beautiful and desirable, my dear de Murcie.'*

14. A beautiful young woman sitting beside Schomburg pinches him on the leg. He jumps, sniggers, then puts his arm round

110

(Opposite) Filming the Passion Play in *La fin du monde*

III

the waist of this woman who has taken offence at what he has just said and who is none other than Isabelle Bolm, his mistress.

15. Little girls from the Order of the Children of Mary, on their knees, saying the rosary, and very afraid. Beside them, a man in ecstasy.

16. A good-hearted priest sobbing.

17. Rapid flashes of different reactions. The ecstatic admiration of two old women; panoramic shot of the incredible concentration of two Parisians who, you can guess, would be sceptical and sarcastic in any other circumstances.

18. In the wings. The man who's doing the thunder: corrugated iron and a bass drum.

19. The wings. The man who plays the devil in the mystery play looking on admiringly.

Sound: the Dies irae, dies illa is being sung.

20. The wings. The singer standing near the organist.

21. The head of Christ: his expression is so convincing and his body so completely still. Isn't he completely dead?

22. The mother of Christ and Mary Magdalene kneeling at the foot of the cross. Mary Magdalene's expression must remain indelibly engraved in the mind.[46]

Sound: a bell.

23. A bell and a choirboy seen from the back. The whole audience kneels as the curtains slowly close.

24. Flash. Some enthusiastic Parisians clap, then stop at ...
– decentre the presentation of Schomburg.

Variant 16 (24b). Flash ... a sign from a good priest who makes them understand that silent admiration is all that's necessary.

25. The stage, behind the closed curtain. The descent from the cross with the help of stage-hands who seem out of place among all these Roman and Hebrew costumes.

Talking

Variant 21 (25b). Surprise: *the actor who was playing Christ, Jean Novalic, has fainted.*

Hubbub. Concern.

They carry him to his dressing room. A young woman looks especially anxious and concerned: it is Mary Magdalene, who is none other than Geneviève de Murcie.

26. Improvised dressing rooms. Various people are already there, laughing and chatting, two priests, de Murcie, some journalists, some Parisians. The hubbub reaches the room. They carry in Jean, still unconscious. Mobile camera. Geneviève's anxiety is very apparent and becoming more and more pronounced.

The person who was playing the devil and who is still wearing his make-up dashes about around Christ trying everything he can think of to bring him round, helped by Geneviève and the good priest, very shaken by this unexpected sequel to the crucifixion. The bystanders have been ushered out.

27–28. Deleted.

29. Jean Novalic comes round. He smiles at Geneviève.

Talking

'*Forgive me, Geneviève. I don't know what happened . . . the emotion . . . the strain . . .*'

30. Geneviève simply replies, in a tone of voice that reveals the depth of her love:

Talking

'*Jean . . .*'

That means 'You gave me a fright. I love you. Nothing is purer or more beautiful than you are.'

Mobile camera. The good priest has brought Jean a little glass of the local wine to revive him. The priest pours one for himself. They clink their glasses. Geneviève smiles. A choirboy gives them some biscuits. The sweetness and provincial naïvety of faith.

31. Martial enters, looking worried and pushing back the people trying to see what's going on. Geneviève:

Talking

'*Your brother is recovering, Martial, there's no need to worry.*'

Martial goes over to his brother with a gesture of deep affection.

Continuation of 29. Jean looks very tired and very distant. He seems already to have that closeness to the infinite that will make him such a moving and mysterious character.

32. The priest notices that love in Geneviève's expression and, visibly embarrassed by this, he covers over Jean's almost naked body. The devil has removed his wig. The priest, called by the people in the corridor who want to know what's happening, leaves the room.

33. Isabelle had come into Jean's dressing room a few moments before with Schomburg, who is eyeing Geneviève. Geneviève lowers her eyes and looks towards Jean. Then Schomburg says to her with a half-concealed irony in his expression of sympathy:

'Don't you think, dear Geneviève, that your friend Jean's heart isn't quite strong enough for such a strenuous part?'

Geneviève is about to reply. Jean makes a little sign telling her not to.

Able to cope with all situations and none too pleased about Schomburg's attentions to Geneviève, Isabelle meanwhile takes the devil's wig (which has a goatee beard attached to it) and deftly places it on Schomburg. *The resemblance to Lucifer will be striking.* This man really is the devil in person, whereas the one who was playing the part looked like a comic fairground devil. (See the head on p.125 of Grillot de Givry's *Musée des Sorciers*.)

Sound: laughter.

Schomburg catches sight of himself in the mirror and bursts out laughing.

Variant 30 (33b). Surprised by the strangeness of this laughter, Geneviève turns round and can't help crying out.

Sound: a cry.

Variant 33 (33c). For the fun of it, Schomburg makes a theatrical movement as if to grab her.

Variant 29. Jean's look stops him in his tracks. Jean's expression. God and the Devil. In a flash, the audience will perhaps grasp the eternal entities [of good and evil].[47]

34. Movement. Isabelle snatches the wig off Schomburg's head and says:

Text: '*Come back from hell, fallen angel.*'
He is really very Luciferian. She kisses him, no doubt on that account. The priest

coughs to show this is not the appropriate place. Isabelle laughs but gradually takes offence at the insistence of Schomburg's look, and noticing that he is watching Geneviève undress. Schomburg can see Geneviève in a mirror – the shapely beauty of this wonderful woman – Isabelle abruptly pulls a screen across in front of Schomburg, who just smiles. Martial is neutral and motionless during these scenes, attracting no attention.

Someone shouts:
Text: '*On stage for the Resurrection.*'

35. The corridor. Everyone hurries back to their seats.

36. The wings. Jean arrives. They all look at him with the greatest respect. He enters as if carried along, in a brilliant ray of light. You can sense that the curtain is opening.

In the distance you can hear César Franck's Alleluia being played on the organ.
His spiritual radiance is even greater than the luminous radiance that surrounds him.

The celestial sound of the music continues.

Behind him, in the shadows, Geneviève gazes ineffably at him.

Fade to blue tint.

37. Iris in, the outside of the hall and the vestibule. Large banners:

Sunday matinée
The sacred Mystery of the Passion
Christ will be played by the typographer
JEAN NOVALIC

38. Movement. Buses, carts, bicycles, cars (1910 vintage), Bugattis, Hispanos. Curious bystanders press in. The last members of the audience are leaving. Many are wiping their eyes and blowing their noses. Some Children of Mary and Sisters of the Visitation form up in rows. Provincial congregations reassemble. The locals are talking about it all. The Parisians criticise or voice their approval.

39. Schomburg is with Isabelle and while they are waiting for Jean to join them, he is filming Geneviève with an amateur Cinex. Geneviève, who is talking to Martial, is taken aback when she realises, but then she smiles, embarrassed at first but then coquettish and charming. She is no actress and yet the gracefulness of her poses is irresistible.

40. Schomburg lowers his Cinex. You can tell he is filming the pretty legs of this beautiful young woman.

41. Close-up. Martial. He notices Schomburg's effrontery and frowns.

42. Jean arrives, surrounded by people congratulating him. Not liking all this attention, he manages to escape, thanks to the considerateness of the priest who answers all their questions.

43. Isabelle gets into the driving seat of a Bugatti, while Schomburg helps in Abraham de Murcie and invites Geneviève to get in too.

Talking

'*No, papa,*' she says, taking Martial and Jean by the arm, '*I'm going back with my friends, on the train.*' She kisses her father and quickly says goodbye to Schomburg, who can't take his eyes off her, and to Isabelle.

De Murcie grumbles. You can see he doesn't like these two young men with whom Geneviève is compromising herself. But given Geneviève's character, there's nothing he can do about it. Jean insists:

Talking

'*Go with your father, Geneviève.*'
'*No, I won't. I'm coming with you, Jean.*'

And she looks at him lovingly. Schomburg vents his frustration by slamming the door in Jean's face.

Martial seems neutral. Isabelle drives off. Jean disengages himself from Geneviève's arm to avoid shocking the onlookers and the three of them walk away.

44. An old woman who had been at the play praying in a corner of the hall kisses the ground where Jean had been standing. People watch her and burst out laughing.

Fade.

There is not space here to include more than a minute sample of the vast correspondence exchanged between Gance and his producers and distributors. In consequence I have limited my selection to letters concerning the production of *Napoleon*.

In his letter to Noë Bloch of 22 April 1925, written during the filming of the Corsican sequences, Gance makes an eloquent plea for his conception of cinema, while protesting against harassment by the production managers. Two letters addressed to Gance, one by Rudolf Becker of Westi, written after Westi's withdrawal from the *Napoleon* syndicate, the other by Hector de Béarn, producer of the 1935 sonorised version, help to contextualise Gance's vitriolic remarks about the degrading effects of commercialism. A fourth letter, from Paul Bernard, is appended, partly because it illustrates the view of an 'enlightened' cinema manager, partly because it is one of the few surviving accounts of a screening of *Napoleon* in a working-class cinema.

Abel Gance to Noë Bloch [48]

Ajaccio, 22 April 1925

Mr Bloch
28 Avenue du Président Wilson
Paris

Dear Mr Bloch,

I have just this moment received your telegram of the 21st on my return from a very hard day's work which has left me completely exhausted, and yet I still have to summon up enough energy to write you this note.

Once and for all – and my words, please do understand, must have and will have a considerable impact *in the future*, long after you and I are no longer here – once and for all I tell you, and no one on this earth can challenge the truth of what I am saying:

I have given to Napoleon my soul, my heart, my life, my health. I have neglected nothing to make it the finest film ever made in this country. I have gone beyond the limit in my commitment to this project, sapping away at my vital forces through overwork.

If after a whole year I have not yet completed the first stage, if I haven't set the audiences of the whole world on fire, it's because all my exertions have been frustrated, I have been prevented from putting my ideas into effect, and the amazing resources that I had been preparing to mobilise with such devoted care have been compromised by an unbelievable lack of concern on your part.

I was made to write three screenplays,[49] with no concern for the intellectual exhaustion that this involved; all possibility of keeping a check on the administrative side of my film was taken away from me. I was not allowed to spread our overheads by incorporating secondary productions when I asked to. By making me work for months on end on a different period from the one I was supposed to be dealing with, you tied my hands and imprisoned my mind, with the result that I couldn't prepare the first screenplay properly and when shooting was due to begin I had to wait months before I could even get started.

These errors became so apparent that, far too late, on my return from Briançon,[50] there was a change of attitude and I was given more and more scope so that I would have the impression I was personally responsible for the time lost and the money spent. At last I had the right to have an opinion. I was able to make some headway against the current that was sweeping us along towards catastrophe, though not enough to avoid the accidents that happened at Berlin[51] and elsewhere and not enough to put the film I dreamed of making back on a completely even keel.

But all this fades into insignificance compared to one thing, something that should be branded on your mind in letters of fire and override all other considerations: my conscience is calm and clear, it denounces resolutely and unflinchingly all the lack of understanding, the pettiness, the back-stabbing; it absolves me so completely from any feeling of remorse that no news, however bad, can make me budge an inch. I do hope you fully realise that.

What you must also understand is that for the last year I have had to fight against such enormous mountains of difficulties that I am still amazed I didn't simply burst out laughing at the sight of them. How can I have agreed to wear such a millstone round my neck? . . .

I always believed that tolerance, patience, goodwill, gentleness, hard work would be enough to restore things to their normal state. I have to recognise that the opposite is true. My project seems to have been carried along on a wave of madness and I have been left alone in the boat without oars or sail . . .

People come up to me with bundles of figures under their arm, not to help me but to accuse me!! It's ridiculous!

I remember Mr Becker's letter in which he dared to write that 'the way Mr Gance goes about things is unbelievably disastrous, etc'.

How can a great work be created in such a Gehenna, for with all this suspicion, misunderstanding, malice and calumny, my life has become a mental hell and each day my work is driven nearer to death.

One detail, not in a hundred but in a hundred thousand. I asked Paris for Cossacks because, as I already remarked before I left Paris, I think my horseback scenes are very weak. In Corsica, I became all the more convinced of this and realised that without exceptionally skilled riders all the sequences involving horses would be much worse than the most mediocre of American cowboy films. And we are particularly counting on sales over there. It is my 'commercial' duty – I gave up talking about *Napoleon* in terms of art a long time ago, for who would understand me? – it is my duty, then, to insist on my request for Cossacks; and I am understandably surprised and pained to read in your telegram: 'Find horsemen on spot. Presume all Cossacks are in Russia.' That's how you would talk to a child, it's just a mockery, and I still can't understand how you could have written it. I suspect it wasn't you.[52]

I can't continue at length because my work is very demanding and I have only a few hours left to sleep. One last word, therefore. I am grateful to you for taking the responsibility for *Napoleon* on your shoulders, and I would like to think that my film will be triumphantly completed in spite of all the mistakes that have been made by others. I would like to think too that one day you will change your opinion of me, as you already would have done if you hadn't been influenced by biased opinions. When that day comes, you will fully understand that for me business, whether it's going well or badly, *always* takes second place to friendship, that you have all of mine and can still work miracles with it. Don't put off that day for too long and don't let the stain of disillusion and disenchantment spread too far in my mind.

The rest isn't worth writing: my work is too great for me to deprive it of any more time.

I remain, in spite of the storms, your devoted *friend*

Abel Gance

Rudolf Becker to Abel Gance[53]

Berlin, 9 October 1925

Mr Abel Gance
8, rue de Richelieu
Paris

Dear Mr Gance,

Thank you for your letter of the 2nd inst. As you requested, I have talked to Mr Pommer,[54] but since in the meantime you will have heard from him directly, it is hardly necessary for me to go into the matter in detail.

You seem to think that my pessimism would melt away like snow in the first rays of the sun if we could see each other more often. Nothing would give me greater pleasure, believe me. Even though I don't share your illusions, that doesn't mean I wouldn't be delighted to have a long conversation with you. I readily acknowledge that you are in my view both a very distinguished artist and a very intelligent and gifted person, but – and please excuse my bluntness – you have no head for business. It's perhaps precisely because of this contrast that I have always had a soft spot for you ever since I had the great pleasure of meeting you. But on a practical level I have become increasingly convinced that I could only ever do business with you if your activity was strictly limited to directing.

Will you permit me to tell you frankly what I think about the future of your Napoleon film? I am convinced that you will manage to complete it but do you know in what conditions? The syndicate will be disbanded, some capitalist or other will buy the whole thing for a pittance and the old shareholders will lose their money. Then the new buyer will force you to make drastic cuts in your manuscript and finish the film on a shoestring budget.

Let us hope I am mistaken, but I really do think things are likely to take this course. That would be very sad, since a unique masterpiece would not then be brought to fruition, and the sceptics who have always told me I was being ridiculous would be proved right. You will understand then, dear Mr Gance, that no one would be happier than I if my prognosis was incorrect.

After all I have just said, you can understand my view that it is logical I should cease all connection with the Société Abel Gance. Although I have so far allowed myself to be persuaded by the kind insistence of all the other participants, I must now put my intentions into effect. I am therefore notifying Mr Bloch of my resignation as member and as president of the Société Abel Gance.

I am firmly convinced that the very frankness of my letter will in no way affect the friendship we have always had for each other. Please present my respects to your wife, dear Mr Gance, and accept my warmest regards.

Rud. Becker

Paris, 27 July 1934

My dear Mr Gance,

I would like to point out a few things to you about your film. You are much too caught up in the idea of creating a masterpiece and not thinking enough about the public. Dreyer's *Joan of Arc* is indubitably a masterpiece but it was totally unsuccessful.[56] Don't get too bogged down in ideology. You tell me: 'The audience has to understand that Napoleon is the inheritor of the Revolution' and in consequence you include two long scenes about the Convention. That would be all very well if you were addressing people who want to be educated or even just a cultivated public, but 999 out of every thousand cinemagoers are morons who only want to see nice pictures.[57] They aren't very interested in your desire for historical authenticity or the ideas you want to drum into them.

Above all, give us a film that is popular, I mean one that makes money.[58] After that, if we get our investment back, we will have every opportunity to use the material you have on Napoleon to make other idealistic films.

For the moment, believe me, I think you would do well to: 1) reduce the Marseillaise sequence by a third; 2) cut the whole of the chase across Corsica, leaving only the beginning and the arrival at the seashore; 3) avoid tiring people's eyes with the storm at the Convention. There are a lot of blurred images here that are exhausting for the spectator to look at; 4) in what I saw yesterday, you have a lot of close shots of milling crowds that are not sharp and are hence unpleasant to watch. Toulon would be perfect if you kept only half of what you screened yesterday.

Don't take these criticisms badly: your film is perfect and, for the most part, it is still technically very modern, but I would like to warn you against yourself and against that feeling of paternity that makes you unable to amputate your offspring. Since you have an upper limit of 3,500 metres and it seems essential to incorporate TOULON, please agree to the sacrifices I am proposing. Believe me, the film will be better and less heavy.

With kindest regards,
Count Hector de Béarn

Paul Bernard
Manager of the Central Cinema
Meudon
Paris, 10 October 1928

Dear Mr Gance,

Your *Napoleon* has been praised to the skies, criticised and roundly condemned. It has even been massacred by vandals who wanted 'to make it more commercial' when it was released at the Gaumont Palace.[60]

I had seen your magnificent filmed poem there, reduced to a skeleton. I saw it again yesterday as you wanted it to be, in a cinema which makes no claim to be fashionable, with an audience in cloth caps, one which has no compunction about demonstrating its approval or disapproval: the honest working people of the suburbs of Montmartre. All the hoodlums of the rue du Poteau and their molls thrilled in harmony with you yesterday, in the little 'palace' in the rue Ordener, the Montcalm-Cinema.

Of course these simple, unsophisticated people didn't understand everything; your great work exceeds their capacities, but what a respectful silence there was, what intense concentration during the three hours' projection of part of the gigantic epic you have conceived. And how sincerely appreciative and not at all chauvinistic the applause for the wonderful tableaux of the Marseillaise.

Your great *Napoleon* flew like an arrow straight to its target.

As a cinema manager, I prefer to avoid publicity screenings and frequent instead local cinemas that I can go to often and where I can study the reactions of a regular and sincere audience. You have given that public something beautiful: it felt that beauty in its simple, ordinary soul.

And I thank you on behalf of these worthy people who can't or don't dare to do it for themselves. And I thank you on my own behalf for all the wonderful hours I owe to you, to *J'accuse* and *La roue* which I have seen ten times, to *Napoleon*, to all of your films.

With my respectful admiration and warmest regards,

Paul Bernard

5 Narrative and History

Rather than a kaleidoscopic portrait of the artist, the texts translated above provide a basis for a contextualisation of Gance's film production. For all their fascination with the great man as poet, philosopher and masterful presence, Buraud and Arroy tell us as much about the historical conditions in which their – and Gance's – romantic conception of the creative Author could circulate as they do about what Gance was like. They don't simply bear witness to the enthusiasm Gance inspired in his friends and associates (Arroy and Buraud are perhaps more fulsome than most, but their responses are not so very different from those of Gravone, Burel, Volkoff and other actors and technicians who worked with him); they remind us of the continuing prevalence of romanticism in the France of the 1920s, of the fervent belief of its adepts in the creation of a new social order replacing the old one swept away by the war, and of their conviction about the radical nature of the role the Artist must play in the construction of that order.

More importantly, the juxtaposition of critical texts problematises the whole notion of ahistorical genius. Gance is shown as a director working within a national film culture at a time of crisis in its development, and whose work is enmeshed in a complex set of debates about the specificity of cinema and its vocation, debates which were pursued with particular vigour in France during the 1920s and which are inextricably bound up with the highly problematical political issues of the inter-war years. The avid discussions about impressionism, the poetry of the image and symbolism are in this sense no less political than the more familiar questions of verisimilitude and truth.

No selection of texts can hope to *locate* Gance as subject in/of history. Simply to take account of aesthetic 'context' would involve broader consideration of his relations with painters like Léger and writers like Cendrars and t'Serstevens, all of whom collaborated with him at one moment or another. Then there are the Russian exiles who, as producers, technicians, assistants and actors, played such an important part in films like *Napoleon*. And there is the impact of German and American film cultures, along with commercial imperatives like the need to ensure international distribution. The importance of the texts selected is that they are symptomatic. Despite the markedly different positions from which they originate, they illustrate in their contradictions and their conformities the interrelation between aesthetic effectivity and social implication.

If there are oppositions between Buraud's presentation of the artist as philosopher and Clair's rejection of his literariness, or Soupault's complaints about the bombastic, all share a concern for the specificity of the cinematic image. Epstein's eulogy of the symbolic, Clair's call for 'pure' documentary, Vuillermoz's appeal to artistic quality and Moussinac's to technical achievement, all construct Gance as innovator in terms of his work on the *forms* of representation.

If Clair's modernism leads him to advocate images of abstraction while the more aesthetically conservative Moussinac looks first at what a film expresses, their arguments run parallel. Clair is interested in the visual impact of the train crash at the beginning of *La roue* but not really in its narrative function. Moussinac condemns the mawkishness of the Violine scenes but admires their visual beauty. More to the point, they castigate Gance for what one calls sentimentalism and the other romanticism, an excessiveness to be found not in the image itself but in some ill-defined space behind it, in 'expression' or 'literary intentions'. Only Soupault, in his condemnation of Gance's naive grandiloquence, links subject-matter to *mise en scène* and performance, but that is in order to reject all three categorically. Gance is polemicised, but politicised only in a selective way, and it is because they are partial that these texts open out a space for an analysis of the political.

Gance's theoretical writings and his screenplays impose a reformulation of the issues. Although he too refers to a poetry of the image, he insists on the integrity of the image-text, on the film-idea from which both story and image are generated. Form, content, social function and emotional impact are thus, for him, inseparable. Furthermore, his films are specifically inscribed in an authorial practice in which the director is expressly designated as the originator of a unified discourse of truth (*Napoléon vu par Abel Gance* ..., Napoleon seen through the eyes of the poet). His system of representations is one which, by occulting contradictions, has as its specific function to construct a unity for the spectator, a unity which should be poetic and popular, appealing not to rationality but to universal emotions. In short, Gance's film practice is founded on a romantic notion of the artist whose vision of the world will be communicated through a universal medium to the hearts of the masses.

It is this subsuming of the political into the socio-aesthetic of the image-text that provides the basis for an analysis, not the evacuation of the political into a world of extraneous content.

When Gance wrote, in 1917, that he was 'penetrated by an invincible conviction of [his] cinematographic powers',[1] he was already aspiring to transform the cinema as it then existed in France, to make films that would be *epic* in their treatment of subjects of universal significance. In this, he was partly influenced by the general mediocrity of film production, partly by his ambition to make his mark in the new world of moving pictures,[2] mostly by a combination of the two, a conviction that cinema could have an impact unique among the arts and that he had something to communicate that nobody else could. Hence the note, also dated 1917, 'The time has come for me to make the great popular epic of the cinema which in a thousand years' time will be our *Chanson de Roland*.'[3] Later he was to describe *Birth of a Nation* as the first *chanson de geste* of the screen,[4] and was clearly influenced by Griffith's work when he embarked on the *Napoleon* cycle. 'There are,' he states in the prologue to *Bonaparte et la Révolution*, 'only two *chansons de geste* in the whole history of cinema since its origins: the first is American, David Griffith's *Birth of a Nation* dating from 1915; the second is French, the film you are about to see, dating from 1925 to 1971.'[5]

The exact terminology is important here, for in his allusions to medieval epic Gance is referring less to a tale of heroic adventures than to the emergence of a new sense of national identity and especially to a new mode of narration in the vernacular, a poetry for the people.

Leaving aside for the moment the implicit nationalism apparent in *J'accuse*, in *Napoleon*, in some of the later films and even in the supposedly internationalist *La fin du monde*,[6] one can immediately recognise the potential centrality of the epic in Gance's work as innovation. It is the ideal form for a popular art.

It is a form that will remain central, from *J'accuse*, originally conceived as the first part of a trilogy which would show the destructiveness of war and the new society that could emerge from it, through to *La divine tragédie* and *Christophe Colomb* which Gance was still talking about filming when he was well into his eighties. Sometimes it is exceptional individuals who, by their visionary qualities, have left their mark on the world – Homer, Jesus, Beethoven, Napoleon – sometimes adaptations of literary works like *Don Quixote*, frequently inventions, fictions that aspire to represent the human condition, as in *La fin du monde* and *J'accuse*, since, as Gance observes in a note probably written in the 1960s: 'The only epic that's possible today is the epic not of an individual but of a people. It's the greatest work that the human mind can undertake.'[7] The list of projects is huge, the number of screenplays that were actually written is extraordinary, the time spent trying to get them off the ground unbelievable.

But epics were not liked by producers, especially when they were prophetic trilogies of inordinate length. Besides which, Gance was not convinced that the viewing public was ready to accept the elevated message he proposed to offer the world (and that his critics dismissed as overblown nonsense).

There was, though, another genre that appealed to Gance as much as the epic – the melodrama, with the possibilities it offered of working through social, psychological and sexual problems within the confined space of the family unit.

Critics have mostly spoken disparagingly about Gance's melodramas, seeing them as early works in an outmoded genre, to be discarded once he had developed his cinematic theory and perfected new techniques, or as stopgaps. Such a view is not simply teleological, constructing Gance as the experimenter who reached greatness with *Napoleon* and from then on was only rarely given the opportunity to show his indisputable genius (in *Beethoven* and *Cyrano et d'Artagnan*, for example); it ignores the prevalence of melodrama throughout his career, and the presence of melodramatic elements in almost all his output.

In the early melodramas he made for Le film d'art (1916–17), Gance was clearly drawing on the dominant modes of bourgeois theatre of the time and was, as Roger Icart points out, particularly influenced by the successful psychological dramas of Henri Bernstein and Henri Bataille.[8] This corresponds very much to Gance's attempts to introduce into the French cinema more elevated subjects (cf. his frequent complaints about the inanity of most film productions of the time). But it is also an attempt to rescue the melodrama as a popular rather than a bourgeois form, in that it appealed essentially to the spectator's emotions. Thus *Mater dolorosa*, a subject he treated twice (in 1917 and 1932) and set on both occasions in a wealthy, professional environment, is described by him as 'an essentially popular theme'. 'I have tried,' he said in a 1932 interview, 'to make a film that I think is touching and human, and which is intended for the general public that frequents the cinema, for mothers, husbands, those who will recognise themselves in the film and improve themselves.'[9]

Similarly, when he decided to make *La roue* in 1919, he consciously chose the melodrama, setting aside more grandiose projects, not simply for commercial reasons but for a whole complex of motives which he attempted to explain at the time in his notebooks:

> I am less and less convinced that cinema can cope with true works of art and I shrink back every day from my great subjects. The equipment is still too imperfect for me to be able to construct my cathedrals of light. Architect, stonemason, priest, I am weighed down by my storms of sunlight ... A little darkness so I can get my breath ... One stair at a time. I am looking for a story that will be at once more melodramatic and of universal significance, set in a world made for the cinema, the world of locomotives, rails, signals, steam ... and in a contrasting world of snow, mountain peaks, solitude; a white symphony following on from a black symphony. Expound the catastrophes of feelings and those of machines together, with each as dramatic, as fundamentally significant as the other; show the ubiquity of everything that beats: a heart and a steam-valve. Since drama is created from the outside, through environments that gradually reveal their heroes, the opposite of theatrical drama, I decide on 30 July 1919, in the gardens of the Caux Palace, after a long conversation with my new little friend, to make *La roue*.[10]

Melodrama does not replace the epic treatment of great subjects, but neither is it a last resort, a gap-filler. That Sisif is an engine-driver does not prevent him from being elevated by love and suffering to the status of epic hero.[11] And though the film is set in contemporary working-class society (or more accurately constructs an opposition between a working-class and a bourgeois-capitalist environment) it can still, Gance insists, evoke universal truths of human relations.

The epic and the melodrama differ little, then, in their object: both are seen as popular forms appealing to popular emotions; both could be ways of expressing universal (and national) truths.

What frequently happens, in many of the films Gance actually made or wrote screenplays for, as opposed to more grandiose projects like *Les grands initiés*, is that forms of melodrama and epic are subsumed into heroic drama of the kind popularised by Edmond Rostand.[12] Often they are simply juxtaposed. Thus it is in *La roue*, a melodrama, that accelerated montage – later to be associated with the development of the epic – is first exploited, while the characteristic *mise en scène* of melodrama, composition in depth with moments of intensity highlighted by close-ups, is frequently used in 'epic' sequences. This juxtaposition, with the shifting patterns of

La roue: Sisif as engine-driver ...

identification offered to the spectator, is in fact a much more fundamental characteristic than superimpression, which Pappas (in his
Cineaste article) sees as the essential feature of Gance's technique.

Gance's *mise en scène* and the positions it constructs for the spectator
will be examined in more detail in chapter seven. Here, I want to
analyse some of the effects of the co-existence of the epic and the
melodramatic in the narrative structures of Gance's films and to look
at some of the political implications.

The plots in most of Gance's films, epic and melodrama, are based
on stereotyped characters and situations. This does not mean that the
characters are two-dimensional or loosely sketched in roles like the
General, the Schoolmaster or the Engineer in some of Renoir's films.
It is rather that the founding instance is the Idea of the film, a
romantic construction rather than a set of realist conventions, the
epic depending for its plot on melodrama while the melodrama
aspires, in its effect, towards the exemplary, the elemental rather than
the purely representative.

Thus Beethoven in 1936 is not so very different from the composer
Damor in *La dixième symphonie* of 1918. Although one is 'historical' and
the other fictitious, both produce their greatest art through suffering,
both are caught up in intense human dramas, both are representations of the artist confronting destiny rather than individuals with the

. . . and epic hero

psychological depth essential to bourgeois literature. And Gance does not hesitate to invent the great love on which his film view of Beethoven is founded. Norma in *La roue* is of a different social class and temperament from her counterpart, Geneviève, in the epic *La fin du monde*, but her situation is similar. Both have an impossible love for a young artist. Both, like Andrée in *Le droit à la vie* and Gisèle in *La zone de la mort*, are forced or tricked into marrying a wealthy capitalist. Both are momentarily tempted by the good life before unhappiness and depth of feeling bring them back to the fold. In both instances, functionality counts for more than individuality.

Stereotyped situations of this kind are not of course unique to Gance. To quote just one example, in *L'âtre*, a film produced in parallel with *La roue* but which Gance neither scripted nor directed, Jean and Bernard fall in love with their adopted sister Arlette. Although she loves Jean, she marries Bernard, creating a conflict which is finally resolved when Jean, on his deathbed, reconciles Arlette and Bernard (echoing the resolution of *Le droit à la vie*). But such situations are strangely insistent in Gance's work.

Clearly, in his desire to produce a popular art, Gance is not simply resorting to sure-fire stories which will make an immediate impact. Nor is he bowing to commercial pressures, to the extent that similar structures recur in the rapidly executed *films de commande* as well as in

Un grand amour de Beethoven

the projects for which he had a relatively free hand. It is rather that
the stereotype is construed as the archetypal, as an intensification of
universal problems contextualised in contemporary French society or
in history. Melodrama, or the melo-epic, thus becomes the modern
equivalent of the myth (Sisif as Sisyphus and as proletarian Oedipus,
the Jean Diaz of *J'accuse* as Orestes and Oedipus) made available to a
popular audience because it is actualised.

The screenplay must only be a pretext, argues Clair, and Gance
tends sometimes to agree, as in an interview with André Lang: 'Don't
you see, I would like to be able to suppress the novelistic, the naiveties
and the repetitions in a film like *La roue*. Naturally, what interests me,
what I am most attached to, are the moments of technical paroxysm,
so to speak, the periods of intensity in the screenplay. But I am not
working just for myself . . .'[14] Yet he frequently complained when
critics discussed only these 'paroxysms', the technical innovations
and spectacular moments. And he insists in 'Le temps de l'image est
venu!' (p.97) that too many spectators just saw in *La roue* images of
trains and stories of railway accidents, whereas for him the tragedies
of human hearts were far more elevated. In his initial project both are
of equal importance, since the true dramatic language of the screen is
a combination of the pathos of things and of men.[15] But the mythic,
the elemental, the melodramatic ultimately count for more. In
Gance's shortened version of the silent *J'accuse*, it is the melodramatic
that survives, at the expense of the epic.

130

Not surprisingly in an archetypal world there are conflicts between heroes and villains, young idealists and depraved capitalists, but if good does in the end triumph over evil, it is not in any simplistic way. The villain is not just effete. His life-style may be decadent – thus giving Gance the opportunity to challenge the censor by inserting scenes of titillating 'indecency' even in a film as austere as *La roue*. But he can't live out his villainy, except in *Napoleon*, where Pozzo di Borgo and Salicetti act out of personal animosity towards Bonaparte and jealousy rather than conviction, and in *La fin du monde* where for once the motivation is explicitly political. Nor is the villain saved, but through his love for a woman he is reduced to the status of instinctive being, punished in his discovery of feeling and a suffering that the heroes have been able to assume and transcend.

Woman, as archetype, is problematical. There is the occasional reverse situation, as in *La Vénus aveugle* in which she is a calculating, self-interested witch, reduced by love and maternity to the instinctiveness of the male villain. More typically, as we have seen, she loves the visionary but is both seduced by the effete capitalist and tempted by the trappings of luxury before she returns to the good cause, too late, in the more interesting screenplays, to live with the man she loves, but able to further his work or at least to recognise its value. Usually absent as mother,[16] fickle as friend in spite of her love, but also the only being able to comprehend instinctively the message of the visionary artist and to transmit it to others, woman remains ambivalent.

That there are political significations circulating in these structures is evident in the opposition capital/art, alongside a sexual politics whose convolutions clearly need to be analysed in much more depth than I have attempted to do here. But it is the conception of the heroic that particularly complicates things in the way it deflects attention away from a male/female or hero/villain hierarchy towards an investigation of the nature of heroism.

It is rare in Gance's screenplays to find a single hero pitched against a single villain, even in the early films. *Le droit à la vie*, for example, does not simply set Pierre Veryal, the depraved master, against Jacques, the virtuous secretary, in a rivalry of love; there is also Marc, the criminal secretary who, by shooting the master in an attempt to save himself and incriminate the other, effects a reconciliation of the two rivals which elevates Pierre, as he dies, to the status of generous hero along with Jacques. Similarly in *La roue*, Sisif and his son Elie, rivals in their love for Norma, are pitched against Hersan.

Divided heroes: François Laurin, the *revanchard*, in the 1919 version of *J'accuse* . . .

And the same kind of scenario, with variations, can be found in a number of other films, right through to *La Vénus aveugle* and *Cyrano et d'Artagnan*.

The effect is a kind of displacement which on the level of screenplay is one of the most interesting aspects of Gance's films. Once set in place as representative of depravity, the villain can be marginalised. His fate remains of interest to the spectator but it is secondary. More usually, what counts is the way his action reflects that of the heroes. More precisely, the effect is to open up a new space in the narrative, shifting attention away from a banal conflict between vice and virtue, towards the struggles between the characters opposed to villainy. And it is towards the resolution of *this* problem that the films usually tend. 'Les frères ennemis' is an old literary and dramatic motif. What's interesting in Gance's appropriation of it is that both brothers are fighting on the same side, inadequately, inviting the spectator to look and work for a completeness.

Thus, in the first version of *J'accuse*, Jean Diaz and François Laurin, childhood friends, are rivals in their love for Edith (François, Edith's husband, is motivated by jealousy, knowing that she prefers Jean). What gradually unites them is their struggle against a common enemy – the war – and the recognition that their love for the same woman is equally strong. The initial thrust of the film may be an interrogation of war and an insistence that the immense sacrifices it has entailed must prove to have produced a regenerated society. The melodramatic intrigue directs attention on the contrary towards the Jean/François axis: François, the brute, the hunter, the *revanchard*, inspired by hatred, jealousy and a thirst for violence, confronting Jean, the gentle, sensitive, inspired author of visionary poems. Even though their love for Edith eventually unites them, neither the brutally instinctive nor the inspired romantic but only a fusion of their

. . . and Jean Diaz, the poet

J'accuse: heroes reconciled in love and war

respective strengths can effect a resolution, in an apocalyptic return of the dead – of François and what he stood for – imagined by Jean in a state of prophetic madness. The new man, fusion of the instinctive and the enlightened, is yet to be, but he has to be if the war is to be justified.

This split of the hero into two distinct positions is even more marked in the two versions of *Mater dolorosa*. In both the villain is marginalised to the extent that he appears only briefly as blackmailer (who, in the 1932 version, redeems himself). Instead, the drama concerns the relations between two men and the woman they both love. Dr Berliac, a paediatrician, neglects his wife on account of his devotion to his work as surgeon and teacher. She falls madly in love with his best friend (1917) or brother (1932), a sensitive writer/ dramatist, who out of respect for Berliac urges renunciation of their passion and is accidentally shot while trying to prevent Mme Berliac from killing herself.

Although the friend/brother dies early in the film and the action apparently turns on the family relationship of the Berliacs, the dramatic structures in fact bring into play the reconciliation of what the brothers stand for. Claude, the ultra-sensitive playwright (in the 1932 version) even produces his art from the suffering that his illicit and unconsummated love produces in him. The paediatrician, motivated by instinctive jealousy and by the calculating nature of science, acts cruelly, risking the lives of wife and child in his desire to learn the truth. His redemption, and the resolution, is the discovery of trust, confidence, respect; through them he becomes complete.

It is in *La fin du monde* that this structure is most fully developed. Jean Novalic, a visionary, and Martial his brother, a distinguished astronomer, both love Geneviève. Jean urges her to marry Martial, which she eventually does (but not before she has been seduced, as in *J'accuse* and *La roue*, by an unscrupulous enemy). It is no longer simply individual happiness which is at stake, however, but the future of humanity: Jean has renounced Geneviève, in spite of their mutual love, so that he can fulfil his mission, the regeneration of society. He loses his already fragile sanity but not before he has recorded his message to the world. Martial, meanwhile, discovers that a comet is about to collide with the earth and, basing his action on Jean's ideas, takes over the press and radios of the world to establish a new order. The comet creates havoc but does not collide with the earth. As it is propelled back into space, the world reawakens to a new existence. (In an epilogue which survives in at least one version of the screenplay, but which was perhaps not filmed, Martial and Geneviève, amid the enthusiastic population of Paris, pay homage to Jean's genius while he, having regained his reason, wanders anonymously through the crowds.) [17]

Even after making allowance for the way the finished product was hacked about by the producer,[18] one can easily understand why this, the most ambitious of Gance's films in its pretensions, was mauled by the critics. Though they mostly complain about inadequacies of technical quality – poor sound, obtrusive use of stock shots, models and so on, it is not difficult to recognise a fundamental objection to Gance's naive universalism. It is, though, an intriguing film for its sometimes voluptuous, sometimes strident overlaying of image and sound and, especially in the present context, for the uneasiness of its merging of melodrama and epic, of the personal and the apocalyptic, the mundane and the fabulous.

In particular, in the explicitness of its dualist heroism, it suggests the need for a reappraisal of the other films. We seem to be confronted with two categories of heroes, each with its own conformities and values. On the one hand the visionary: artist, writer, poet or musician (Elie, Jean Diaz, François Rolland, Claude Berliac, Jean Novalic); on the other the materialist: man of science, doctor, astronomer, engineer (Emile Berliac, Gilles Berliac, Martial Novalic), along with anti-intellectual characters like François Laurin and those who have predominantly physical skills like Sisif.

Indeed, the whole issue seems to be neatly explained in an unpublished 'schéma dramatique' of *La fin du monde* written in March 1929:

Jean Novalic was born to be a prophet, an idealist, a poet, a mystic. Self-sacrifice, poetry, love for mankind, beauty are his daily bread. Unhappiness must, therefore, be his lot – in spite of the divine optimism that inspires him.

Martial Novalic, on the contrary, is a clear-sighted, practical positivist, brought up on science and an adherent of the school of reality, a chemist, a physicist, a distinguished astronomer who, in spite of his good fortune, is a pessimist, realising that science after all doesn't bring happiness to man and that the dangers of war, of revolution, of science are greater and more serious than they have ever been, in spite of the hypocritical promises made by one nation to another.

The exactness, the prodigious memory of Martial, the scientific atmosphere in which he is immersed, confer on him a kind of Napoleonic genius for action, which his disgust for the present state of affairs prevents him from using.

If Jean Novalic was born to be a prophet, Martial Novalic was born to lead. And it is the extreme difference in their natures, even though these meet in the magnificent paroxysm of their intellectual tension, that has not yet allowed them to understand what they could gain by complementing each other instead of working in divergent ways.

The scientist lacks the poetry necessary for him to be able to construct. The idealist lacks the practical sense needed to accomplish his aims.

The interest would seem then to be less in the conflict than in the lack and its elimination in a necessary unity inspired by the poet but effected by the man of science (with the help of the woman who loved the poet and who learns to love the man of science).[19]

We need, however, to beware of reducing these conformities to a simple model as though we had identified a 'deep structure' revealing the inner workings of the poet's mind. There is also the danger of taking *La fin du monde's* schéma and analysing it as though Gance had been working intuitively towards the definitive resolution of a problem that can only be identified retrospectively.

That there are conformities has been demonstrated, and that there is a progression of sorts can also be shown. But it is not a simple teleological progression, and the differences in the conceptualisation or representation of unity are perhaps more important than the conformities.

In some of the early films, the unity is merely sketched out, accomplished only in the future, after the action of the film has ended. In the first *J'accuse*, for example, Jean and François both die and it is only in Jean's vision of the new post-war society that the fusion of the instinctive and the inspired can be effected. In *La roue*, the closing images show Sisif dying, having at last attained fulfilment. And in the 1917 *Mater dolorosa*, Emile Berliac's conversion is in effect the resolution, heralding a new life which is shown only as coming into being (there are changes in the remake but the resolution is basically the same).

Increasingly, though, attention is focused on the unified hero himself. *Napoleon* ends with a vision of the future, but the unity of the character has been established early on. Martial Novalic's discovery of unity in *La fin du monde* is an important moment, but most of the film concentrates on the activity that this unity makes possible and the attempts of others to thwart him. François Laurin, in the 1938 *J'accuse*, is present only in the prologue, and although the plot is no less melodramatic than in the 1919 version, Jean Diaz is the undisputed focus of attention.

What also happens in Gance's films of the 1920s is a shift in the nature of the unified hero. It is increasingly not the visionary but the man of science who, inspired by the former, achieves unity as man of action. No gentle philosopher, then, or sensitive poet, but a dynamic presence, enflamed by a sense of mission, energetic and resolute, prepared to have recourse to whatever means are necessary to defend an emergent new society, a friend of the people but quite uncompromising in his action against its enemies. He may appeal to reason and to the heart, but first of all there must be order, discipline, authority. Converted by Jean, Martial Novalic in *La fin du monde* does not need to question. His mission is to impose Jean's views in order to save the world.

By the late 1930s, there has been a further shift. Jean Diaz in the remake of *J'accuse* is man of science and a visionary but his science is powerless. The formula for 'steel glass' he has invented is stolen by a corrupt capitalist and merely leads to the development of more powerful weapons. Only the visionary in him can save the world, but it is by instilling fear, terrifying the populations of the world by raising the dead, the victims of the Great War who would have died in vain if there were another European war.

These conformities and variances can, in their way, be ascribed to an authorial practice but only if the 'author' is construed as subject in

The visionary Diaz in the 1938 *J'accuse*; and (below) the return of the dead

history. The Romantic Hero is not a monolith nor the author an autonomous producer of meanings since fictional systems of representation or symbolisation exist within specific struggles, and authorial constructs are part of a complex of political, intellectual and economic debates. Like the capitalist villains, our divided heroes and their unification are historically inscribed.

That question of 'context' will be the next major stage in the analysis, but account must also be taken of the emplacement of the spectator within the narrative process, and with regard to the world the films produce. That the spectator is aligned against the villain is already apparent, as is the ambivalent placing of the woman as object of desire and devotion. (In films in which the roles are reversed, like *La Vénus aveugle*, this ambivalence is, with modification, the attribute of the male.)

The problem for identification arises from the shift of the centre of attention away from a conventional struggle between good and evil towards the interrogation of heroism. The spectator inscribed in the early films discussed above cannot fully identify with either of the incomplete heroes since neither is in total possession of the knowledge (or strength) needed to effect a resolution of the narrative enigma. Instead the spectator is led into an alignment with the narrative process, aspiring towards a unification, which takes place only at the moment of resolution or beyond it, in a world outside the fiction of the film. But the spectator has been mobilised to desire a specific form of unification, a symbiosis of the attributes that have been presented through the fragmentation of the hero. When, later, the hero does emerge entire within the narrative, he is constructed from that already generated desire, as though called forth by the spectator to act on his or her behalf.

Remembering Bazin's observation about the response of the spectator in realist cinema, emerging from the fictional world with a new understanding of the real one and motivated by a desire to change it, it is all the more important to take account of this positioning in films like Gance's, which construct not a realist but an essentially narrative space, directing us towards an ideological position which exists not in the world of our experience but in that of our desires mobilised in and by the film and cast out beyond it, into a world which has itself, in the process, been politicised. Hence the need to move through from story and narrative to *mise en scène* as stages in the positioning process, and also to attend in the narrative construction to implication as well as to explication.

6   Politics and the Aesthetic

POLITICS AND POPULISM

The image of the unified hero that gradually emerges in Gance's films clearly owes a great deal to a whole romantic tradition typified by the Schillerian ideal of the aesthetic man, and to Nietzsche, whose impact in France was immense. (Reading *Zarathustra* for the first time in 1915, Gance describes the experience as like seeing the sun for the first time.)[1] The need to reconcile art and science was also being forcibly argued in France by writers like Paul Valéry, a generation older than Gance and already an established intellectual presence. But what makes Gance interesting historically is his rejection of the cult of the self so essential to reactionary writers like Maurice Barrès and in which, in Gance's view, even Nietzsche remained too entrenched.[2] Gance's hero is not a divided individual seeking completeness in and for himself (self-interest is the attribute of the calculating villain). As fusion of energy and sensibility, of visionary and scientist, of two quite *distinct* personas, he is essentially a hero *for others*, a 'man of destiny'. This, and the increasingly authoritarian nature of the hero's power, have a particular resonance in the France of the 1920s and 1930s.

Other influences could be invoked, like D'Annunzio, a poetic authoritarian and patriot greatly admired by Gance when he was still aspiring to a literary career; and especially Elie Faure, a dominant presence for a whole generation of radicals during the 1920s and the major source for *Napoleon*. The important point, though, is that the Gance hero is not a nostalgic harking-back to a mythical unified society but an address to specific problems of an epoch, seemingly outmoded in the unrealised projects of the 1960s, but very actual, as the vigour of the critical debates shows, in the years 1918 to 1939, and founded on the need for radical social change. In short, Gance's romanticism is specific to the inter-war years in France, and as such, in spite of his disclaimers, is both committed and essentially political in its effects.

The basis for this desire for change is the belief, widely held among artists and intellectuals of the Third Republic, that bourgeois materialism had created a decadent society. Shared by most of Gance's avant-garde friends, notably Blaise Cendrars, his assistant for *La roue*, it is a view that emerges frequently in their insistence on the need for a new anti-bourgeois art. It informs much of Gance's writing on the aesthetics of cinema, as well as his vehement attacks on the commercialism of producers and distributors, who are held entirely responsible for the holding back of technical progress and the prevalence of mindless products. The arguments, too, if reduced to essentials, are familiar ones. Bourgeois parliamentary democracy has constructed a society based on conformism and individual self-interest. It is dominated by corrupt capitalists, avid only for self-aggrandisement and financial gain. Its materialism engenders depravity among the dominant and moral blindness in the exploited working classes. If the Great War had any possible justification, it was to sweep away the old social order along with its positivist and rationalist underpinning and herald a new era of concord and class solidarity. Some, like Jean Guéhenno, even believed that the war had achieved this aim: 'I really thought that a completely new man had been born, a man whose senses were quite different: a sense of the people, of the world, of the future. I wasn't far from thinking that we had witnessed a Passion of humanity which, like that of Jesus, would be the beginning of a new era.'[3] There are reminiscences here of *J'accuse*, in which the attack on the horror of a *revanchard* war is twinned with an appeal to what war must achieve if it is to be justified. But Gance also has a less naive view of regeneration.

In a 1913 project for a serial, along the lines of *Fantômas* and provisionally titled *Diaz le briseur de fortunes*, Diaz is a worker who, having gained entry into middle-class society, takes on as his mission to kill the bosses who exploit their fellow men. By 1919 the Diaz of *J'accuse*, though still of humble origins, has become the prophet of the new age, driven mad by the horrors of a capitalist war. His successor, Jean Novalic in *La fin du monde*, who has *chosen* to live among the poor, loses his sanity because he is attacked by a hostile crowd after trying to save a child from maltreatment by drunken parents. In between comes *La roue*, in which the representation of social evils is much more developed than is generally realised, since the most explicit scenes were usually excised from the distribution prints. Hersan, the precursor of Schomburg as representative of a capitalist establishment, combines moral and sexual decadence, giving wild parties, tricking Norma into marrying him, passing off Sisif's inventions as his own. The railway bureaucracy is shown, in some bitingly satirical scenes, as incompetent, insensitive and anxious only to produce a report on the train accident that absolves the company of all responsibility. The railway workers are degraded by working conditions and alcohol.

141

J'accuse: the prophet driven mad by the horrors of war

Radical reform cannot come then from the established order. As Elie Faure wrote in 1921, echoing a long line of anti-democrats: 'Democracy, in France at least, necessarily means the assertion and solidarity of mediocrity and incompetence.'[4] But neither can Revolution emerge directly from the masses, since they too are depraved. The people remain the source of a new energy (to quote Elie Faure again, the working class is alone in trying to take France back to the path of creative dynamism),[5] but this can only be galvanised by a powerful authority with high ideals and strength of purpose. Hence the need for the unified hero whose power derives from the masses but whose inherent qualities confer on him a natural leadership, who is resolute enough to stand above corruption and to overcome the forces of self-interest. Some cataclysmic event, the Great War, the Revolution, the imagined End of the World, the Return of the Dead, may still be necessary before the need for regeneration can be recognised, but it is the visionary man of action who restores order and shows the way ahead.

Even if cinema can operate only in the realm of fiction or of history revisited, it is intricately linked to this conception of the political. The film-maker, as artist, also aspires to be seer, who like Jean Diaz brings the dead back to life, acts on popular imagination, appeals to their intuition, imposes his authority and convinces that his vision is the poetic truth of the world.

This emphasis on the people as source of impulsion and on the need for a strong creative force to guide and inspire them, on the role of the prophetic artist, is, in effect, an elitist populism that merges art and politics, making art, allied with science, the effective political force.

Divergent forms of populism have never been easy to locate within conventional modes of analysis, and this is particularly the case in the complex political and aesthetic conjunctures of between-the-wars France, when radical shifts of allegiance were almost commonplace.

Satire: the railway authorities in *La roue*

In his insistence on the social importance of cinema, Gance distances himself from what the Marxist Emmanuel Berl called the petit-bourgeois anarchism of the avant-garde surrealists,[6] who in their turn reproached Gance for his sensationalist commercialism and fidelity to bourgeois narrative forms. As the critiques of Clair, Buñuel and Soupault show, the avant-garde was much more concerned with the development of a new art as a counter to bourgeois hegemony rather than as a renewal founded on forms of popular culture. In this respect, and in his belief in the people as the source of a new energy, Gance seems closer to the Marxist left. Indeed, he counted among his friends a number of communist intellectuals, notably the novelist Henri Barbusse, and for a time, in the early 1930s, he was attracted towards militant groups of writers and artists. But Gance's mysticism is a long way from historical materialism and, as Moussinac's criticisms show, his cult of the hero was viewed as highly dangerous by a generation of left-wing activists for whom the struggle against fascism was already becoming the major issue.

It would be tempting to equate his attacks on bourgeois corruption and his insistence on the need for order and strong authority with the views of extreme right-wing nationalists like Georges Valois, who saw Napoleon as the only true Leader and instinct as the only source of creative energy.[7] But there were many varieties of Napoleonists, ranging from hard-line militarist patriots to fellow-travellers like Elie Faure, who in a 1932 letter to a Marxist colleague describes Napoleon as the Lenin of his time.[8]

In fact, Gance was reviled by the extreme right. L'action française, for example, published two extremely hostile reviews of La fin du monde, condemning it as the ludicrous work of an eternal schoolboy: 'We hardly dare to add that Abel Gance is a Jew, which would nevertheless clarify the issue. Some Israelites might quite correctly take offence at being placed in the same category as this primeval maniac. And Gance's Messianism is of too puerile a form for us to assimilate it to the destructive machinations and revolutionary currents which accompany the wandering race.'[9] Gance had rarely been treated so disparagingly, except by François Coty, a Corsican and leader of an extremist patriot party, who publicly attacked him in his newspaper Le Figaro for making Napoleon with German money, but omitted to mention that he himself had categorically refused to participate in the French syndicate Gance had hoped to launch early in 1924.[10] The film, he claimed, would simply be anti-French propaganda, showing France as a militarist nation avid for conquest and bloodshed (but the point was that it might stimulate attacks on France's rearmament policy).[11]

What Gance's argument most closely resembles in many respects is that of Spengler and the anti-Marxist Prussian socialists who also insist on the decadence of parliamentary democracy caused by industrialism and intellectualism, on the need for regeneration of the masses led by a natural aristocracy. But there were parallel movements closer to home, among syndicalists inspired by the anarchist Georges Sorel: here too there is an uneasy juxtaposition of patriotism and internationalism, authority and spontaneity, reformism and anti-intellectualism.[12] And there were the different elements of the *Jeune droite* which came to prominence in the early 1930s, led by writers like Jacques Maritain, Emmanuel Mounier and Drieu la Rochelle, criticising the individualism of bourgeois democracy and Marxist notions of class struggle, and advocating a natural patriotism as the basis for a new universal and spiritual social order.[13]

If, in order to find a way out of this apparent confusion, we were to apply the criteria adopted by Zeev Sternhell, we would be led to classify Gance as a member of a new left which emerged from revolutionary syndicalism and which in its rejection of bourgeois rationality and historical materialism entered into a relationship of symbiosis with a radical new right. This fusion, Sternhell argues, forged that seductive, dazzling and challenging ideology that can be defined as fascist, even if its adepts never wore a brown shirt. 'That is what made it possible for a large number of intellectuals to be fascists without realising it.'[14] As a well-documented attempt to clarify a complex situation, Sternhell's analysis is an impressive one, but it is primarily based on statements produced from declared political positions, and his notion of symbiosis evades the problem of the contexts within which specific statements were made. Similar ideas could and did circulate within radically heterogeneous discourses. In particular, his classification cannot explain why Elie Faure, the archetypal figure of an 'unpoliticised' new left and not mentioned by Sternhell, should have thrown in his lot with the communists and gone to Spain in 1936 to support the Republican cause, while Gance, intellectually so close to Faure, was quite happy to accept the Franco régime. Both, in Sternhell's terms, would have to be condemned as proto-fascists, along with very many contemporary artists and writers.

In spite of flirtations with Marxism, Gance's cult of the hero, his appeal to popular intuition and insistence on the need for spiritual regeneration do, it seems, bring him closer to a radical right than to a revolutionary left. But convenient labels like 'proto-fascist' remain unhelpful. They are not just ill-defined, they tend to deny history, failing to differentiate between an appeal for a new order and authority in, for example, 1923 and 1935, or changes in the nature and function of the authority that is called for.

We need, then, to revert to the broader but more easily definable notion of élitist populism. As a form of political romanticism – political in its address to the question of the social formation, romantic in its advocacy of a spiritually united force guided by a superior being – it can be categorised, in Marxist terms, as reactionary in its denial of struggle and its appeal to a natural unity. But the complex issue of historical inscription cannot be resolved simply in terms of preconstituted political parties or movements. *Napoleon* does indeed, in this very narrow sense of the term, place itself outside the political, in spite of its blatantly authoritarian line. It is precisely populism's attempts to deny that it is political that have to be analysed here.

Following on from a discussion of *Napoleon*, the analysis of two films dating from the mid-1930s and early 1940s may further clarify this issue of historical inscription: an epic, the sonorised *Napoleon Bonaparte* of 1935, usually dismissed as an act of sabotage inflicted on the 1927 silent version, and *La Vénus aveugle*, a 1941 melodrama. Neither film refers explicitly to contemporary political events, yet both need to be read in terms of quite specific conjunctures: hardening positions of the left and right in 1935 and the formation of the Popular Front; the Nazi occupation and the Vichy government in 1941. Basically both produce and appear to be produced from a Pétainist position. More precisely, Pétain seems to have become the only figure in an aleatory present who might preserve popular energies. The aesthetic remains the dominant concern, and it is this subordination of the political that must be considered as reactionary. It is also what makes *Napoleon* exemplary.

NAPOLEON THE EXEMPLARY

Any discussion of *Napoleon* is complicated by the fact that the screenplay went through many versions and that the 1927 film was not, in its conception, an autonomous work but the first part of a cycle which was never completed. In the first outline screenplay submitted in September 1923 to Giuseppe Barattolo, head of the Unione Cinematografica Italiana,[15] Gance envisaged a single film of 6,000 metres, covering the whole of Napoleon's career from Brienne to Saint Helena. The project quickly grew. By December of the same year the scheme submitted to Barattolo was for four films of 2,000m each[16] and by the time a production syndicate had been formed in the early summer of 1924,[17] the number of films planned had been increased to six (of 1,500 to 2,000m, provisionally entitled 'Arcole', '18 brumaire', 'Austerlitz', 'La Campagne de Russie', 'Waterloo' and

'Sainte-Hélène'). And finally, when the syndicate insisted that three full screenplays should be written before shooting began,[18] Gance upped the total to eight (of 2,500m each).

What Gance in fact did was to expand the prologue (*Brienne*) and split the remainder of the first film into two, *Vendémiaire* (or *Bonaparte et la Terreur*) and *Arcole*. The three completed scripts were submitted to the syndicate in December 1924[19] and it was on that basis that shooting began early in January 1925. After that a programme of recontraction set in. The withdrawal of Westi, the principal backers, in June 1925 brought production almost to a halt[20] and although Gance eventually succeeded in obtaining new sources of funding, the new production company (the Société générale de films) insisted that the three screenplays be welded back into a single script, which was completed in December 1925.[21]

Since as much of the existing footage as possible had to be used, it was mostly *Arcole* that was cut – almost in its entirety, resulting in a radical change in orientation. Instead of a prologue and two films, one culminating in the saving of the French republic at Vendémiaire[22] and the other in the liberation of the north of Italy and the proclamation of the Cisalpine Republic, there was now a single film ending with the first skirmishes of the Italian Campaign and Bonaparte's dream of the future. Gance turned these commercial and material constraints to good advantage, introducing the triptychs to reinforce the impact of the visionary ending. He even produced a powerful argument as to why the first epoch of his epic should end with a sense of anticipation (the French Revolution carried beyond its frontiers) rather than of completion. The effect, even so, was to replace a series of narrative climaxes by a visual one, to substitute the aesthetic for the political, a problem we will need to return to.

More important is the absence of the planned continuation. *Arcole* was never filmed, although the screenplay survives in manuscript.[23] And when Gance began writing again, in the autumn of 1927, he directed his attention to the final episode, *Sainte-Hélène*, a script that was eventually adapted and filmed in Germany, by Lupu Pick.[24] Only one other of the films originally planned was ever made, *Austerlitz*, shot by Gance thirty years later in Yugoslavia with Nelly Kaplan as his collaborator.

What has disappeared, then, is not simply *Arcole* but a whole concept of Napoleon. As Gance wrote in a preliminary note to the first outline script: 'With Napoleon, I am taking on the greatest drama of all time,' adding that, as a result, he must at all costs respect 'the immortal truth.'[25] And in the preface to the *Sainte-Hélène* screenplay, he describes it as a kind of titanic bourgeois drama, a realist and intimate poem in a 'colossal' style, an interiorisation in which the grandiose aspects of Napoleon's life are transformed into everyday concerns, monotony, boredom, memory and remorse.[26] The texts Gance wrote to present his film to the public in 1927 also speak of his desire to present a bioptical portrait of Napoleon, master of his destiny as saviour of the Revolution, slave of that same destiny when entrapped by the proclamation of the Empire, not wholly opposed to war, but having to fight incessantly in the illusory pursuit of lasting peace. Napoleon as hero of a romantic drama (as opposed to absolute hero), man of destiny, born to lead, outflanked by hostile forces and tainted ambition, unable to maintain his youthful idealism.[27]

Vendémiaire suffered less than *Arcole*. It was redrafted in 1925 with the loss of some scenes, relating notably to the fall of the monarchy and to the leaders of the Revolution,[28] but its main strategies survived through to the completion of filming on 1 September 1926. Much more was lost, though, at the editing and distribution stages. As Moussinac stresses, the version of *Napoleon* shown at the Opéra in April 1927 was little more than a loosely connected anthology, lacking the entire Brienne prologue and many other important scenes.[29] (Gance states in contemporary correspondence that it was about 5,000m in length, subsequently reduced to 3,700m.[30])

Immediately afterwards, Gance edited a complete version in six episodes of 1,800 to 2,000m each[31] (elsewhere he states that the total length was 11,000m).[32] This was shown twice, to an invited audience of friends, critics and trade representatives in May 1927 at the Apollo cinema, but when the film began its ten-week run at the Marivaux cinema in November 1927, it was again a short version that was shown: not the Opéra print but a modified version of it, with the prologue added and other sequences cut. As a letter of complaint from Suzanne Charpentier to Gance (CF/AG 3) shows, almost all the Violine scenes had been removed – and a number of others had been pruned. This was partly, says René Jeanne (*Rumeur*, 18 November 1927), because Gance wanted to tighten up the film, partly because the distributor (G-M-G) had insisted on cuts, and partly because the censors objected to certain of the scenes representing the Revolution. But an almost complete Apollo version, with the triptychs, was offered to provincial cinemas. Some of these followed the Marivaux pattern, screening a short version in two parts, showing, for example, Brienne, Toulon and the Italian Campaign at the matinée, and the Marseillaise, Vendémiaire and the Italian Campaign in the evening. Others did, though, show the long version.[33] Then, after the disastrous release of a massacred print at the Gaumont cinema in March 1928, described by Gance as 'a parody of my film',[34] Gaumont-

Metro-Goldwyn agreed to restore a 'complete version' that was screened in twelve Paris cinemas from 28 September 1928. It (or parts of it) was also extensively shown in suburban and provincial cinemas at least until the autumn of 1929, as the letters of appreciation received by Gance demonstrate.[35]

Of all these different versions of the film, to which should be added the Pathé 17.5mm release and 16mm prints of varying lengths,[36] only one can be considered complete, the Apollo version. It is not extant. Indeed just over a third of it is missing in Kevin Brownlow's reconstruction, extended since its screening at the 1980 London Film Festival to five hours thirteen minutes at 20fps (about 7,200m) as opposed to eight hours for the Apollo version at the same speed. The Harris/Coppola/Universal version distributed in the United States is even shorter – four hours at 24fps, about 6,600m compared to the 11,000m of the Apollo version.

The effect, particularly marked in the American version, is to focus attention very much more on Bonaparte as authoritarian leader, capable of restraining every sentiment which does not advance the cause to which he has committed himself: the solitary hero working for the cause of humanity, working to create a new order and discipline which will make possible the construction of a new France and a new world.

It is the 'péripéties' that are lost, the incidentals, the filling out of the story, a good part of the fiction which Gance thought it necessary to include in order to attain a 'poetic truth'. Outlines, manuscript screenplays, the scenario published in 1927 and accounts of the Apollo version make it clear that these were essential to the basic structure of the film. They, to a great extent, constructed its mode of address. *Napoleon* was in its complete form and in its planned continuation *the* melo-epic, the uneasy fusion of the heroic and the melodramatic.

If it is the melodramatic that has largely disappeared, privileging the heroic, sufficient elements are preserved in the restored version, screenplays and notes to show what the spectators of 1927 were supposed to witness. And to show that this integrated structure was not so very different from Gance's other films of the time in its appeal to popular emotion. In his investigation of history Gance rediscovers the archetypal.

Thus woman, as represented by Josephine, is problematical. She both fears and admires Bonaparte, but she is fickle. She is capable of inspiring – and exciting – love, but her motives are ambivalent. Ultimately, she is serving her own ends rather than living, like Bonaparte, for a cause; and, having passed from her first husband (a *noble* reactionary) to Hoche and to Barras, she will move on in the opening sequence of *Austerlitz* to an affair with her hairdresser.

Then there is the problem of the family. Bonaparte establishes his own identity alone, impoverished in Paris. Before he returns to Corsica he has already determined what his destiny will be, to re-establish order in the chaos of the Revolution. In Corsica he is the loved son (as in *J'accuse*), the protective brother, taking over the role of the absent father. *Austerlitz* shows the emergence of jealousies within the family, but in *Napoleon* its sense of unity is strengthened by external threats, by a hostile faction led by Pozzo di Borgo. In principle the struggle is a political one over the future of Corsica. Pozzo is for England, Bonaparte for France, but they are opposed in family conflict, in historic rivalry as much as in political difference. In this clan warfare, reminiscent of Mérimée's *Colomba*, feuding takes precedence over principles (the attack on the Bonaparte town house in Ajaccio, the burning of their country home) and as in some archetypal Western it is the united family that survives.

The villains too are melodramatic archetypes, not just Pozzo but Salicetti, also a Corsican caught up in rivalry with Bonaparte. In spite of their differences – Pozzo is counter-revolutionary, Salicetti a Commissar of the Republic – they team up against Bonaparte, attacking all that he defends, sworn enemies who stop at nothing, less to serve their own ends, for they are shown as not having any, than to frustrate those of their opponent. When Salicetti goes to Robespierre to ask for Bonaparte's head, political reasons are only a pretext; it is personal hatred that inspires him. Similarly, when Bonaparte, the better horseman, escapes his clutches, Pozzo swears eternal enmity against the man, not the cause he represents.

The villains, then, are simply and decidedly villainous, any political convictions they might have being subordinated to jealousy, rivalry, self-interest (all the features of the romantic anti-hero) rather than to political causes. As in the melodramas, they attack the hero for his virtue but are eventually pardoned when Bonaparte displays his magnanimity after Vendémiaire.

Since a number of the Pozzo and Salicetti scenes are lost, they appear in the reconstructed film as episodic characters. They can be recognised even so as standard villains of melodrama, espousing reactionary causes to serve their own interests. What has not survived, although it was included in the Apollo version, is their depravity, their attempt to rape Violine Fleuri (thwarted by Bonaparte), to betray her by sending her a fine dress so that she can be arrested as an aristocrat, to have her shot at Toulon – all because she resists their advances.

Villains: Salicetti and (below) Pozzo di Borgo – with snake – in *Napoleon*

Violine as 'aristocrat' in a lost sequence of *Napoleon*

It is in fact the role of the Fleuris[37] which changed most in the different transformations of the text. In the 1923 outline Tristan and his daughter are, after Napoleon, the two most important characters in the whole film. As soldier, cook and manservant of the Emperor, Tristan follows Napoleon through all his campaigns. But he is not simply an amiable buffoon, he also has a secret identity: servant during the day, he is a phantom grenadier at night, carrying out daring exploits that amaze everyone. Not until Waterloo does he reveal his secret, putting on his uniform during the day in a last heroic attempt to change the course of the battle. Wounded, he is recognised by Napoleon, whom he follows to Saint Helena, where he is the Emperor's last confidant. In the final scene, as Napoleon dies, Tristan hurls himself from the top of a cliff, dressed in his grenadier's uniform. His daughter, called Camille in this version, falls deeply in love with Bonaparte the first time she sees him, in Paris in 1793. She becomes Josephine's servant (but is obliged to leave when her secret altar to Napoleon is discovered), then becomes a canteen woman so that she too can follow the Emperor during his campaigns, and finally dies of love and exhaustion during the retreat from Moscow, watched over by Napoleon, who recognises *in extremis* the depth and purity of her feeling.

The function of these characters, in what is already an immense project, is clearly indicated in this outline. They will provide contrast and human interest while allowing Gance to concentrate on historical authenticity in his portrayal of the Emperor. The truth of history will establish a hold over the mind of the spectators; the passionate and dramatic fiction of the Fleuris will engage their hearts. Above all, the Fleuris will be the representatives of the People in what is construed as a double epic – the monumental story of Napoleon and the humble and obscure adventures of the phantom grenadier and his daughter, both impelled by 'the same deep spirit of love and sacrifice'.

The whole of the Revolutionary period is dismissed in a few lines in the 1923 outline; and when, with the contraction of the 1924 screenplays into one, the almost exclusive focus of the film became the years 1792–6, the role of the Fleuris had also to be transformed. Tristan could no longer be either a phantom grenadier or the Emperor's confidant (in fact, he was completely written out of the *Sainte-Hélène* screenplay, although in the final moments there is a phantom presence who raises the dead heroes of the Napoleonic campaigns to be present at the apotheosis).

Instead, he remains in Bonaparte's shadow, but is never explicitly recognised. Still the same clumsy, lovable fool, if he is heroic, it is usually accidentally, as for example when he saves Bonaparte's life at Vendémiaire. Camille, renamed Violine, remains the incarnation of innocence and a pure, mystical love, but she too is more closely integrated into the action. What happens, then, is that the Fleuris' roles are expanded rather than cut, with a consequent development of the fictional and archetypal elements of the film. While continuing to provide moments of comic relief and a sentimental dimension, they take on new functions which are essential to the film's balance and to its discourse.

On an immediate level, the Fleuris have a basic narrative function. Although Gance does occasionally place Bonaparte in purely imaginary situations (at the Bal des Victimes, for example, or, more noticeably, his appearance before the ghosts of the Revolution assembled in the Convention chamber), his striving towards 'authenticity' seriously limits the possibilities of invention. With the Fleuris, on the other hand, precisely because they are fictitious characters, he can simply invent, making them witness scenes at which it is historically impossible for Bonaparte to appear – the fall of Robespierre, for example, or Josephine's imprisonment in the Carmelite convent.

More importantly, and again because they are fictitious characters, they can be made to move at will through time and space, obeying no other logic than fantasy and coincidence. Thus, in 1792, Violine is a maid in the household of Dr Guillotin when he presents his new invention to Robespierre, Danton, Marat, Saint-Just etc., and is sacked because she shows her disapproval of the crimes committed in the name of the Revolution. The lodging house in which she takes refuge happens to be inhabited by Pozzo di Borgo, Salicetti – and Bonaparte (it is there that the attempted violation takes place). Meanwhile, Tristan has for some unexplained reason been appointed 'arroseur public du roi', which allows him, after stupidly ruining Bonaparte's cardboard boots, to save Violine by turning his hose against the *tricoteuses* who are dragging her off to prison and, incidentally, to prevent a battle between Sans-culottes and the Swiss guards by soaking their cartridges. His enlistment as a Volontaire de l'an II does not prevent him from taking refuge in the suburbs of Toulon to escape from the September massacres, or from being the proprietor of the inn at which meetings of the army chiefs of staff are held and the cook who prepares Salicetti's victory celebration. Back in Paris as one of Fouquier-Tinville's clerks, he saves Bonaparte's life by tearing up his file, but is obliged to accompany Danton in the cart driving him to the scaffold.

Subsequently, he serves under Bonaparte at Vendémiaire, is master of ceremonies at the Bal des Victimes and is in the front line of the Army of Italy infantry at the end of the film. In the meantime, Violine has been proprietress of a shop selling caged birds, at a moment when the Revolutionary government has ordered all birds to be killed; a waitress at her father's inn; the cloakroom attendant at the Bal des Victimes, assisted by her brother Marcellin; and ultimately lady's maid to Josephine, as in the original outline.[38]

Some of these scenes, like the Guillotin dinner party and the bird shop sequence, were excised when the screenplay was cut back in 1925. Most, however, as contemporary accounts and publicity stills show, were included in the Apollo version and in the longer release prints. The absence of some of the most significant of these scenes in the restored print now gives a distorted view of the completed film. Enough survives, though, to illustrate the importance of the Fleuris, over and above their immediate narrative function.

They remain points of identification, centres of humorous and sentimental interest as in the original 1923 outline. But since they are present in all the major sequences, except in Corsica where Bonaparte's *real* family takes over, they also bind the action of the film together, integrating it into the 'political' melodrama of the Nation as family. More than that, they are epic characters, epic in a Brechtian sense, representatives of a position in a complicated play of identification and distanciation, at once caricatures and essential presences, always unexpectedly there, ridiculous and touching figures who change roles but not their faith. In the last resort they are the only epic characters on a narrative level, since Bonaparte's grandiose future is represented only in dreams and visions.

They illustrate, more perhaps than any other characters in Gance's films, the fusion of epic and melodrama as aspiration towards a popular form of cinema. While providing a point of entry into history, they construct the truth of fiction.[39]

The Fleuris also illustrate the extent to which the film can be located within a populist ideology. Bonaparte, as he is presented 'historically' in the film, has a natural authority already apparent in the Brienne prologue, but he owes his position as much to circumstance, the incompetence of his superiors and the intrigues of Barras and Josephine, as to his talent. And since Bonaparte has already been shown as the opponent of incompetence and corruption, the Fleuris help to resolve what might otherwise be a troublesome contradiction, by providing the foundation for his power. While the masses have been depraved by centuries of misery and listen all too eagerly to bourgeois demagogues promising revenge, the Fleuris stand for humble virtues, fidelity and natural enthusiasm. Opposing the excesses of the Reign of Terror, they recognise the achievements of the Revolution and the need for an authority which will preserve those achievements, an authority exemplified by Bonaparte.

The Fleuris are, in short, one of the three forces[40] in a grandiose heroic drama, the force of the populace pitched against the excesses of the bourgeois demagogues and convinced that Bonaparte alone can save the Revolution from anarchy. It is their instinctive recognition that Bonaparte is serving the interests of the people by reconciling freedom and order that legitimates his actions. Their naive enthusiasm and devotion confer on him the status of Saviour, subject to the law of the state as individual but superior to it through his vision of a social order that will be the realisation of popular aspirations. As incarnation of the fundamental principles of the Revolution, Bonaparte is a secular Jesus and the Fleuris represent his true family, the uncorrupted people of France.

Hence the importance of the mystical marriage of Violine. In an unfilmed scene inserted in the published screenplay at the beginning of the Toulon sequence, Violine had imagined herself as a modern Joan of Arc before realising that it was Bonaparte who would save France. On the night of his marriage to Josephine, she decks herself out in an improvised wedding-gown and, after praying at the altar she has dedicated to the object of her devotion, embraces the shadow of a cheap effigy – 'a threepenny Bonaparte' – cast on to the wall by a candle. It is a scene that some have found overbearingly sentimental and others an extraordinary visual success, a symphony of white on

Napoleon: the mystical marriage of Violine, with the 'threepenny Bonaparte'; (below) Josephine prays with Violine at her Bonapartist altar

white, as Moussinac says. It is, in any case, an essential scene, as symbol of the alliance of Bonaparte and the people, confirming the legitimacy of the one and the fidelity of the other.

Although in the completed film the scene is set in counterpoint to Bonaparte and Josephine's embrace seen through a series of white veils, its significance is much greater than a simple opposition between the ambivalence of Josephine's attraction and the purity of Violine's love. That there is more at stake is emphasised in the following sequence. While Bonaparte, on his way to take command of the Army of Italy, stops to reflect in the deserted Convention chamber and solemnly swears before the assembled ghosts of the Revolution that he will uphold its principles, become its leader, liberate enslaved peoples and work towards the establishment of a universal Republic, Violine prays once again at 'the first of the altars that popular enthusiasm will little by little set up in every household in honour of the new Alexander'.[41]

In the 1923 outline Camille was sacked when Josephine accidentally discovered the secret altar. In the 1927 film Josephine kneels to pray alongside Violine, consecrating the class unity Bonaparte will construct.

Preventing this unity are the leaders of the Revolution, Marat, Danton and Robespierre, rivals locked in contradiction, endangering the young Republic. All three claim to speak in the name of the Revolution, but none can speak with its authentic voice as Bonaparte can when he proclaims after Vendémiaire that, from today, he *is* the Revolution. The leaders of the Revolution are not condemned outright, as some critics of 1927 thought. Robespierre is admired for his disinterestedness, Danton for his appeal to the masses. Even the 'bloodthirsty' Marat is occasionally remembered as the champion of the underprivileged. And there is Saint-Just, the visionary, the prophet familiar in other Gance scenarios, playing John the Baptist to Bonaparte's Jesus and, like Jean Novalic in *La fin du monde*, acted by Gance himself. When Violine goes to the Convention with her young brother, determined to shoot Robespierre, she exclaims, after listening to Saint-Just's defence of their politics: 'They are too great for us.' All these figures are caricatured, as hostile critics were quick to point out. But all are shown as ambivalent, as in the suppressed scene quoted in chapter 4, with its 'torrential flood' of images evoking turn by turn hecatomb and progressive decrees. They all have greatness but, divided into warring factions, they are unable to control the forces they have unleashed. They establish the principles of a new social order while endangering its future. Bonaparte learns from their failings as much as from their virtues.

The leaders of the Revolution: (above) Danton and Robespierre; (below) Marat and Saint-Just

The members of the Committee of Public Safety fight against the enemies of the Revolution but they are indiscriminate, feeding the guillotine by daily quotas, massacring poets, scientists and men of honour – André Chénier, Lavoisier, Beauharnais. Saint-Just makes a stand for principles at all costs but he too falls victim to a factionalism that opens the way for a bourgeois decadence, a betrayal of the Revolution.

It is in fact for the society of the Directory that Gance reserves most of his vehemence. Decadent and superficial, it is exemplified by the *jeunesse dorée*, concerned only with luxury and pleasure while the rest of France starves. Even Fleuri is taken in, flirting with a transvestite at the Bal des Victimes while Bonaparte, disapproving of the display of indecency, is entranced by Josephine's charms.

As in *J'accuse*, the ultimate question is not whether slaughter should have been avoided but whether it has served a purpose. The Revolution, like World War I, is the signal of a new era. Its sacrifices must have been useful.

This is Bonaparte's significance, less as militarist dictator than as saviour. He has observed the progress of the Revolution, its achieve-

'From today I *am* the Revolution'

ments and its errors and is determined to put it back on the right path. Without him, it would be overthrown by reactionary forces or its achievements frittered away by a decadent bourgeoisie. It is a romantic view of Napoleon promoted by a number of early twentieth-century historians (not to mention Carlyle and Emerson). But it is also a Napoleon for the 1920s, addressed to the post-war generation, a stand against the new *jeunesse dorée*, an appeal to popular imagination.

Although Napoleon will later be entrapped by his family, his ministers and his enemies into a defence of a bourgeois order (*Austerlitz*), the young Bonaparte is a man for the people, for the future. As Gance explained forty years later, 'not a Bonapartist but a Republican'.[42] As a Republican, his power derives from the people, who in turn recognise in him a natural authority. He, understanding their desire for liberty and order, will establish both, restoring order to protect liberty and, eventually, to bring peace to the world. This, reduced to essentials, is what *Napoleon* is about, the unity of people and leader, of the social and the natural. Few cinema heroes have been so archetypally romantic or so resolutely populist.

The naturalness of Bonaparte's authority is apparent from the beginning, in his leadership in the snowfight, in his righteous indignation when Phélippeaux and Peccaduc conceal stones in their snowballs, in

159

The young Napoleon and his Corsican eagle

his physical power and his superior tactics, in the muted approval of Pichegru and the other masters, in the enthusiasm he inspires in Tristan Fleuri, especially in the bond he has established with his Corsican eagle, released from its cage by his enemies and returning to console his master after his expulsion from the dormitory.

Later, his look is enough to daunt his enemies, with the eagle's beak frequently in superimpression to reinforce the point, as in the Corsican episode. His resolute gaze, his bearing, a gesture disarm even the

The power of the look: Bonaparte in Corsica

most determined opponents, like the chiefs of staff of the Army of Italy who, choosing to ignore the young upstart, are captured by his look and unable to play out their pre-arranged scenario. But that same look can also show understanding and forgive. In a crucial scene, which exists only in the single-screen version of the final sequence,[43] Tristan Fleuri is in the front line of the infantry being reviewed by Napoleon. Overcoming his timidity at last, Fleuri steps forward so that he can be recognised as the kitchen-boy at Brienne, who has followed so closely and contributed in his own way to the General's rise to fame. Bonaparte, on horseback, halts, looks and orders the front line to take one pace forward. Fleuri, trembling at the knees, finds himself back where he was without having moved. Order is restored and a serious infraction of military discipline allowed to pass unnoticed. It is not even clear whether Bonaparte has recognised Fleuri. There are just the piercing look and abrupt command that make allowances for this man of the people. Although he almost faints and then wanders off to console Marcellin who has been caught out yet again in his attempt to be a soldier ('Too short!'), Fleuri is soon back in the front line as enthusiastic as ever and cheering wildly as Bonaparte harangues his troops.

It is almost as though Bonaparte were looking at an estranged member of the family whom he can't quite place. And, indeed, there are resemblances between the Bonaparte-Fleuri relationship and the pairings of brothers, fathers and sons, lifelong friends which provide the basic narrative structures of *J'accuse*, *La roue*, *La fin du monde* and *Mater dolorosa* – especially if one takes the 1923 outline of the complete project into account. Although Tristan has none of the crude brutality of François in *J'accuse*, he is, like him, elemental when set against the visionary qualities of a Jean Diaz, or a Bonaparte. Like François and Sisif, he is a down-to-earth manual as opposed to intellectual, artist or poet. He may seem stupid but he is steadfast and his qualities are only revealed in secret, like Sisif, who drives engines during the day but invents mechanical devices at night. Since we have only the first 'epoch', we see no more than the merest hint of the process of recognition, and nothing at all of the interdependence of Napoleon and Fleuri after Waterloo, their fusion in a bond of friendship and confidence, their living and dying together. What we are left with underscores the political nature of the narrative link: the Fleuris complement not Bonaparte's character but his policies, constructing the unity of a *nation*.

Bonaparte as man of feeling is revealed in his love of nature and his family. He is also a man of superior intellect with exceptional powers of concentration, forgetting to eat, sleep and even to go to his own

Concentrating on affairs of the world: Napoleon forgets his wedding

wedding, so intent is he on preparing plans for the Italian campaign. As man of letters, he is the admirer of Racine and Rousseau, and the friend of Talma; as man of science, he resolves difficult mathematical problems in his spare moments and while in prison designs a canal at Suez. He is, like the Napoleon of Elie Faure, a poet of action, a man whose importance lies both in the power of his imagination and in his effect on the imagination of others. Gance may be convinced that he is presenting an authentic view of the young Bonaparte; the myth, even so, counts for as much as the history. Hence, like the Fleuris, we are called upon to recognise his appeal to the imagination, to be like them the representatives of the nation the hero could create.

Curiously, given Moussinac and Vuillermoz's contention that *Napoleon* was an apologia of dictatorship, the film was not nearly as successful in Italy in 1928 as Gance had anticipated, notably because Mussolini's censors insisted on the removal of the Marseillaise sequence and the whole of the Corsica episode. On 29 March 1928, Gance wrote to D'Annunzio asking him to intercede, enclosing for good measure a letter addressed to the Duce himself.[44] After asking Mussolini to look at the film so that he could form his own opinion, Gance adds: 'I would like to think that this incident will turn to my advantage by proving to Your Excellency that there are a few French productions that are working silently in the same spirit as yours for the whole of humanity,' and concludes: 'Please find here, Excellency, the deeply felt assurance of my devoted and respectful admiration.'

Three months later, Gance approached the right-wing patriot François Coty again, overlooking the latter's former hostility in his desire to obtain money for the continuation of the *Napoleon* project. Asking for an appointment, he writes: 'The cinema is indeed too powerful a weapon for you not to realise the interest it can hold for you during the next few years, and it would be unforgivable of me not to have been one of the first to indicate to you the direction that it must take.'[45] When this and an approach during the summer to Ufa, the German distributor of *Napoleon*, came to nothing, he relinquished the completed *Sainte Hélène* screenplay to Lupu Pick (September 1928) and turned his mind to publications, to revivals of *La roue* and *J'accuse*, and to other cinema projects. A version of the scenario of *Napoleon* had appeared at the end of 1927[46] but negotiations for the publication of *La victoire de Samothrace, Arcole, Sainte-Hélène* and the *Napoleon* triptychs fell through.[47] Instead, he published *Prisme* (1930), the edited and structured selection of his 'daily thoughts' initially entitled *Moi*, and an extraordinary example of early twentieth-century High Romanticism. Of his many projects, which include a scheme for the use of film within the production of a play at the Comédie Française, three merit special mention.

The first, dating from the spring of 1928, concerned the establishment of a cinematographic section of the League of Nations, which would make films for worldwide distribution, encouraging international and mutual understanding between nations. It was to be accompanied by a 'Section for the observation and practical utilisation of universal psychological forces by the League of Nations', and was well received by Gance's well-placed friends at Geneva, notably Albert Thomas, director of the ILO, considered by Gance as 'like a brother'. The reports to the League were written by Gance's assistant Georges Buraud, but Gance pursued the project with great enthusiasm.[48]

The second project, dating from early 1929, was for a series of films entitled *Les grands initiés*, beginning with the Passion of Christ, continuing with films devoted to Buddha, Moses, Krishna, Mohammed and Confucius, and 'crowned' by *La fin du monde* and *L'annonciation*. The complete cycle would be 'a synthesis of all the religions, seen as different kinds of heat all emanating from the same hearth'.[49] This soon became a vast enterprise in Gance's mind, involving the transformation of the SGF into a Société mondiale de films with Moslem,

164

Jewish, Hindu and Far-Eastern subsidiaries, all working together under his supervision.[50] Only *La fin du monde* was ever made and, apart from its opening sequence in which the prophet, Jean Novalic, played by Gance, identifies himself with Jesus, acting out in a Passion play his sacrifice of himself for the sufferings of the world, it is construed principally in terms of the political internationalism of the League of Nations project.

The third project, dating from 1931, seems at first the most surprising: the setting up of a company for the release in France of Soviet films[51] (in return for which Gance would be provided with facilities in the Soviet Union for the making of *1812*, a film which would present Napoleon, Gance declared in a 1932 interview, as 'already enfeebled, already corrupted by power').[52] Although it was criticised for the condition of the prints it circulated, the company did have a degree of success and was responsible for the introduction into France of a number of previously unknown Soviet films. *1812*, of course, was never made, and the parallel group, a 'Society for the expansion of the influence of the French cinema, under the direction of Abel Gance', also dating from 1931, seems to have been little more than a convenient letterhead.[53] A fourth project ought perhaps also to be noted: a series of films on the French colonies, planned in 1931 for the colonial exhibition of 1932 and sponsored by the French government.[54]

All this seems like grist to a variety of mills: political inconsistency (cf. Kramer's reply to Pappas), naive pacificism, delusions of grandeur, the subordination of mercantile and moral considerations to the cause of Art. Again, however, context and conviction count for as much as opportunism. Although it eventually came to nothing, the League of Nations project reflects the universalism apparent in the later sequences of *Napoleon* and by no means exclusive to Gance. *Les grands initiés* was to add a spiritual dimension to this universalism while giving Gance, as artistic director of the transformed Société générale de films, extensive powers to impose his view of cinema worldwide.

The Russian project coincides with the launching of the *Comité international de défense de l'Union Soviétique,* which Gance joined in February 1931, and the influential *Association des écrivains et artistes révolutionnaires* founded in the following year. Many members of these groups were committed Marxists or fellow-travellers but others were like Gance, pacifists and internationalists attracted to them as much by Western belligerence as by interest in the Soviet experience.

All these projects, then, can be read as variations on the romantic theme of a universal understanding, inspired by art and needing a resolute authority to combat warmongering, depravity and bourgeois self-interest. As is more than hinted in *Napoleon* and *La fin du monde*, an enlightened France should provide the example of the new social order, with art pointing the way ahead, reconciling the patriotic with the internationalist, peace with authority.

Apart from *La fin du monde* and a few shorts, notably some experiments with triple-screen polyvision,[55] Gance completed no films after 1927 until the remake of *Mater dolorosa*, released in December 1932. After that he embarked on a series of adaptations of novels and plays, working from original screenplays only in *Napoleon Bonaparte* (1935), *Un grand amour de Beethoven* (1936), the remake of *J'accuse* (1938) and *La Vénus aveugle* (1941). Contracts were signed for films for which Gance would have been wholly responsible (for example *Il était un petit navire*, 1931, and *Le vaisseau fantôme*, 1932), but at the last moment the producers found themselves unable to raise the necessary cash.[56]

After the bankruptcy of the Société générale de films in 1933, Gance was able to repossess the original negatives of the 1927 *Napoleon*,[57] and in May 1934 he signed a contract with Hector de Béarn, a leading shareholder in the SGF, for a new, shortened and sonorised version of the film, due to be completed by August of that year.

Many of the original actors were re-engaged for the recording sessions and the shooting of the necessary additional footage. Filming went on much longer than planned, however, and the new version, having grown to 3,850m instead of the 2,500-3,000m specified in the contract, was not released until May 1935. Justifying the delay, Gance explains in a letter to Béarn in December 1934 that parts of the original negative were unusable because they had shrunk, and that in consequence more new footage had to be filmed than had been budgeted for.[58] But there was a more important reason for the delay: as later with *Bonaparte et la Révolution*, Gance was making a new film. The result, accompanied by a vibrant musical score composed by Henri Verdun, was enthusiastically received, in spite of the awkward matches between new footage and dubbed silent footage projected at 24fps, and discrepancies in the appearance of the actors.

But it was a new film, and one which had a specific impact in the political circumstances of 1935, as the autograph dedication inserted immediately after the credits suggests: 'To all those who still believe in the destinies of France, I offer this film in homage. Abel Gance.'

Instead of beginning at Brienne and ending at Montezemolo, the film has a framing narrative which takes place at Grenoble in March 1815, just before the Hundred Days. Stendhal is delivering the manuscript of the first volume of his *Life of Napoleon* to Crécy, a 'printer, soldier and poet', committed to the Napoleonic cult. He meets the radical poet Béranger and both are taken by Crécy into a Bonapartist club which he operates. There they encounter Georgin, whose simple woodcuts of the Emperor inspire Béranger to remark: 'Do you know, young man, that there is more poetry in your naive pictures than in many celebrated paintings?'[59] This leads into a discussion of the power of the image over the minds of the humble masses. In the meeting-house a prayer is intoned: 'Our father Napoleon, may your reign return, in the name of the Father, the Son and the Holy Ghost.' And when Stendhal asks whether he really believes Napoleon will return, Crécy replies: 'No, but you have to make people think he will . . . People are dying in France of a lack of enthusiasm.'

This extensive prologue sets the tone of the whole film, in which all the Bonaparte scenes except the finale are shown in flashback, 'narrated' by those who have admired his exploits and his virtues. Thus it is Tristan Fleuri, blinded at the battle of Marengo, who recounts the events of 1792, the Brunswick Manifesto, the singing of the 'Marseillaise', the rivalries between the leaders of the revolutionary factions (neither he nor Violine has very much place within the flashbacks). Fleuri is preceded by Théroigne de Méricourt, a crazed visionary who has boundless enthusiasm for Bonaparte but an unmitigated hatred for Napoleon: for her, Bonaparte died at Saint-Cloud during the coup d'état of the 18 brumaire, year 8. And he is followed by Santo Ricci, one of the shepherds who served under Bonaparte in the Corsican *maquis* in 1793; and so the narrative proceeds, producing a tone of nostalgia for a lost energy and sense of direction.

The significance of the Revolution, not as an absolute but in the direction that it needs to take, is also markedly changed. Saint-Just's speech is extended and given a more prophetic tone: 'We will often be cursed in the future, but later, when the whole of Europe has become a single family, united by the same laws, people will perhaps remember that *we* constructed the footbridge of liberty across the frontiers. That is all that matters.' And there is Marat's call, at the fall of the Girondins, for a leader, a soldier, a military tribune who will sweep away the wicked. Other statements present in the 1927 intertitles are given a new emphasis in the sound version, like Bonaparte's call for order, his authoritarian words to Barras and his vow pronounced before the spirits of the Convention to work towards the construction of a universal Republic. Even Bonaparte's impact in the last reel (there were no triptychs, but 'stereophonic' sound) is reinforced by Crécy's comment: 'It's the greatest flow of strength that history has ever known.' Then after a montage of images of Brienne, Toulon, Bonaparte's visions, the film shifts to the present, ending with a shot of the Arc de Triomphe and of the victories inscribed on it.

The authoritarian aspects of the film are hardened. There is the need for a new sense of direction, and for order, indicated in the dedication and repeatedly pointed out in the film. And there is nostalgia for the true principles of the Revolution which, as the Revolutionaries themselves admit, can only be restored by a powerful leader. The Fleuris and their melodramatic counterparts in the 1927 film were looking to the future. The narrators in the new version look back nostalgically to what might have been and wish for the great man's return. What they long for most is the enthusiasm Napoleon engendered, the sense of vision lacking in the society in which they live, leaving them only with the possibility of re-imagining the past.

This call for a new society based on what has been lost, a strong authority and its appeal to loyal, devoted subjects, is, in 1935, not far short of a call to arms to restore virtue in a decadent world. Jarringly at odds with the efforts of Renoir and the October Group to promote the conciliatory policies of the Popular Front, it could have been dedicated to Pétain. In retrospect, one could indeed construe Renoir's *La Marseillaise* of 1938 as a direct response to the sonorised *Napoleon* (still in distribution when *La Marseillaise* was filmed), presenting a democratic form of populism that is diametrically opposed to Gance's heroic elitism.

La Vénus aveugle was indeed dedicated to Pétain and, at the gala premiere at Vichy in 1941, prefaced by a speech in honour of the Marshal. Before we can look at the implications of the speech or analyse the film, we need, however, to examine the complex circumstances that led up to its production.

After *Napoleon Bonaparte*, Gance made three 'commercial' films, *Le roman d'un jeune homme pauvre*, *Lucrèce Borgia* and *Jérôme Perreau* (all 1935), only the first of which was based on his own screenplay. Then came *Un grand amour de Beethoven*, in which 'man conquers Art through the sheer force of his willpower',[60] followed early in 1937 by another commercial adaptation, *Le voleur de femmes*, based on Pierre Frondaie's novel, and the remake of *J'accuse*, begun in June 1937 (just after the release of *La grande illusion*) and completed late in the same year.

The new version did not just have a very different story and a more resolute, energetic hero than the original. It was much more strident in its indictment of war and of the capitalists who stood to gain from it. In contrast to Renoir's benign humanism, Gance's message was urgently and *aggressively* pacifist.

Gance then turned his attention back to the epic treatment of heroic figures. Briefly, early in 1938, he flirted with the idea of making a film about Jaurès based on a script by the socialist politician Paul-Boncour,[61] but this was soon supplanted by a more grandiose project: a life of Christopher Columbus, to be filmed in Spain and produced by Gilbert Renault-Decker, a Pétain supporter and future Resistance hero who had also produced *J'accuse*, and with Victor Francen, the Martial of *La fin du monde*,[62] as Columbus. While Renault-Decker went to Burgos to negotiate with the Nationalist authorities, Gance wrote to Franco in terms of high praise, urging him to support the project.[63] Then, waiting for the necessary authorisations, he made a filmed version of Charpentier's operetta *Louise* (October–November 1938), and in April-May 1939 directed *Paradis perdu*, a popular romance with elevated sentiments. But by April he was able to announce that filming of the Columbus film would begin at Granada on 12 June 1939 and that there would be three versions, 'French, Spanish and American', of what by now had become yet another trilogy: Columbus would be followed by the Cid Campeador and Ignatius of Loyola.[64]

Columbus, wrote Gance, was one of the most extraordinary personalities in history. He described him in terms that closely resemble the unified hero of earlier films: the great visionary, resolute man of science. 'In him, the poet sees and the scientist achieves. He inherited a supreme degree of intuition – that memory of the future – and trusting in it, he developed within himself that very rare quality: a will for the future. What a lesson of energy for us all, we who have hardly any will even for the present!'

'Why am I making this film?' he asks. 'Because cinema is above all a machine for resurrecting Heroes. Its teachings must be lessons of energy, elevation and courage which all humanity so greatly needs at the present time. Cinema does not exist simply to aid the digestion of materialist minds by its blandness, but also to open the window of the soul on to the exhilarating breeze of dreams and legends. [. . .] The legendary, the magical and the historical interpenetrate in Columbus, amalgamating to form a poetry which surpasses anything that could be created by the imagination.'[65]

Nothing came of the scheme, probably because Renault-Decker's London backers were concerned about its ambitiousness, though Gance claimed the film had been stolen from him.[66] Back in France, he began work instead on a screenplay entitled *Bleu, blanc, rouge*, a virulent attack on Nazi militarism and an appeal to the national cultural values of France.[67] It was, he says in a letter to Barattolo in December 1939, commissioned by the French government, though the real point of his letter was to sound out Barattolo about the possibilities of making a film in Italy in the following spring.[68] During a short visit to Paris in April 1940, he again affirmed in an interview that he was to make propaganda films for the government, adding that he had seen Pétain in Spain and was going to urge Paul Reynaud, the Premier, to recall him to France.[69]

The rapidity of the German invasion made *Bleu, blanc, rouge* and a related project, *La patrie en danger*, redundant,[70] along with other schemes, including a contract for an unspecified film signed with Scaléra Film of Paris in April 1940 and a screenplay to be written in collaboration with Jean Anouilh. Gance returned to the south where, in August, in what was now the Free Zone, he signed a contract to make a film initially entitled 'Messaline, drame des temps modernes vu par Abel Gance', and later renamed *La Vénus aveugle*.[71]

Summarily dismissed in Roger Régent's study of French cinema during the Occupation[72] as a ludicrous melodrama, saved only by some atmospheric images of a seaport, *La Vénus aveugle* is in fact one of the most interesting of Gance's later films. Paul Bertrand and Henri Mahé's decors, Burel's cinematography and Gance's direction produce images that are not 'gratuitous' (Régent) but compelling, essential ingredients of a *resolutely* melodramatic film, one of the best illustrations of Gance's populism. In particular, the film draws together some of the apparently conflicting strands in the earlier abortive projects: a sense of collective identity and resistance to external threats, the struggle against calamity, the triumph of elevated sentiments over materialist self-interest. Above all the need for a poetic vision of the future, the imaginary voyage of 'Vénus' and her friends echoing Columbus' discovery of the New World.

That there are further parallels to be drawn between the unrealised epic and the 'humble' melodrama is indicated by a text Gance wrote to present *La Vénus aveugle* to the public:

[. . .]*La Vénus aveugle* is at the crossroads of reality and legend. It is swathed in music and thus enters more fully than any imitation of real life could into the domain of cinema, which in the evening opens a window for us on to dreams that everyday life so resolutely suppresses.

The heroine of *La Vénus aveugle* gradually sinks deeper and deeper into despair. Only when she has reached the bottom of the abyss does she encounter the smile of Providence that life reserves for those who have faith in it, and she can then go serenely back up the slope towards happiness.

If I have been able to show in this film that elevated feelings are the only force that can triumph over Fate, then my efforts will not have been in vain.

One must never forget that there is always a rainbow even at the end of the most violent storms of life.[73]

The implicit political dimension of the film is already hinted at in this text – given the circumstances of production and the commercial necessity of distribution in the Occupied Zone, politics could only be referred to metaphorically, as in Grémillon's *Lumière d'été*. One of the principal functions of the Vichy speech, underlying the obligatory eulogies, was to explicate.

'For us French people,' Gance begins, 'two great names rise up over our future: Joan of Arc and Philippe Pétain. Joan had saved France at Rheims; it is from Vichy that our Marshal is saving France.' Not all the speech seems to have survived, but two further extracts were quoted in a contemporary review of the film:[74]

I am aiming not for the audience of minds but that of hearts. And, since the true dramatic language of the screen is the pathos of things brought down to the same level as in people, it is in the style of a popular lament, basing myself on simple themes, with images that are frequently naive, that I have constructed this fresco of modern life, this modern *chanson de geste*. [. . .]

The cinema opens a window for us on to dreams that we often need today in order to escape momentarily from our troubles. And since everything is possible in the immortal garden of France, and since misfortune makes us disregard all that isn't useful, I will try to build better, bigger and stronger things in the great shadow of the Marshal and the Admiral.[75]

The dedication, a simple handwritten caption inserted before the credits, reads: 'It is to the France of tomorrow that I wanted to dedicate this film, but since France is now personified in you, Marshal, allow me to dedicate it in all humility to you.' Not surprisingly, the caption was excised from prints released in the Occupied Zone.

The basic plot of *La Vénus aveugle* is quite complex and in the shortened version that is usually seen parts of it are almost incomprehensible. Clarisse (Vénus), a dark-haired beauty, refuses tempting offers of fame and fortune in order to remain with Madère, her lover, whose dream is to restore a laid-up cargo boat of which he was once the captain. She also looks after a crippled sister, Mireille. Discovering that she is going blind, Clarisse decides to break with Madère, sacrificing herself in order not to become a liability to him. Madère is seduced by Giselle, an ambitious and self-seeking blonde

Blind Venus ...

and leaves with her on a round-the-world trip. Clarisse gives birth to a daughter and to support her becomes a singer in a dockside bar, where she is the star attraction, expressing her sufferings and those of her listeners in her songs. Madère and Giselle return; they have married and she too has a child, a son. Clarisse's daughter dies, and she goes completely blind. Turning against men, she and her sister support each other as best they can. When Giselle moves on to better things (as a film star), Clarisse refuses to see Madère in spite of his contrition. Then, as the film moves gradually towards resolution,

Madère embarks on an elaborate stratagem of generous deception. With the help of Clarisse's friends and admirers, he restores the old cargo boat and disguises it as a luxury yacht. Concealing his identity, he becomes her protector and takes her on an imaginary cruise. Gradually Clarisse 'sees' through the pretence, accepts his presence and his love – and regains her sight.

There are many elements here that are reminiscent of *La roue, Mater dolorosa, Beethoven* and other melodramas. Abridged, the sentimentalism can easily seem excessive. But there are powerful dramatic

. . . and deaf Beethoven

moments: the scene in which the self-sacrificing Clarisse convinces Madère that she doesn't love him; the confrontation between Clarisse and Giselle, rivals, mothers of the same man's children but reaching a certain emotional understanding of each other; and especially a scene at the church where the funeral service for Clarisse's child and the baptism of Giselle's coincide and dramatically clash, pathos carried to an extreme but hard to resist.

Alongside these there are elements that for 1941 are stridently progressive, like the solidarity of Clarisse and Mireille as crippled women in a man's world, and Clarisse's aggressive exhibition of her body and of her sufferings as woman and mother in songs performed for a predominantly male audience. And, like many films of the time, *La Vénus aveugle* resorts to a discreet political symbolism in Clarisse's depth of feeling, blindness, despair and resilience, in her handicapped sister, in the struggle between Clarisse and the calculating blonde, and so on. Like Sisif and Napoleon, these ordinary people become figures of myth or, to use Gance's preferred phrase, characters in a modern *chanson de geste*.

The film is strikingly populist in its introduction of a collective hero, the friends of Clarisse and Madère who admire and support her, who join with him in repairing the boat, who become the attentive crew during the imaginary journey, who at the end share in a collective rejoicing. Once Giselle has been excluded, there are no villains, just the working of a community towards happiness. Gance's New France may still be a dream of the future but it can at least be imagined by the people who work together for its construction. *La Vénus aveugle* expresses hope amid catastrophe, a specific hope for a regenerated world. The characters are ordinary people confronting exceptional difficulties, covering what Gance refers to as the whole span of human emotions. Their response is not only resolute, it is also aesthetic. That, basically, is what the ideal of the New France consists of, an aesthetic renewal achieved collectively, guided by a powerful vision of the future.

Although some of Gance's more adulatory phrases may be no more than extravagant flattery, there are too many remarks of a Pétainist persuasion for them to be viewed as mere opportunism. It is also clear that Gance did for a time hope that *La Vénus aveugle* would bring him support from the Vichy regime, either to make more films in France (*Sainte-Hélène, Voyage au bout de la nuit* and a trilogy based on Balzac novels are among projects under discussion) or to be given an official posting abroad. That the film and its director were well received at Vichy is amply confirmed by the press of the time and by a letter from Gance to Fernand Millaud of 3 November 1941, in which he announces that he has been appointed by the Pétain government to a diplomatic mission for the expansion of Franco-European cinema in South America.[76] Funds for this mission were authorised on 3 January 1942 thanks largely to the personal support of Admiral Darlan. But, yet again, the scheme fell through, and with it hopes of reviving the Columbus project in the New World (Gance claimed after the war that the German authorities had refused the necessary visas and that, in any case, his main objective had simply been to escape from France.)[77] Instead he returned to Paris and in August began filming an adaptation of Théophile Gautier's novel *Le capitaine Fracasse*, interesting for its experiments with theatricality (including the famous duel fought out in Alexandrines) and for its renewed appeal to noble sentiments. In the summer of 1943, he left for Spain pursued, he claims, by the Gestapo, and spent the remainder of the war there.

There is ample evidence, then, to show that from the mid-1930s through to the early 40s Gance became increasingly committed to Pétainism. In this respect, he resembles a large number of French people who saw a strong government as the only answer to internal instability and, after the outbreak of war, Pétain as the only man who could defend French patriotic values against the Nazi invader. It is important to record this, not so much to demonstrate that disparaging remarks of the Jeancolas type are superfluous as to parry the defensiveness of devotees – no head for politics, always getting mixed up with people with whom he had nothing in common, and so on. Gance was, by the late 1930s, a man of the Right, just as in the 60s he was a de Gaulle supporter. In neither decade did that prevent him from taking an active interest in the cultural productions of the Eastern bloc. What did perhaps differentiate him from a majority of Pétainists was his romantic notion of the leader as enlightened hero. He may not literally have believed all that he said about Pétain as the personification of the immortal garden of France, but he did expect the soldier to salute the artist who would sow the seeds of regeneration.

There may seem to be a conflict between the inherent nationalism of the 1935 *Napoleon* and *La Vénus aveugle* on the one hand, and the League of Nations scheme and projects like 'Columbus' on the other. In fact, Gance increasingly aspired towards a kind of internationalism apparent in Bonaparte's commitment to a Universal Republic, developed in *La fin du monde* and the *Grands initiés* project and still present in *La divine tragédie*, an ambitious post-war project for which, in addition to various members of the Roman Catholic hierarchy, Gance enrolled as patrons President Hoover, Lord Halifax and Sir

Stafford Cripps.[78] But national feeling was the basis of unity. As Saint-Just says in the 1935 *Napoleon*: 'Patriotism is not a question of political parties, it is a matter for the heart.' Once firmly implanted in popular loyalty, liberty and a new order could spread beyond national frontiers, carried by the enthusiasm of the people and their orchestrator.

It was as poets of action that the Columbuses and the Napoleons had transformed the way the world was apprehended. The Mussolinis, Francos and Pétains of the modern world might not have that same genius, but they could create the order, the space in which the artist could operate. Art and politics could be fused in the ideality of history, with the visionary artist as romantic historian there to signal the message, but in an actual situation the political had to be able to guarantee art's conditions of existence. While needing politics, art was superior to it and was in its way more fundamentally political in its appeal to the imagination. As in the 1935 *Napoleon* and *La Vénus aveugle*, it could provide an aesthetics of and for the people.

ART FOR THE PEOPLE

As singer, Clarisse in *La Vénus aveugle* is very much like the artists in earlier Gance films, the composers in *La dixième symphonie* and *Un grand amour de Beethoven*, Elie, the violin-maker in *La roue*, Claude Berliac, the playwright in *Mater dolorosa*. As with all of them, and especially with the deaf Beethoven abandoned by his love, her art is produced from the depths of her grief. She, like Beethoven, is transfigured by it, becoming an aesthetic person. But the beauty of art lies more in its effects on those who witness it. Clarisse is an artist of the people, representing their sufferings and transforming them too into aesthetic men and women through their intuitive response to her art.

In this respect, the members of the Napoleonist club in the 1935 *Napoleon* and the clients of the dockside cabaret in *La Vénus aveugle* are not so very different. Napoleon, the artist, the poet of action, brought to his devotees a new vision. He changed the world politically, but what they mostly remember him for is his aesthetic presence and his action on others, the enthusiasm he inspired, which is sadly lacking in the France of 1815 and 1935. Clarisse asks for nothing, but the devotion she engenders results in a new enthusiasm, and the discovery of a new sense of community. In neither film is the new society actualised since the imaginary voyage in the one is matched by the nostalgic recollections of the Bonapartists in the other. But both epic and melodrama evoke for the spectator what the world might become through the aesthetic unity of people and leader. In presenting the silent *Napoleon* at the Opéra in 1927, Gance stated that it was not politics that was at issue but art. In fact it is both, or rather a merging of the two into an aesthetic politics which informs even more markedly the films of the 30s.

In its insistence on the myth, on the people as source of latent energy, and on the intuitive as basis for regeneration, this aesthetic politics may seem to belong as much to a Bergsonian tradition as to a Sorelian or Nietzschean one. It has, though, a more immediate parallel in the writings of Elie Faure, whose book on Napoleon was, as we saw, a major source of inspiration for the 1927 film and whose élitist populism is similar to Gance's. For Faure, the quality of a great leader is a fusion of strength and lyrical intuition, mobilising the energies of the masses not by inflammatory slogans but by appealing to their desire to emulate. The function of regeneration is to restore intuitive qualities, especially the collective sense of rhythm that bourgeois materialism and individualism has repressed in all but some of the black races.[79] Blaise Cendrars takes this further, seeing in Gance's *La roue* a symbol of the rhythm that generated the world and which is impervious to rational explanation, adding in *Moravagine*: 'In the beginning was rhythm, and rhythm became flesh.'[80] Rhythm survives, Faure insists, through dance, which preserves the harmony of instinct, intellect and a sense of the sublime.[81] This too is a view shared by Gance – and by Céline. After experimenting with expressive dance as a visualisation of music in *La dixième symphonie*, Gance used a dance of the people as the resolution of *La roue*. Norma, invited by the mountain guides to their annual celebration, joins hands with them in a round and, as they dance higher and higher up the snow-covered mountain, is gradually absorbed into their communal rhythm and harmony with nature. Worth noting, as well, are Gance's projects in the early 1940s to make two films on dance, *La Fiametta* and *La danseuse de Pampelune*.

What dance had done throughout history had become the function of cinema in the modern world. Like dance, it appealed to the intuitive, it was essentially rhythm. Here, we need to refer back to Gance's theory of cinema and his insistence that it had to become an art form for the people, an art of regeneration, replacing lost enthusiasm and lost energies. For Cendrars and Gance, the cinema is like a communion, an idea developed by Faure who defines it as 'the principal instrument of collective rhythm of social movements', adding, significantly: 'If the cinema is mobilised in the service of a unanimous social effort capable of delivering us from *individualism* by exalting all the spiritual resources of the individual necessary for the promotion of this effort, then we are right to see in it the most incomparable

177

instrument of communion that has yet been available to man, at least since the age of great architecture.'[82]

What is at stake here is not simply the shared experience of a group of spectators sitting together in a darkened room, or even the rediscovery of the intuitive through the rhythmic succession of images, but the appropriation of cinema, the production, through its agency, of a specific social change. This helps to explain why Gance insisted that while watching *Napoleon* the spectator had to become a participant in the drama. He/she is in a sense captivated by the flow of images but through them is engaged in an action, and should be transformed by it. In spite of all that Gance says about art as suggestion,[83] as what is not shown, as the relation between images, the spectator is also drawn towards what those images contain. The cinema is there to appeal to the intuitive and to mobilise.

Here, there may be a difference between the modes of identification which operate in the melodrama, with the shared response it generates to the poignant relation between archetypal individuals, and the epic. But in both the feelings evoked are already present within the frame, and it is from there that we are moved into a space outside the frame, the space of the film's performance. The object is the construction of the *spectator* as aesthetic person; art surpasses the politics on which it is founded.

7 Image, Spectacle, Position

From very early on in Gance's career as director, two main trends are apparent in his experimentation: a concern with deep space and with innovation on the level of distorted images, superimpression etc. The former, opening up the possibilities of composition in depth and the exploration of character relations, might initially seem to be particularly associated with the melodramatic and I will refer to it as the narrative space of melodrama. The latter, operating a change at the surface of the image and seemingly more appropriate to the epic, will be called, provisionally, the discursive surface of the epic. More important than any generic distinction, however, are the different effects which these techniques produce in terms of their positioning of the spectator, and what we need to move towards in analysing these effects is how, through their manipulation of the look, they construct the spectator as subject, or victim, of spectacle.

Films like *J'accuse*, *La roue* and *Napoleon* had an immense impact when they were first screened because they seemed to break with mainstream cinema. In retrospect this impact was, not surprisingly, attributed to those features, like superimpression, rapid cutting and the lateral montage of the triptychs, which were the most innovatory, a view which was then enshrined in histories of the cinema tending to valorise originality. The result has been a curiously distorted view of Gance's output, privileging the exceptional at the expense of the dominant. In much the same way as progressive form was set against reactionary content, the radically different has been filleted out, leaving aside images that because they work within, and operate on, mainstream practices can be dismissed as secondary. The overall effect of the interaction of different kinds of images has thus been overlooked.

Gance's concern with the status of the image is apparent not just in 'The cinema of tomorrow' but in numerous other texts dating from the 1920s, in which he insists that cinema should not be representing what we see but should be showing things differently, enriching our sensibilities, using the visible to suggest the invisible.[1] What counts is not the individual shot but a flow of images and what is in between them. It is thus that cinema becomes rhythmic, intuitive, impulsive.

We may recognise here a sub-text, the appropriation of a literary debate which opposes the poetic, elevated and energetic to the drab sentimentalism of the novelistic. This could sometimes be construed as a plea for the abrasive 'masculinity' of the image and was nearly always a veiled attack on the effeteness of bourgeois concepts of art. More immediately, it was an attack not just on the literary but on the theatrical, a stance against filmed theatre in favour of a cinema of powerful emotions.

But for Gance, this was never an argument for the complete denarratisation of the image. When he writes in 'Departure towards polyvision' that the impotence of cinema was a result of an exclusive preoccupation with narrative, he goes on immediately to stress the need even in a 'polyvision' film for a good story. Narrative is necessary but it has to aspire towards the poetic. This echoes a statement first printed in the programme for the gala presentation of *Napoleon* at the Opéra in 1927: 'I had thought since *La roue* that one could always appeal to emotion over and above the dramatic significance of the image. Hence the need for new techniques of filming to make cinematic style more flexible.' It is the *over and above* that is important here. Narrative is not effaced, but like Flaubert's conception of the real, it is a springboard. Superimpression and rapid montage sequences may indeed operate *over and above* the drama (or plot), but only to the extent that they have first been located within a narrative before taking off on the 'wings of poetry'. Even in the 1930s films, where the occasional montage sequence intrudes conspicuously into an otherwise realist *mise en scène*, the overall *intention*, whatever the effect, is to intensify rather than to produce radically heterogeneous meanings. Narrative is not a discrete entity, separate from a poetic image; it is the image, as process mediating a story, that constructs narrative and exceeds it.

To focus this argument, we have to retreat further into history, to November 1915, when Gance wrote in a note addressed to himself: 'I should make my films in much bigger sets, have a larger field, higher sets.' Earlier in the same note, he had observed: 'I must convince myself that the *mise en scène* is more important than the scenario. The detail, the really appropriate object, the picturesque, authority, are the primordial qualities. If along with these there is a good subject, success is guaranteed.'[2]

We might note here the impact of Feuillade[3] not just on some of Gance's early screenplays but on his strategies of direction and

La dixième symphonie: audience transfixed as Damor plays

emphasis on *mise en scène*. There is also an obvious reaction against the
theatricality of much French film production of the time and a complaint against the confined studio space in which young directors like
Gance had to work. But it is the terms of the protest that are most
interesting, the shift away from filmed story to a narrative *mise en scène*.
Like action, dialogue and description in a realist novel, screenplay,
decors and acting are all subordinated to a metadiscourse, to the
authority of the director exemplified in Gance's text 'The producer'.
Film is narrative image aspiring towards poetic truth in the 'over and
above'.

The importance of going back to 1915 is to demonstrate the initial
integration of the poetic and the narrative, of the 'theatrical' and the
performance of the image, as in *La folie du Docteur Tube*, whose
anamorphic images are happily located within the story of a doctor
who discovers a light ray that distorts the objects it strikes. Estranged
images are thus recuperated into an acceptable narrative (acceptable,
that is, to the director and his imagined public but not to the producer, who refused to release the film because it was too unconven-
tional).

More pertinent is a film like *La dixième symphonie*, in which superimpression and a discrepancy between 'sound' and image are combined
with experimentation with depth of field. Here already, as in the later
silent films, the image does not simply capture the performance of the

actors but neither does it break entirely with conventional modes of filming. When Damor plays his symphony on the piano for his guests, images of a woman dancer in an idyllic garden setting convey to the spectator the imaginative power of the music, but these images are keyed into the narrative by periodic returns to the performer, composition-in-depth shots of his transfixed audience, and the look of the 'guilty' wife: the poetic remains subservient to the narrative. The last image of the film shows not the fictional composer but Gance himself taking a bow as author of story, *mise en scène* and image, as ultimate performer, creator of a narrative experience.

We can't, then, take superimpression, montage or apparently denarratised images as separate categories as most criticism has tended to do, as if they have autonomous effects or form part of a teleological development of cinema. They function in individual films as constituent elements of a cinematic practice, juxtaposed, uneasily perhaps, but all subordinated within a discourse of 'truth' passing through the narrative in its aspiration towards the poetic.

As the example from *La dixième symphonie* shows, depth is not simply, even in the early films, a 'descriptive' device, a way of introducing into the frame the significant detail or the picturesque, as the 1915 quote suggests. The relation between character and setting and the contrast between settings and lifestyles are indeed highlighted both here and in the 1917 *Mater dolorosa*, but more particularly it allows the marking out of dramatic spaces and the mobilisation of a play of looks within the frame. Thus when Damor discusses his daughter's marriage with Fred Rice, her suitor, unaware that the latter is his wife's former lover and a profligate blackmailer, the two women observe in the background, revealing to the spectator their opposing anxieties. It is in ways like this that composition in depth constructs the ideal space of melodrama, producing the intensification of enclosed relationships within the confines of the frame. It also functions to hold and direct the spectator's gaze.

The best example of this is perhaps a scene from the remake of *Mater dolorosa*. Deep sets have already introduced the harsh, unfeeling atmosphere of the children's hospital which Gilles Berliac directs and the stark modernism of his home. We then cut to the apartment of his brother Claude. The large *salon* is furnished traditionally and comfortably with antique pieces strategically placed to enhance the depth as well as indicate Claude's artistic tastes. Claude, wearing casual clothes and a dressing gown, enters through a doorway in the far left-hand corner of the set, hurries down a small flight of steps and across to a door at the centre-right of the set to let in a visitor – not Marthe, Gilles' wife, as the spectator might anticipate, since we know

Composition in depth in *Mater dolorosa*

she is in love with Claude and anxious to see him, but Gilles himself. They cross to a table in the centre and towards the foreground of the set, around which most of the action takes place. Although there are changes of camera placings and inserts, the scene is basically a long take with the two brothers mostly close to the camera, but with an emphasis on depth and with the back of the set in quite sharp focus. Early in the conversation, Gilles idly picks up a pair of ladies' gloves from a dish on the table, looks at them, and replaces them in the dish, seeming not to register their significance or to notice Claude's uneasiness, and talks about the stunning beauty of Rita, the leading lady in Claude's new play. The conversation, dominated by Gilles, turns to the morality of the play, the child that Marthe is expecting, the friendship between the two brothers and their differences of temperament, with Gilles explaining, in terms that resemble those of Martial in *La fin du monde*, why he is indifferent, in his struggle against illness, to all except physical suffering. This is punctuated by the sound of a woman weeping, coming from beyond the doorway through which Claude entered and dismissed by Gilles as the result of a petty dispute with Rita, who he assumes is Claude's mistress.

Positioning the spectator: the 1932 *Mater dolorosa*

The encounter between the two brothers is vital to the action of the film. It is the only scene in which they are alone together and the only time that the central issue of the complementarity of science and poetry is explicitly raised. But the attention of the spectator is also being directed throughout by Claude's hasty entrance, by his uneasiness, by the gloves, by the weeping, towards the doorway at the back of the set. In fact, the spectator 'knows', from the moment that it is Gilles and not Marthe who is ushered in through the centre-right door, that Marthe must already be in the apartment, beyond our, and Gilles', field of vision; and as the intensity of the scene mounts, his/her look is increasingly drawn, through the action, into the deep space of the set, towards her invisible presence.

One could argue that, working on a cheap remake within the constraints of early sound studios, Gance is merely reappropriating here a device that had been used countless times in the days of fixed cameras and which was in any case borrowed from bourgeois theatre.[4] It nevertheless exemplifies how the space of the melodrama is created and how the spectator is drawn into that space. It illustrates the basis of the narrative hold which, as I've suggested, is what

184

underpins Gance's cinematic practice not just in the melodramas but in films that aspire towards the epic.

Perhaps its essential feature is that the spectator's look appears to be unmediated – as if there is nobody here looking but me – effacing the frame and the surface of the image, producing an absorption into the narrative. As a result, a particular form of empathetic identification is produced through the search for the desired object of the look, absent in this instance yet present beyond the visible field rather than in a subsequent shot or a reverse field.

Even if innovation were to be valorised in itself, Gance is remarkable for his pioneering attempts to explore the possibilities of depth, constructing the principal set for *La roue* in the middle of a marshalling yard at Nice so that the passing engines would be continual reminders of the world of the characters, and working always to draw the spectator into the space of the action. Hence his early experiments with stereoscopic vision which also date back to the filming of *La roue*, when Gance wrote enthusiastically to Charles Pathé (28 June 1920) that he was almost certain that he had discovered a stereoscopic process. (One reel of *Napoleon* was in fact shot in 3D, but was not included in the final print since, according to Gance, the seductive effect of the image would distract attention from the content, fascinating the eye instead of the heart.[5])

Drawn into the frame by composition in depth, the spectator's gaze is not then left free to wander as if in some mythical Bazinian film. Like most depth directors, Gance constructs a hierarchy of spatial relations which organise the look. But even that is not insistent enough for an 'author' as directive as Gance. Depth provides a basic narrative space, a dominant mode (which does not need to be presented first in a sequence of shots but simply to be established as dominance). Other strategies orientate the look and direct responses.

It may simply be that the camera tracks in, directing the look towards the point of identification, or tracks out to relocate the focalised person or object. More often it is expressive effects of, for example, light and shade that manipulate the spectator's response. When, in the 1932 *Mater dolorosa*, we are finally shown Marthe's reaction to what she has overheard, she is back-lit, heightening her beauty and her suffering. (In the silent version, Gance plays even more on extremes of light and shadow to create an emotive effect.) And the struggle for the gun with which she accidentally shoots Claude is conveyed more by cutting and jerky camera movements than by the performance of the actors. Although there is a shift here towards the performance of the film as opposed to what it represents, the represented remains dominant. *Mise en scène* is at the service of the

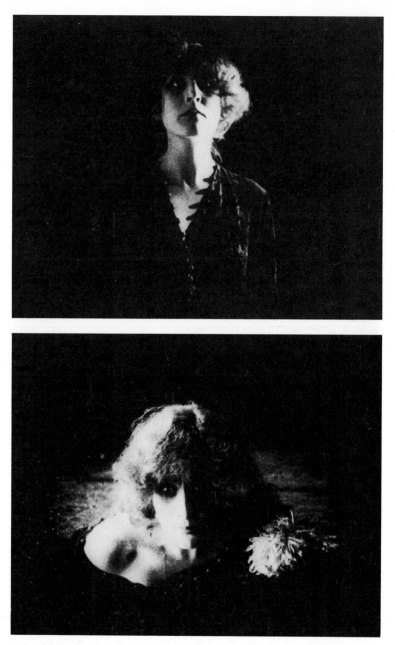

Light and shadow in the 1917 *Mater dolorosa* (above) and (opposite) *La dixième symphonie*

action, confirming the positioning of the spectator through an emotional hold, mobilising feeling, directing it towards empathy with the protagonist(s), providing, in Gancian terms, access to the invisible through the visible.

Point-of-view shots, which Gance pioneered in his early films, often quite obtrusively, may *seem* to establish a different position. When, to quote *Mater dolorosa* again, Marthe is being taken by Gilles to her child who she thinks may be dead, the car seems to be heading straight towards a cemetery and only at the last minute does it turn towards the house in which the child is hidden. The camera, placed inside the car, gives exactly Marthe's point of view, intercut with reaction shots showing her emotion. The subjective shots here are quite disturbing for the spectator, partly because of the reverse angles. The effect is perhaps even more marked in the 1917 version, where the same strategy is used – the camera, again in the car, heads directly towards the cemetery and then tracks along the side of it, past the entrance – in a film in which, otherwise, there is relatively little camera movement. But in neither version is the basic pattern of identification changed: it is simply intensified, as though our gaze has been drawn further into the frame to take up one of the positions within it. Subjective shots, although frequent even in the early films, are usually quite short. As in *Au secours*, when a hand-held camera conveys Max's trepidation as he approaches the haunted chateau, or in *Napoleon*, when the camera mounted on a horse's back gives the point of view of Bonaparte's pursuers in the escape from Corsica, the spectator is not drawn into the drama as 'participant' but momentarily given a privileged viewpoint which is quickly recuperated back into the overall strategy of the narrative hold, of the unmediated look. When the spectator of *Napoleon* does indeed become a participant, it is not in the action, but in a celebration of the film and its impact.

Most of what has been said about subjective shots could also be applied to the use of close-ups, which occur much less frequently in narrative scenes than production stills would suggest. Sometimes they are used as reaction shots; mostly, as Charles Ford points out, they indicate the high point of a scene,[6] and are thus also subservient to a broader strategy.

What matters, then, is the apparent effacement of the discursive,[7] of the film as performance, the absorption of the spectator into a story-experience, in a way that seems not to conform to the general view of Gance's cinema.

This is not to say that the discursive is ever entirely effaced. Other strategies foreground it, but these are typically separated out from the narrative. One example is the use of intertitles, the mark for René

Napoleon: the death of Marat, modelled on the painting by David

Clair of Gance's literary pretensions. Although these frequently serve to advance or clarify the narrative, they are often commentaries on the action in the form of quotations or general observations, conferring on the narrative a broader significance. A more important strategy is the recourse to the symbolic, or rather the iconic. I am referring here less to Epstein's view of the wheel as symbol of the human condition than to Gance's equation of Napoleon with Prometheus in his presentation of the film and of Sisif with Oedipus. The iconic, that which occurs within the image, is exemplified in *La dixième symphonie*, when a mask of Beethoven is superimposed on to Damor performing his symphony and juxtaposed images equate Eve with the Victory of Samothrace. More dramatically, in the two versions of *Mater dolorosa*, the heroine poses beneath the same painting depicting the sorrowing mother, bare-breasted and holding her dead child. There is an address here which operates over and above the narrative, a change in the status of the look to one of recognition. The same shift operates in *Napoleon*: Marat's death reconstructs the David painting known to French spectators if only through reproductions in school history books, like the animated representation of Rude's 'Chant du départ' which 'illustrates' the spirit of the Revolution at the end of the Marseillaise sequence. The effect is not to highlight authenticity, as in the widely used publicity photograph of the Gros painting of the

Heroine and icon in the 1917 *Mater dolorosa*

young Bonaparte on horseback in which only the face was changed –
Dieudonné's for Napoleon's. The iconic may serve as guarantee, but
it is more important as an establishment of complicity, as direct
address to the spectator, invoking, through recognition, a confirmat-
ory response.[8]

As the films tend towards spectacle, two other major strategies
intervene to further shift the narrative hold:

– the mediation of the spectator's gaze, directing it through a look

located within the frame, transferring identification from the protagonist to the observer of an intra-diegetic spectacle;
– the holding back of the look at the surface of the image, the
construction of a spectacle that supplants the diegetic.

THE MEDIATING LOOK

There are occasions in the melodramas when the spectator's look is in
conflict with another look, inscribed within the frame but not that of
the protagonist. In the opening sequence of *La dixième symphonie*, for
example, after we have watched Eve shoot the sister of her profligate
lover, we become aware that Fred, the lover, has also witnessed the
event. Our look as he emerges from the shadows is thus set up in
opposition to his: while we search for understanding and redemption,
he seeks only to exploit his knowledge. It is as though Fred's villainy is
established by his stealing of a look that seemed at first to belong
exclusively to the spectator. Towards the end of the film, when Eve
returns to Fred in order to save her stepdaughter, the stepdaughter
looks on. Again the spectator's look is separate, directed towards the
same object but with a greater understanding.

In the two versions of *Mater dolorosa* there is an interesting shift of
the intra-diegetic look. The trusted manservant, present at the acci-
dental shooting of the poet/playwright but sworn to secrecy as to the
cause of death, looks on, unable to speak out as Eve/Marthe suffers,
like a pre-echo of Stefan's dumb servant in Ophuls' *Letter from an
Unknown Woman*, though he does eventually reveal the truth and effect
a reconciliation. Like John, he does not direct the spectator's look, he
represents it, encapsulating the desire for a resolution that neither he
nor the spectator can bring about. Later, in films like *Beethoven* and *La
Vénus aveugle*, these lookers-on become more important, forming in the
latter a chorus devoted to the blind heroine's salvation, seeing what
she can't see.

It is this kind of look, or play on looks, that becomes the foundation
of the epic, through an insistent mediation. Although our first view of
Jean Novalic in *La fin du monde* is a direct one (this view will be
examined later in terms of spectacle), it is almost immediately mediated through Geneviève, whose love for Jean is transparent in the way
she acts out the role of Mary Magdalene. We are invited to love and
admire along with her, resisting the view of those who are eventually
revealed among the audience who scoff at *him* and eye *her*. The look,
here, is directed in a totally different way, towards an identification
not with Jean but with Geneviève, the stand-in for the spectator.
Although we do sometimes look directly at Jean later in the film, the

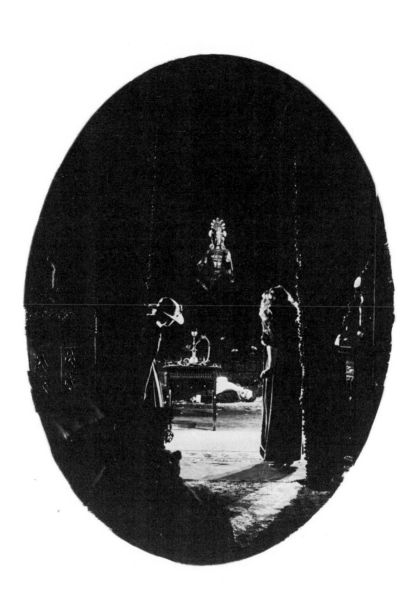

The look directed in *La dixième symphonie*: Eve and her stepdaughter discover Fred's suicide

pattern of the mediated look is maintained in most of the sequences in which he appears. We look on with Geneviève, with Martial or with those who take care of him during his illness. Jean is too unworldly, too unapproachable for us to identify with him. Instead we are led to the position of those who believe in him – and who will bring about the resolution.

Again, *Napoleon* is exemplary, indicating how the mediated look changes the status of the image, impelling it towards spectacle. Sometimes it is Bonaparte who is the mediator, especially in the early sections of the film. In the Cordeliers sequence, the spectator might feel some bemusement at the appropriation of the 'Marseillaise' by the ambitious Danton. But Bonaparte is there on the sidelines. While he does not join vigorously in the singing like the assembled crowds, the Fleuris and, in some of the early screenings of the film, the audience, his presence and his penetrating look guide and reassure.[9] His seal of approval confirms that the spectator's enthusiasm is a correct response and his 'Merci pour la France' addressed to Rouget de l'Isle carries with it the gratitude of the public within and without the frame. In contrast, the violence that surrounds the fall of the monarchy is clearly designated by Bonaparte's look as excess, as is the depravity of the new bourgeoisie at the Bal des Victimes. In these instances, Bonaparte directs and authorises responses. It is through his look (and it is often just a look rather than a statement of opinion) that the spectator is led to a specific view of the Revolution.

Much more frequently, though, it is Bonaparte himself who is the object of the mediated look, observed within the frame by his family, his aides and enemies, Josephine, especially the Fleuris. Bonaparte's return with his sister Elisa to the family house in Corsica begins with location shots explained by intertitles or, in the sound versions, by voice-overs. His arrival at the house is signalled as a return to origins in family and nature by one of the most self-consciously aesthetic and romantically effective series of images in the whole film: the swarm of bees, the brilliant sunshine, the threshold seen from inside the house framing the unexpected homecomers, the display of feeling. With Napoleon's delayed entry, watched by Elisa then by the mother, the sequence moves into what will remain its dominant mode, composition in depth, a hierarchy of spaces, expressive lighting, the play of looks within the frame between the protagonists, all the standard elements of the melodramas. And the sequence does indeed function as melodrama bonded into epic, humanising Bonaparte, establishing him as Man of Feeling. But the spectator's gaze, drawn into the frame, is led towards spaces that are already occupied by minor characters whose looks are directed towards the hero. The younger

The homecoming: Bonaparte, the family and Santo Ricci in the Corsican episode of *Napoleon*

brothers and sisters look on admiringly, confirming him as surrogate father, head of a family that stretches beyond the confines of the frame. More significantly for the film's politics, Santo Ricci looks on, first in the background, then as spiritual father and representative of the people, directly interpellating Napoleon, seeing in him the only man who could save Corsica from its betrayers.

Both narrative and spectacle seem to remain in play here. On the one hand we observe, as if without mediation, the reinsertion of Napoleon into the family. On the other, our look is mediated. As head of the family and as political leader, he is, like Jean, distanced from us. Our admiration is channelled through and identified with the response of the observer within the frame.

It is in this latter respect that the Fleuris are particularly important as presences in the film. They are not just there as *narrative* points of identification, as the 1923 outline might seem to suggest, that is as characters who help the spectator to understand the action, to avoid his/her becoming confused by the complexity of the events. Like Geneviève, but more insistently, they are stand-ins, mediators within the frame, constructing responses.

At Brienne, the young Napoleon takes on his adversaries in the snowball battle. There is never any doubt about the outcome: although the enemy cheats, Napoleon wins through resoluteness and a superior strategy, while the masters, including Pichegru, predict for him a brilliant future.

Increasingly, as the intensity of the struggle is heightened, we are held back at the surface of the image, caught up in the performance of the film as spectacle, but Tristan Fleuri is there to locate our look. Like a cheerleader on the sidelines, he urges Napoleon on, approving, eventually triumphant – and caught out by the stray snowball which strikes him full in the face, making him drop the tub of food he is supposed to be preparing. He is our representative, constructing for us in his naive way the enthusiastic response that we are summoned to experience. Because he is naive and is caught out, we do not align ourselves with him, but neither can we identify innocently with the young Bonaparte. It is rather that our look, channelled through Fleuri's, is enthusiastically conditioned, mobilising our approbation, establishing a system of recognition. We have a place from which to observe and interpret, sharing Fleuri's joy and able to go beyond it, feeling what he feels intuitively but able to rationalise.

This look, establishing both complicity with the person looking and a certain distanciation, becomes dominant in *Napoleon*, interpreting our gaze, converting it to a look directed towards spectacle. We applaud along with Fleuri but are made to feel superior to him, sharing his emotion but not his simplicity.

At Toulon, Fleuri is again on the sidelines, looking on admiringly but unrecognised at Bonaparte's prowess, unlike young Marcellin who is always caught out by Bonaparte's look. Violine, too, is unrecognised, except by Josephine who momentarily shares her fervour as they both pray at Violine's improvised altar. Otherwise she, like her

The mediating look in *Napoleon*: at Brienne and (below) at Toulon

father, is essentially mediator, indicating how we should interpret the events of the Revolution, recognising on our behalf the achievements of the Robespierres and the Saint-Justs, while turning us against political excess. Mostly, like her father's, her look is addressed towards Bonaparte, in person or in effigy.

A system of representations is thus established in which the spectator's look is guided. Like Jean Novalic, like the leaders of the Revolution, Napoleon is 'too great for us'. He is elevated to the unapproachable, the great leader whom the Fleuris intuitively recognise as Saviour. The Fleuris' function is insistently to tell us that; to keep us in our place as spectating subjects. Once they have been established as figures of melodrama who direct our look, mediating and thus constructing distance, the direct look again becomes possible, as look at spectacle. We look as subjects of *his* look, positioned by it, identifying not with him but with those who look on as we do. Bonaparte is constructed as object of desire, as realisation of what we cannot attain, leaving us as inferiors, able to glimpse an order of things, a potential in which we can imaginatively participate, a sense of unity in which we momentarily share as collective audience, but aligned with the Fleuris, summoned with them to adore the hero of the spectacle – and its author.

196

Although the mediated look is similar to the apparently unmediated one in that it too draws the spectator into the space within the frame, its principal effect is to operate a shift of identification, away from the protagonist towards the sympathetic onlooker. What the Fleuris do, in this respect, is provide an individualisation of a collective response. At some moments it is with a collective in the image that we are invited to merge, with the singers of the 'Marseillaise', with the soldiers at Toulon, with the Army of Italy, but the individual mediator is still there to confirm that our response is correct. As in *Lola Montès* we are impelled to take up a position with regard to what is already there, but whereas Ophuls' inscribed spectators were wooden cut-outs, distanciating us, Gance's extras were factory workers on strike, living out the fantasy of a new society. Like them we become participants in a performance, while our response is directed towards the author of the performance, Danton, Bonaparte – or Gance (in reports of the filming of the 'epic' scenes, cries of 'Vive Abel Gance!' predominate). The essential point is that, in scenes which are in themselves spectacular, the look, passing through intra-diegetic spectators, is constituted in such a way as to construct the hero as spectacle.

Spectacle cannot, then, be analysed in any monolithic way, but only as play of looks and discourses. Apparently there is a hierarchy with at its summit the hero, the unattainable object of all the looks, the source of enthusiasm and of meaning. Then the intermediaries, often in themselves spectacular but subservient. And lastly the cinema audience emplaced by the other two instances. But the problem with a ranking of this kind is that it elides the performance of the film as essential feature of spectacle, a problem which some examples may help to clarify.

Towards the end of *Paradis perdu* (1939) there is a sequence that seems at first to come close to 'pure' spectacle. The setting is a luxurious nightclub during its opening party. An immense set with elaborate decors, a lavish floor-show, singers, dancers and orchestra all combine to make this scene a high point of the film, a moment of visual pleasure, registered by the inscribed audience's expressions of delight. Even so, it is the performance of the camera rather than what it records that constitutes the sequence as spectacle. Sophisticated camera movements and placings, extreme angles, skews, close-ups of dancers' legs, inserts and shots filmed through the spokes of the ship's wheel which is the centrepiece of the decor become a kind of celebration of the filmic event that surpasses the one being filmed. It is as though we were being held back just a little so that we can enjoy the virtuosity of the film-maker.

The narrative is not elided or pushed back into the wings until the spectacular number is over and done with. On the contrary, as increasingly insistent cutaways remind us, this is also the culmination of the melodramatic plot. For Pierre, the hero, a gifted painter turned fashion designer and creator of the nightclub decors (an art for the opulent), this was to have been the celebration of his marriage, but he is gradually convinced that he must renounce his own happiness for that of his daughter. Spectacle and narrative are, then, set in counterpoint, intensifying the melodrama through an appeal to conflicting emotions. But our desire as spectators is continually drawn back towards the spectacle, to the celebration in and of the film.

In this instance, the spectacle is presented as innocence, as something there simply to be enjoyed while we shed a tear for the generous hero. But spectacle also interpellates and its mode of address may thus produce more radical conflicts, as in the Bal des Victimes sequence in *Napoleon*. Here the Carmelite convent set is quite narrow but has a depth that is frequently exploited as the camera tracks or as characters move towards or away from it. There is also a complex play of looks since the Fleuris, Bonaparte and Josephine are all present. In terms of the look located within a narrative discourse, Violine is there as representative of a people who adulate Bonaparte, Tristan as the man seduced momentarily by effeteness, Bonaparte as austere judge. Perhaps it is because *his* look is captivated by Josephine's ('What are the weapons you fear the most, General?' – 'Fans, madam.') that his authority is diminished, but even before that there has been a conflict between the disapproving look of Bonaparte, appalled by this display of a sensuality verging on depravity, and the visual excitement of the scene. Intertitles or voice-overs are insistent but ineffectual. The spectator's look has itself already been captivated, taken at first by surprise (Fleuri looks as if he is going to read out the names of victims for the scaffold), then seduced by the *mise en scène*. Bonaparte, for once, has been outflanked by the scantily dressed dancers on their swings, by the charm of camera movement and montage, by a spectacle that is in itself seductive. Bonaparte's disapproving look shows how we *should* respond, but it is subverted by the performance of the film offering itself as spectacle with images that contradict the mediating look.[11]

Because the sequence is contradictory, it opens up a gap between mediation and performance, a space the films tend to deny, offering themselves instead as the unity exemplified in the opening sequence of *La fin du monde*. As the screenplay emphasises, we need to be

Contradiction and the seduction of the look: Bonaparte outflanked in the Bal des Victimes sequence in *Napoleon*

convinced initially that we are witnessing a real event, that our look is unmediated. A hand expresses intense suffering; the face, the dislocated body agonise. We are present at the crucifixion, which must even so be a representation since we are watching a film, but it is as though we are direct observers. As the camera tracks back, it reveals first Mary Magdalene, directing our look, and the rest of the group surrounding the cross, then stage, auditorium and, by implication,

The artist as Messiah: Abel Gance as Jean Novalic as Christ in *La fin du monde*

ourselves as spectators. It is as if there are two contrasting tensions, one holding our look as participants, the other pulling it back valorising the film itself as performance, an effect intensified by an orchestral accompaniment of Bach at his most luxuriant. The two are held together by the ubiquity of the director, exhibited bodily as Messiah, suffering for his art and for humanity, and present invisibly as the force behind the camera, expressly designated as author of the spectacle by the title Soupault found so ludicrous ('La fin du monde, vue, entendue et interprétée par Abel Gance'). Of the two, it is the second that eventually predominates, the performance of the film rather than the metonymic spectacle the film contains.

The hierarchy has, then, to be revised. The narrative look of melodrama draws the spectator into the frame; the mediated look directs within the frame, constructing the protagonist as spectacle; the film, as performance, operates not just as metadiscourse but as ultimate spectacle. Indeed, we could define filmic spectacle as that which arrests the spectator's look at the surface of the frame as opposed to what is within the frame. In other words, mediation is a passage from one direct look to another, from into the frame to at the frame, from melodrama to epic and from hero to author. We pass from the aspiration towards unity as resolution of melodrama, through the unified hero poet of action, to the film itself as authority, energy and unity.

Earlier we examined images that operate over and above narrative while still located within a predominantly narrative hold. Their effects can now be reviewed in terms of spectacle.

Two of the most striking instances occur in *La roue*. In the Alpine sequence Elie looks out of the window and sees Norma's face in superimpression on the mountain peaks. He closes the window, places a cloth over it and then puts his cloak over that, but still the image of Norma remains. This echoes a scene from much earlier in the film. Sisif, glancing through the window into his tiny garden between the railway tracks, catches sight of Norma on a swing. His look is drawn towards her as a sexual presence, and especially towards her legs. A mask draws the shape of the image in, making it first round, then oval and centred, eye-shaped, on Norma's legs as if in close-up. Sisif hastily draws the curtain but can't resist holding it aside and continuing to look. Eventually he turns away and covers his eyes but the oval image of Norma's legs is still there, intercut with shots of Sisif.

These scenes are apparently entirely recuperable into a narrative system. The image of Norma superimposed on mountain, window, cloth and cloak is Elie's, just as the look at her legs is Sisif's and the closing in of the image simply reinforces this, emphasising feelings of desire and guilt which are his, not ours. As such, these are remarkable pieces of 'subjectivity', but their fascination for the spectator lies at least as much in the performance of the film, as though we were being summoned to celebrate inventiveness. The eye-shaped mask closes off the depth initially constructed by the narrative look. The closing of the window, the cloth and the cloak draw the image of Norma forward until it seems to be held at the surface of the frame, typifying the interplay between narrative and performance. As examples of subjective images generated within the narrative, they resemble the scene in which Sisif's reflection in the mirror he is holding becomes increasingly blurred, signalling his failing eyesight (a similar strategy is used in *La Vénus aveugle*). There is, even so, a change in mode of address brought about by performance and especially apparent in superimpression. Once Norma has accepted the idea of marrying Hersan, she begins to reflect on the advantages of wealth. A superimposed series of images representing the accoutrements of luxury gradually fills the periphery of the frame around a mid-shot of Hersan. They are fragmented visualisations of her thoughts but once again they remain on the surface of the frame, as though they come between us and the initial image of Hersan. The statement is less a naturalised 'Norma thinks . . .' than an address of the kind 'Here are the temptations that beset Norma'. The mask of Beethoven superimposed over the image of the composer Damor, already referred to above, carries this move a stage further towards the discursive, an effect which is even more apparent in Gance's use of montage.

Bazin dismisses Gance in the briefest of references, lumping him together with Kuleshov and Eisenstein as one of those directors who do not show events but simply allude to them, producing an abstract result.[12] Although this view is not surprising, given Bazin's hostility to montage, it may be based more on ignorance than on prejudice – his only explicit reference to *La roue* is to the montage sequence of engine wheels, and looks suspiciously second-hand. As a representation of Gance it is also entirely misleading. For whatever reason – polemic, political difference or the absence of opportunity to see the films – Bazin, like most of his successors, completely overlooks the linkage in Gance's films between montage and what has come to be called narrative realism.

Like superimpression and expressive shaping of the image, montage is initially dependent on a narrative hold and often has a predominantly narrative function. The rapid flow of images in *La fin du monde* which signals Jean's madness is supposedly interiorised, representing the confusion of his mind. Rapid montage is also used to convey Sisif's account of the train crash which sets in motion the action of *La roue*. In both instances, there is an apparent source of the image within the frame. They are like the speeded-up sequence which conveys Machefer's garbled and breathless account of another accident later in the film. But even when there is not an inscribed point of origin, there is usually a narrative justification. The assemblage of shots of engine wheels from a multiplicity of angles, not necessarily the most memorable elements of *La roue* but those which have been

La roue: Elie's death

handed down as the mark of its originality, are from nobody's point of view. Yet they function narratively as integral parts of a sequence, constructing the idea of excessive speed and impending disaster. They break out momentarily into spectacle but are quickly recuperated back into narrative.

Not surprisingly, perhaps, it is when the subjective and the unlocated narrative viewpoint are fused that the spectacular becomes most apparent. Elie, wounded by Hersan, clings with one hand to a branch over an abyss. Norma, at first leading Sisif, rushes on ahead in an attempt to find Elie and rescue him. Rhythmically, the sequence begins slowly but as the tempo gradually accelerates, time seems to be stretched out interminably. Alternating montage cuts between Norma running and Elie's hand and face. The duration of each shot is reduced until we reach thirty frames and less. Then, as Elie loses his grip, we move into an extraordinary sequence of split-second shots of three to five frames reduced to two and eventually to single frames.

Elie's death:
single frame montage

204

Close-ups of Elie are intercut with images of Norma from earlier in the film, of their childhood, their adolescence, their love for each other, images which summarise his life.

The effect produced for the spectator is, at the end of the sequence, an extraordinary shock, a shock due only in part to the fact that our expectations have been manipulated. Within the conventions that Gance exploits, Elie should of course be saved and we are led at first to believe that this will indeed be the case, that suspense is building up towards a release as Norma arrives in the nick of time. But why is Norma taking so long? What will happen if she does arrive in time, since Elie is hanging by one hand from a branch below the cliff top and Norma hasn't the strength to pull him to safety?

These questions are elided by the performance of the film, as the sequence moves beyond narrative into spectacle. The protracted cross-cutting, too long to be acceptable as narrative realism, establishes a rhythm, building up from a slow beginning to the single-frame montage of the climax. The impact derives at least as much from this heightening of the tempo and its abrupt halt as from Elie's fall to his death. In visual terms, the spectator's look is drawn increasingly towards the surface of the frame as long shots give way to close-ups, especially as the rhythm of the montage accelerates. In the shots of three, two and single frames which conclude the sequence, we can no longer clearly distinguish what the images contain, and it is only if the film is viewed in slow motion that we can really establish that the images of Norma are Elie's memories of his love for her. Performance exceeds narrative, and in terms of narrative would simply seem to be excess, but it has momentarily changed the spectator's position, constructing a look *at* the film. The silence and slowness that ensue impose a reluctant return to narrative.

The space of spectacle is already marked out here. All that is lacking is the mediator who, bridging the gap between depth and surface, operates the easy transference from spectacle within the image to the image itself as spectacular.

The 'Cordeliers' sequence in *Napoleon* is basically similar in its strategies. It begins slowly, even in confusion, gradually establishing order and harmony and culminating in a rhythmical montage which also builds up to a series of single-frame close-ups at the climax, with for good measure the iconic representation of 'La Marseillaise' in superimpression. Deep space mobilises our look, drawing us along with the Fleuris into the spectacle represented within the frame. Bonaparte's approval confirms the correctness of the desire to participate. Then we are pulled back to a hold at the surface of the frame. The deep space is effaced; only an assemblage of close-ups and superimpressions remains. Instead of applauding Danton or Rouget de l'Isle along with the participants, we are called back into the present, as spectators of the performance of the film in a cinema, sharing in a collective response in the here and now.

This kind of positioning has been anticipated in the Brienne sequence. Initially Fleuri organises our approval, but as the snowball fight intensifies the narrative look becomes increasingly inadequate as the action escapes a narrative control. Hand-held cameras may for a moment create an impression of involvement in the action, but the overall effect is that of a camera so close to the action that it is unable to make sense of what is going on. Excitement is again constructed at the surface of the image, and intensified by rapid montage: the climax accelerates rhythmically from shots of twenty-two frames of the main action intercut with inserts of the young Napoleon of half that length down, in stages, to single frames. As in the earlier examples, we can no longer distinguish between the frames. There is only the impact of the film as spectacle.

In the pillow fight that ensues, the division of the frame into separate images of varying size and number, accompanied by super-impressions and a white halo encircling the frame, similarly produces a spectacular effect, through the look at the frame and not at any individual image.

Like the other sequences examined, the finale of *Napoleon* begins slowly and undramatically, as Bonaparte's arrival at the Albenga encampment passes almost unnoticed by a demoralised, dejected and ill-fed Army of Italy. Indifference gives way to a struggle for the look, between the soldiers and Bonaparte, defended by Fleuri, especially between Bonaparte and the chiefs of staff whose silent revolt he quells. No words are necessary: authority is imposed on soldiers and generals alike by the power of his look. From then on we look not with him but at him, with Fleuri and the whole army as mediators. When, within the hour, order is restored and a new enthusiasm created, the whole scene becomes spectacle, with Bonaparte at its centre, as in the Cordeliers sequence when we are called up to identify not with Danton but with the assembled populace.

As the centre camera irises in, followed by those to left and right revealing a high-angle panorama of the army ready for inspection, the feeling of exhilaration is intensified, as though the complete space of spectacle is being offered to our gaze, a space controlled by Bonaparte. It is a critical moment in the film since as the commander-in-chief reviews his troops, riding up and down the lines of soldiers through the depth of the frame and then across the three screens, the admiring look of the spectator is directed towards both the great

Dividing the frame: the pillow fight in *Napoleon*

leader and the performance of the film. From there on, mediation becomes increasingly unnecessary: as the film gradually supplants the hero, the narrative hold is relaxed and panoramic views give way to triptychs. The next morning, Bonaparte harangues his troops, centre-screen, with panoramic views of the soldiers intercut showing their enthusiastic response (at the Opéra premiere, the speech was delivered by an actor, as though the audience was also being inter-pellated). Then the army marches off, left and right with, in the centre, images of the people cheering them or of Bonaparte's authority. Montenotte is taken (again a combination of panoramas and triptychs), opening the gates of Italy, as intertitles inform us, since much of the narrative has by now been relegated to the intervals between the images. And the army continues its march, centred now, and flanked on either side by Bonaparte on horseback, guiding his troops along the path to glory, galloping towards history, while in Paris a huge crowd gathered at the Convention applauds the victory.

Then, the apotheosis. As Bonaparte stands on the heights of Montezemolo, dreaming of the future, the crowds, the army, even Bonaparte, are gradually effaced. The images are narratively ascribed to him, but that is quickly lost sight of. It does not even particularly matter that these supposed visions of the future are in fact images of the past, an assemblage of superimpressions on the triple screen of shots from earlier in the film. It is probably not even noticeable that some of them are upside-down. As the rhythm increases, only the flow of images counts, culminating in the mael-strom and the tricolour, here and now in the cinema, inviting an applause which will prolong the experience of communion.

But what *do* we applaud? Bonaparte as militarist hero, the spectacle within the frame, or the film as spectacle? Mostly the last, in a celebration of cinema as apotheosis of the artist. The final image could be, as in *La dixième symphonie*, Gance as author of the spectacle,[13] the hero for today who has mobilised enthusiasm there where *we* are.

Spectacle may not always take precisely this form. In the Double Tempest sequence, for example, there is no mediating look and both narrative and explanatory commentaries are relegated to intertitles, leaving superimpressions (in the surviving version) and triptychs (in the original Opéra version) to 'speak' for themselves. More usually, as in most of the examples analysed above, narrative and spectacle occur in conjunction. But it is precisely because this is not the case in the *Napoleon* finale that it illustrates so well how spectacle functions. As the film passes from narrative (the look into the screen) through mediation (the deviation of the look) to the look across the screen, it is as though it is shifting tense: the narrative and the mediatory have been necessary for the film as spectacle to become part of a continuing present acting on the audience. In other terms, the 'narrative space of melodrama' has positioned the spectator through identification and an appeal to feeling. It, and the mediating presences that come to occupy it in order to organise our response, can now be dispensed with, leaving only what I called earlier 'the discursive surface of the epic' but which can now be redefined as the dominant mode of spectacle. A mode which, through its rhythmical flow of juxtaposed or superimposed images, engenders a collective response to the film as performance. Its appeal is to what Gance refers to as intuition, though early romantics might have called it enthusiasm – being in harmony with a superior spiritual presence.

Gance sometimes claimed that he invented the triple screen because he needed more space for his crowd scenes. That may have been initially the case, but it is not the way he mostly exploits it. Panoramic shots form only a relatively small part of the *Napoleon* finale, largely because André Debrie's synchronised cameras were not available until shooting was almost completed and were used only for the Albenga and Montenotte sequences. Like the missing triptychs of the Double Tempest and the Bal des Victimes and most of Gance's later experiments, the greater part of the finale is, to use Vuillermoz's term, in polyvision, the lateral montage of three separate images shot with an ordinary camera, or, more frequently, matching images to left and right with a different but complementary one in the centre. Elie Faure, as art historian, saw in this juxtaposition a defence of the plastic against the continual encroachment of naturalism, a new musicality or harmony of images.[14] And indeed, Gance's montage, whether lateral or linear, is rarely dialectical. Images do not conflict but confirm each other, constructing a unified meaning.

Grafted on to *Napoleon* at a late stage, the triptychs were seen as the high point of the film, especially the Double Tempest sequence which was for Elie Faure the mark of Gance's symphonic genius. But they serve principally to intensify what is still apparent in the single-screen version. The opening out of the space of spectacle completes the process by which the values incarnated by Bonaparte are conferred on to the film. Images of power are transformed into the power of the image. In short, the aesthetic experience of the spectator absorbs and supplants the political rationale established within the image. It is the whole audience which, in its collective response to the film, is summoned to experience that romantic unity which Bonaparte exemplified in the past. As Gance explained in his presentation of the film at the Opéra, the audience should be swept along in the rhythm of the images.

a

b

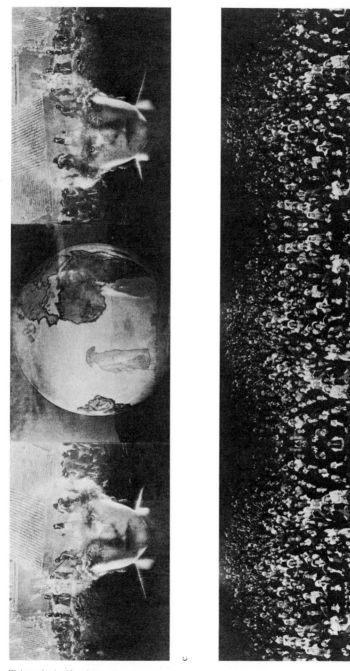

Triptychs in *Napoleon*: a) panorama; b) symmetry; c) symmetry and superimpression; d) the crowd at the Convention (triplication of single image with centre frame reversed)

All the statements of Gance, his admirers and critics about the spectator as participant in the action need then to be reappraised in terms of position or, more precisely, of a play of looks which construct positions. Although the action may capture our interest, we are essentially placed not in it but with regard to it, mobilised by narrative, held back as spectating subjects. At certain key moments, it is as though the film duplicates its own process of signification, as in the opening sequence of *La fin du monde* when the overhead track reveals an audience looking at an image that we thought was only for us. In the Cordeliers and Albenga sequences in *Napoleon*, we, as spectators, look on at other spectators who are themselves spectacular. Our response should be like theirs with regard to the heroic, but they are also objects of our look. While they cheer, we applaud not just them as performers, nor their hero, but an experience that resembles theirs, as though the content of the image was representing metonymically the feelings of the cinema audience. What we participate in is, once again, less the action than the performance of the film as spectacle.

In the melodramas – including melodramatic scenes in the epics – we are drawn in as though our look was an individual one directed towards individuals. Even so, our experience is a collective one, shared by all the spectators. Spectacle tends to negate what survives of that individuality, leaving only a collective response, hence the importance of the representations of unity within the frame. Placed as universal subjects, we are led towards regeneration through a communion instituted by the spectacle. Gance's often repeated ambition was to have massive performances, with an immense screen and with an audience of 20,000 or even 80,000 spectators all of one heart and one mind.

It is in fact the heart, here, that takes precedence over the mind in the construction of unity, given Gance's desire to create a cinema of powerful emotions. Other directors of the time did, to be sure, hold similar views on the predominant role of the emotive in cinema – not least Eisenstein. But few privileged it to the extent that Gance did, casting out rationality in favour of what he calls the affective faculties. Thus spectating is not simply an act of communion, it also constructs each individual as completeness in tune with collective rhythms. Through the imaginative, the spectator becomes an aesthetic person. The irrational, whether it is designated as instinctive, intuitive or poetic, constructs a unity through its domination over minds that have been perverted by the bourgeois ethic of calculating self-interest.

We are invoked, then, to be unquestioning; uncritical spectators who recognise the authority of the spectacle as poetic truth. The film, says Gance in one of his 1920s texts, must exert an absolute hold over the public.[15] And in the 1970s he was still arguing along similar lines: 'For me, a spectator who maintains his critical sense is not a spectator. I wanted the audience to come out of the theatre amazed victims, completely won over, emerging from paradise to find, alas, the hell of the streets.'[16] (The same phrase, 'victimes émerveillées', attributed to Malraux, appears in the 'Preface to the readers' of *Cyrano et d'Artagnan* published in the *Cahiers du cinéma* in April-May 1968.) Subjectiveness thus gives way to the subjected, one could almost say to the unthinking, positioned to accept the truth of human experience communicated by the artist through the heart – Gance as author of the spectacle reincarnating the greatness of Bonaparte.

Through this experience the spectator is politicised, not directed explicitly towards this party or that, but led to a desire for a politics of the aesthetic as the foundation of change.

We cannot then simply classify Gance as Late Romantic inspired by a general desire to create a better world, any more than we can innocently celebrate him as visionary artist whose films generate excitement and unite the audience. Nor can we choose to overlook certain 'regrettable' tendencies in the portrayal of character on the grounds that content matters less than the power of formal innovation in the creation of cinematic experience. The aesthetic is never apolitical or ahistorical.

Even in his disclaimers ('not morality or politics, but art'), Gance frequently goes on to explain art's social function. More usually in his writings, as in his films, he is explicitly political in his attack on representatives of a specific class, a profit-oriented bourgeoisie held responsible for national unrest and international strife. If his films preach peace and concord to ordinary men and women, they do so through an insistence on the need for order, and a class unity that only a strong authority can bring about. Struggle is thus dismissed as arising purely and simply from individualism and self-interest.

The problem is that the spectator also lives within history, not just in an aesthetic space designated by the film. Emerging from the cinematic paradise into the hell of the streets, the spectator is confronted by specific struggles that he or she is invited to resolve by responding to some visionary and resolute authority.

The publication in the spring of 1968 of the preface to *Cyrano et d'Artagnan*, with its overtones of authoritarian lyricism, is probably a historical accident – the text was written several years before and the film had been released in 1963. The prologue added to the 1971 *Bonaparte et la Révolution* is, on the contrary, quite explicitly directed at post-1968 youth. *Napoleon* is updated for a new generation, showing Bonaparte as an opponent of the established order (*'contestataire'*), important as an example of revolt against corruption and incompetence, but mostly as an illustration of the need for a concerted effort. The two versions of *J'accuse* clearly address immediate issues; but so, on another level, do the two *Mater dolorosas*, in their positioning of the spectator with regard to social values. Even a modest commercial film like *Le roman d'un jeune homme pauvre*, adapted from Octave Feuillet's novel and released in 1935, has to be historicised in terms of the spectator. Gance says he made it in order to show that noble and generous sentiments still existed in France, but the location of these sentiments within the old order (an impoverished aristocracy) contrasts strikingly with the efforts of other film-makers to create a cinema supportive of the ideals of the emergent Popular Front.

The construction of Bonaparte as authoritarian hero was less suspect in 1923, when Mussolini was still admired by some sections of the Left, and in any case the complete project would have presented a more ambivalent view. By 1927, though, political positions had hardened considerably, and the apotheosis of Bonaparte, without the rest of the series as moderating force, had a quite other resonance. In 1935 the appeal to a militarist leader who would restore order, morality and enthusiasm was not far short of an endorsement of the anti-democratic, para-military Right. And we have also to take account of the film's effects in the 1980s, not just at the Rome Colosseum or in Paris, where 'extremists' came along to applaud patriotic and authoritarian values, but more generally the power of the film in its construction of a unified response, creating a shared belief in the need for heroic leadership and engendering an enthusiastic subservience.

It is not just a question of superior individuals incarnating specific values. The Napoleons and the Martials are exemplary in that they already possess the understanding which the melodramatic characters are searching for, but it is how we look at them historically that counts, as subordinated elements in a process. The process of spectacle constructs the spectator as a 'man of the people' marshalled into a pre-established order, respecting a natural authority. Like the extras recruited in 1926 for the Cordeliers sequence (who, according to Vuillermoz, would at Gance's command have stormed the National Assembly), we are called upon to believe implicitly in the represented as authentic truth and in the authority of the director. Order, communion, the unification of the individual realised through shared experience are not just *in* the image. They are constructed *by* it through the absorption of content and performance into spectacle.

The dominant aesthetic is source of desire for change, and its power constructs subjects desiring specific forms of change. It is from this, the construction through spectacle of uncritical subjects, interpellated as though the political as actuality does not exist, except in aesthetic unity, that the films derive their potency. That is what makes them reactionary in their effects.

8 Conclusion

Concluding remarks can be brief. Basically there are five points that need to be taken up in relation not just to Gance's films but to film theory in general.

The first is the central issue of reactionary innovation. As the analysis of spectacle shows, it is no more possible to separate out progressive form from reactionary content in cinema than it is in any other domain. Nor can innovation be held to be progressive just because it challenges established *forms* of representation. It is part of a *system* of representations and especially of a positioning process. The radically new may indeed be more reactionary than the traditional. That does not necessarily make it any less dynamic or 'impressive'. It simply means that innovation has to be politicised through a consideration of its effects. To valorise the innovatory *per se* is to fall into yet another idealist trap. If in cinema this has been less widely recognised than in other spheres, it is perhaps because of the importance of technology, the need to perfect the apparatus so often referred to by 1920s critics and theorists. But it also has something to do with the quest for recognition of cinema as an autonomous art form (the *new* art form of the twentieth century) and as an object worthy of serious study.

Linked to this is the way the term 'reactionary' is used in debates on cinema. Particularly in discussions about realism it often seems to designate simply a defence of the status quo, a representation of bourgeois hegemony as if it were the logical way of ordering the world. What this elides is any notion that the reactionary might be as emphatically opposed as the 'revolutionary' to the existing state of affairs. Gance, in his insistent attacks on the alienating effects of bourgeois conformism, reminds us that the reactionary is also oppositional, demanding change, seeking to overthrow a corrupt liberal democracy. What distinguishes it is nostalgia, the desire to restore values and virtues that the bourgeoisie, in furtherance of its own aims, has undertaken to destroy. The reactionary is not, as is sometimes claimed, 'irrational'; it is an attack on bourgeois rationality. In some instances this may indeed lead to a profoundly cynical conception of

216

the political, as in Fascism. But what matters in the more prevalent romantic or élitist populism is the privileging of the intuitive as re-establishment of a mythical unity of heart and mind, a natural harmony in which the élite naturally knows best.

The third point is the relation between politics and pleasure. Demonstrating that a film like *Napoleon* is reactionary is not tantamount to denouncing it or placing it on some kind of Index. On the contrary, it is an attempt to come to terms with its impact, to recognise the film's power and all that that entails. In other words, it is of the seductiveness of *Napoleon* that we have to take account: not to deny the pleasure but to politicise it through a recognition of the particular kind of subjection which it imposes. The problem has been highlighted by responses to the reconstructed *Napoleon* and the collective euphoria it has generated; but, once again, who or what is being applauded? *Napoleon*'s pleasure is not there to be accepted or rejected, it is offered as shared experience. What counts is to recognise the position we occupy when we do share in it, applauding ourselves along with artist and hero as integral parts of that experience. It is not enough to enjoy and be vaguely worried about the enjoyment, as though we should not be there. As much in the innovatory spectacular as in the most orthodox Hollywood dream-machine, we have to realise where we are being placed. Authoritarian populism derives its potency from its calling upon the audience to be present. The message can be adapted to suit particular moments, as in the remakes of *Napoleon*, but the address is the same: you, the audience, are the force of history. The film is here to tune you in to intuitive responses, to point you in the right direction, to make you accept the intuitive interpellation that has to be recognised as a political form of pleasure.

The fourth issue concerns the way the history of cinema has been constructed. There is still a tendency to operate on the basis of a series of polarities, like the Bazinian opposition montage/composition in depth, as if they were discrete practices. Although they may invite new distinctions, Gance's films tend rather to elide them. Impressionist cinematography, rapid montage and 'realist' depth of field are all present, ready and waiting for us to take up the positions they offer. All that counts is the explicit manipulation of the spectator. That is the declared object of all the strategies. Deep space and the surface of linear or lateral montage may come into conflict as techniques, but their object is the same. Their concern is not with the real but with the truth, a truth imposed through interpellation. Gance's cinema has little to do with the illusion that the spectator might possibly be in control. Even in those sequences where the look is drawn into the depth of the frame, that look is directed, controlled, positioned. The image is never transparency, just authority. It is, in that sense, anti-realist in its emphasis on the involvement of the spectator in an *actual* experience of the real. As such these strategies impose a reinterpretation of that illusory space within the screen which is called realism.

The last issue is the polarity art cinema/popular culture, so enshrined in film criticism and which Gance's populism explodes. As well as imposing a redefinition of the relationship between the mainstream and the avant-garde, his films complicate a political debate that has too often used Griffith and Eisenstein as original reference points. That is Gance's centrality: neither a conservative liberal nor a materialist, but an anti-bourgeois populist whose belief in the power of the cinema is radical, dynamic, mystical and inscribed in a broader history than that of cinema. Carlyle might have envied Gance his powers of persuasion. Céline did.

Notes

1 Introduction: Politics and Criticism

1. 'Abel Gance. Il n'aimait tenter que l'impossible', *Télérama*, 18 November 1981, p. 33.
2. For a more explicit attack, see Richard Philpott, 'Whose Napoleon?', *Framework*, 20, 1983, pp. 8–12.
3. *Le Havre libre*, 15 November 1982.
4. Guy Dumur, 'Eviva Bonaparte', *Le nouvel observateur*, 19–25 September 1981, p. 103.
5. Alain Rémond, 'Au rendez-vous des chefs', *Télérama*, 18 November 1981, p. 103.
6. *New Yorker*, 16 February 1981.
7. This is not of course to deny the importance of work that has been done, for example Alain Weber's 'Idéologies du montage' (*CinémAction*, 23, 1983).
8. Louis Nalpas to Gance, 19 February 1923 (CF/AG 33).
9. Notably Truffaut and Rivette's interview with Gance, *Cahiers du cinéma*, 43, 1955, pp. 6–17. Articles by Gance had already appeared in issues 27 (1953) and 41 (1954). Another, on Epstein, was published in no. 50 (1955). Gance notes (CNC) that his *Cahiers* supporters were Domarchi, Rivette, Malle, Truffaut, Marcorelles, Astruc and Rohmer.
10. Roger Boussinot, *L'encyclopédie du cinéma*, Paris, Bordas, 1967, I, pp. 624–5.
11. *Abel Gance*, Paris, Seghers, 1963, p. 78.
12. *Abel Gance*, Lausanne, L'âge d'homme (still unpublished at time of writing).
13. 'Abel Gance ou le défi épique', *Lumière du cinéma*, 5, 1977, pp. 48–55. 'A la découverte de *La roue*', *Cahiers de la cinémathèque*, 33–4, 1981, pp. 185–92. 'La représentation de Napoléon Bonaparte dans l'oeuvre d'Abel Gance', *Cahiers de la cinémathèque*, 35–6, 1983.
14. 'The superimposition of vision: *Napoleon* and the meaning of fascist art', *Cineaste*, XI, 2, 1981, pp. 4–13.
15. *Cineaste*, XI, 3, 1981, pp. 48–9.

2 Gance and his Critics

1. Arroy also published two interviews with Gance (1925 and 1929) and two articles on his work (1923 and 1927). He compiled the elaborate press book for *Napoleon* and edited *La roue* as a *ciné-roman* in 1930.
2. A verse tragedy, completed in 1913 but never performed. It was one of the works Gance was planning to publish in 1929.
3. The third screenplay in the *Napoleon* series, *Arcole* was written in 1924 but not filmed. *Sainte-Hélène*, the final screenplay in the series, was written in 1927–8.

4. Lupu Pick's film (1929) is an adaptation of Gance's screenplay by Pick and Willy Haas. Gance had originally wanted Pick to play the part of the Emperor in the film.

5. Never published, though Gance returned to the idea of a book on the cinema in the 1960s and 70s.

6. Published, by Gallimard, in 1930, in one volume.

7. Best known as an art historian, Elie Faure (1873–1937) also wrote extensively on literature, politics and cinema. As a populist intellectual and aesthete, he had a considerable impact on the young generation of the 1920s, particularly André Malraux and Gance, who quoted him frequently in his writings on cinema and adopted Faure's conception of Napoleon in his 1927 film. It was Elie Faure who had recommended Buraud to Gance in 1927. His preface was written in April 1929 (correspondence with Faure, CNC).

8. This screenplay does not seem to have been completed, although there are reminiscences of it in *La fin du monde*. Gance returned to the basic idea in the 1940s with *La divine tragédie*.

9. I have reproduced only the opening section of Arroy's text.

10. See below, note 12.

11. Cf. Vuillermoz's account later in this chapter.

12. Byron's dramatic poem (1817). *Vittoria nostra, non sarai mutilata* is a pamphlet by D'Annunzio published in October 1919 promoting Italian claims on Istria and Dalmatia. Cf. Arroy's reference a few lines above to D'Annunzio's occupation of Fiume.

13. *Ecce homo* and *Le royaume de la terre* were two of the titles of a trilogy Gance had planned to make in 1918.

14. *Théâtre et Comoedia illustré*, March 1923, reprinted in *Réflexion faite*, Paris, Gallimard, 1951, and *Cinéma d'hier, cinéma d'aujourd'hui*, Paris, Gallimard, 1970, pp. 87–9.

15. 'La roue, sa valeur plastique', *Comoedia*, 16 December 1922, p. 5. Translated in *Functions of painting*, edited by Edward W. Fry, New York, Viking Press, 1973, pp. 20–23 ('A critical essay on the plastic quality of Abel Gance's film The Wheel'). Léger wrote to Gance the day after the publication of this article urging him to make drastic cuts in the film so that the innovatory aspects would be privileged (CF/AG 33).

16. 'Pourquoi j'écris le roman de *La roue*', *Comoedia*, 29 December 1922, p. 5.

17. 'Conférence de Madame Germaine Dulac faite à la séance des Amis du cinéma [...]', *Cinémagazine*, 19 December 1924, pp. 516–18.

18. Paris, Editions de la lampe merveilleuse, 1922.

19. Quoted from Moussinac's manuscript (CF/AG 33). A revised text was published in *Le crapouillot*, 16 January 1923.

20. Cf. 'As a glorification of France on the screen, Abel Gance's *Napoleon* is the most wonderful hymn to France. It's the Marseillaise of the image.' *La semaine à Paris*, June 1927, quoted by Jean-Philippe Domecq, 'Napoléon vu par Abel Gance: une épopée', *Positif*, 256, 1982, p. 2.

21. *Revue des études napoléoniennes*, XVIII, 82, 1928, pp. 53–6.

22. 16 August 1924 (IDHEC).

23. For an account of the Opéra version, see Kevin Brownlow, *Napoleon, Abel Gance's classic film*, London, Cape, 1983, pp. 150–60.

24. After attending a private screening, Moussinac wrote to Gance on 25

March 1927 (IDHEC), suggesting cuts that could be made given that the film had to be reduced by 3,000m. In addition to the prologue, he proposes cutting Bonaparte in Paris, parts of the pursuit in Corsica but none of the Convention scenes. Toulon could be abridged, but then nothing until the reaction after the Terror. The love scenes and the Bal des Victimes sequences could be pruned, and the Violine scenes (even the mystical marriage he liked so much) plus the appearance of Bonaparte before the ghosts of the Convention could be cut.

25. Critics of Gance's films often compared them to the romantic verse dramas of Edmond Rostand, a highly successful turn-of-the-century playwright. Georges d'Esparbès was Keeper of the Palace of Fontainebleau and an enthusiastic writer about Napoleon. Gance had been invited by d'Esparbès to write his screenplays at Fontainebleau in 1924, and later hoped d'Esparbès would write a book based on his cycle of films.

26. Ingres is of course the nineteenth-century painter – and amateur violinist. The term 'violon d'Ingres' refers to a hobby or pastime.

27. The home of boulevard theatre in Paris.

28. *Le temps*, 8 January 1927.

29. Rostand and d'Estarbès are referred to above (note 25). Dumas is of course the prolific romantic novelist. Victorien Sardou was an author of popular nineteenth-century melodramas.

30. Frédéric Masson was the author of a long series of books on Napoleon and his family which were enormously popular in the early part of the century.

31. The preceding paragraphs are an appreciation of Gance's technical mastery, as is the article on the same visit he published in *Le temps*, 27 March 1926.

32. The Cordeliers sequence.

33. Francisco Aranda, *Luis Buñuel, a critical biography*, London, Secker & Warburg, 1975, p. 272.

34. *L'Europe nouvelle*, 678, 7 February 1931, pp. 179–80. Republished in Philippe Soupault, *Ecrits de cinéma*, texte présenté par Odette et Alain Virmaux, Paris, Plon, 1979, pp. 197–8. The original is translated here but, apart from a few minor details, the two texts are identical.

35. *Revue du cinéma*, 20, 1931, pp 64–5.

36. 'La fin du monde, violente et pathétique', *Pour vous*, 15 January 1931, pp. 8–9.

37. Notably in his appreciation of *Magirama* in *L'écran, revue mensuelle de cinéma*, 3, 1958, pp. 76–8.

38. Or rather the astronomer Camille Flammarion, whose widow Gabrielle gave Gance permission to adapt her husband's story. Gance in fact only used Flammarion's basic idea.

39. Soupault had reviewed King Vidor's *Hallelujah* and Sternberg's *Blue Angel* on 27 December 1930 and 10 January 1931.

3 Gance on theory

1. 'Qu'est-ce que le cinématographe? Un sixième art!', *Ciné-Journal*, 9

March 1912, reprinted in Marcel L'Herbier, *L'intelligence du cinématographe*, Paris, Corréa, 1946, pp. 91–2.

2. Radio interview with Jacques Chancel, 29 February 1971.

3. Gance returns frequently to this point, for example in an article published in *L'intransigeant*, 19 April 1936 ('Where I imagined a church, they have built a bazaar'), and in the preface to *Cyrano et d'Artagnan* in which he reproaches film directors for their blatant commercialism (*Cahiers du cinéma*, 200–01, 1968, p. 11).

4. *Scénario*, 1921, p. 749. Letter dated Arcachon, 19 March 1921. Cf. 'Images will have to take the place of words that have lost most of their depth and their specific meaning and which, it must be admitted, no longer have the same impact on popular imagination as they did in the age of Homer or even in medieval times.' ('La porte entr'ouverte', *Paris soir*, 17 March 1927.)

5. Jean Mitry, 'Abel Gance nous parle de *La roue*', *Cinéa-Ciné pour tous*, 15 December 1923, p. 8.

6. 'Comment on fait un film', *Conférencia*, 16, 1928, pp. 197–209.

7. Ibid., p. 200.

8. 'Le cinéma c'est la musique de la lumière', *Cinéa-Ciné pour tous*, 15 December 1923, p. 11.

9. *Le film*, 1918, reprinted in *L'intelligence du cinématographe*, pp. 199–212.

10. *Prisme*, p. 60. Cf. interview in *Cahiers du cinéma*, 43, 1955, p. 11.

11. Roger Lion, 'Un grand artiste français: Abel Gance', *Filma*, 15 May 1920, pp. 5–8.

12. See chapter 6.

13. *Prisme*, p. 166.

14. In order to differentiate between *cinégraphique* and *cinématographique*, I have used 'cinematic' for the former, keeping 'cinematographic' for the latter.

15. *L'art cinématographique II*, Paris, Alcan, 1927, pp. 83–102.

16. *Cinémagazine*, 10–12, 1926, pp. 485–6, 524–6, 588–90 (also published in the Bulletin of the Institut général de psychologie).

17. I have omitted the introductory section and, later, a few remarks presenting film extracts that were screened during the lecture.

18. A play on the titles of two early Lumière films.

19. Ernest Schoedsack and Merian Cooper (1927). The film was frequently compared at the time to Flaherty's work.

20. Maurice Maeterlinck, *La vie de l'espace*, Paris, Fasquelle, 1928.

21. A file in the CNC archive and some letters in the CF collection show that Gance had experimented with this process while filming the last sequence of *Napoleon*. Cf. Kevin Brownlow, *Napoleon*, p. 135.

22. One of Gance's earliest projects was to make a film about Merlin.

23. Edouard Herriot (1872–1957) was a writer and member of the Académie française as well as a radical-socialist politician and cabinet minister. In addition to a series of books on literature and politics, he had also written on music, e.g. in *Esquisses*, Paris, Hachette, 1928.

24. Gance ends by thanking the organisers and presenting the single-screen version of the *Napoleon* finale.

25. For more details, see chapter 6 and the filmography.

4 Gance as author-director

1. Charles Ford, *On tourne lundi*, Paris, Jean Vigneau, 1947, pp. 149–54; René Jeanne and Charles Ford, *Abel Gance*, Paris, Seghers, 1963, pp. 113–17.
2. 'Comment on fait un film', *Conférencia*, 16, 1928, pp. 197–209.
3. 'A la découverte de *La roue*', *Cahiers de la cinémathèque*, 33–34, 1981, pp. 185–92.
4. The heading indicates that these are shot numbers 928 to 992 but no breakdown is given.
5. *Plan américain*: basically the equivalent of 'medium close shot', cutting off the actor(s) at or just above the knees.
6. It was in fact possible. Burel, the cinematographer, was very proud of these superimposed titles, all done in the camera.
7. Sisif was the crack engine-driver, Jacobin his unscrupulous rival.
8. In the prologue, Sisif discovers a little girl lying on the railway embankment after a train crash. His only clue to her identity is a half-burned letter (which he destroys) and a medallion inscribed 'Norma – London'. Bringing her up as his own daughter, he falls in love with her and when she marries Hersan, the villain of the piece, he transfers his affections to his engine, baptising it Norma Compound and hanging up the medallion in the cab. His son Elie is also in love with Norma.
9. Buveurdot (Machefer), the fireman, is a clownish character who drinks too much and always has his nose in a book.
10. What Gance published was basically the screenplay as revised in 1925, omitting unfilmed sequences but not taking account of later modifications and changes in order. For details of the different versions, see chapter 6, *Napoleon the exemplary*.
11. A contemporary breakdown of the 'Apollo' version of the film indicates that a sequence devoted to the *Tenth of August* and the *Fall of Louis XVI* measured 394m (about 17 minutes) but this may have included other scenes like Violine's arrest.
12. Kevin Brownlow (*Napoleon*, pp. 110–11) mentions the billing of the appeal on the studio walls and quotes the text from a copy in the CNC archive. It should be added that it was also published in the press at the time, and again in 1971 in *Matulu*. All these are in fact a modified and slightly shortened version of the original inserted in the 1924 screenplay and quoted by René Jeanne and Charles Ford, *Histoire encyclopédique du cinéma*, Paris, Laffont, 1947, I, p. 339.
13. Gance's heading is 'Prim[ordial] Tech[nique] gén[érale]'.
14. The typescript reads 'bannières', clearly a misreading of 'barrières' in the original manuscript.
15. It was at Fontainebleau in July 1924 that Gance completed his first screenplay – the prologue and *Vendémiaire* (1792–6). As we saw, he had been invited to stay at the palace by Georges d'Esparbès.
16. *Forty* leagues in the printed text.
17. I.e. the whole of this sequence. A scored-out note in the typescript shows that at one stage Gance planned to begin the sequence here and that he would indicate the date – 3 July 1792. With the modifications, all the numbering has been changed and on the handwritten pages there is no numbering at all.

18. Gance used Rude's sculpture on the Arc de Triomphe, usually called 'Le chant du départ', as the basis for the climax of the Marseillaise sequence.

19. Marginal references in the typescript: 'Hugo '93, p. 87, 88, 89. Madelin, Révolution française, p. 230'.

20. These technical indications do not figure in the typescript.

21. Added in pencil in the margin of the typescript.

22. Although it seems long, this whole sequence, with shots reducing from about $2\frac{1}{2}$ seconds to a tenth of a second, would last less than a minute.

23. Originally Gance planned to introduce here a shot of Bonaparte sitting alone at the back of the room. Instead he is with his young sister, a situation which highlights the parallels between the Bonapartes and the Fleuris.

24. 'Danton sits down', scored out in the typescript.

25. Léon Cogniet (1794–1880): *La Garde nationale part pour l'armée* (Musée de Versailles).

26. I.e. renderings of the 'Marseillaise'.

27. Already in love with Bonaparte, Violine had been mortified when, in an earlier suppressed sequence, she had seen him walking along with Elisa on his arm and had assumed that she must be his fiancée.

28. This remark was initially placed at the end of the 10 August sequence.

29. The first two pages of the version published in *Le rouge et le noir* are a half-size and barely legible facsimile of a handwritten text. They are also in the wrong order (p. 8 should precede p. 7). I have checked the text against the first draft (CF) and a typescript copy with manuscript additions (CNC).

30. Shot indications are abbreviated in the facsimile and the printed text but not in the typescript and only occasionally in the manuscript. For the sake of consistency, I give expanded versions.

31. The title is preceded in the facsimile by the heading 'The Tenth of August 1792' with a partly scored out note indicating that this should come before the 'last sunrise' scene. In the first draft there is no clear divide between the two scenes. Instead there is a sequence of rapid shots of bell-ringers waiting for the appointed hour (they have been instructed by Danton to sound the Tocsin in all the churches of Paris at six in the morning). In the typescript Gance has added in manuscript the title 'The greatest day of the Revolution: 10 August 1792. Fall of the Monarchy'. A note in the margin reads: 'Of all the *Days* of the Revolution, the 10th August was the one which had the most serious consequences. Robespierre thought it more important than the 14th July 1789. Sagnac (*Chute de la monarchie*) p. 327.' There are also some marginal notes in the facsimile pages, mostly abbreviated references to technique and only partially legible in the reduced format.

32. The facsimile ends here. The shots so far are numbered 308 to 314 but in the printed text shot numbers are omitted. Since numbering in manuscript and typescript is inconsistent and incomplete, it has not been possible to reconstitute it.

33. The signal for the uprising (see above, note 31).

34. In the CF manuscript and the CNC typescript this is followed by a note scored out in pencil: 'From this point on, the scenes will progress with an increasing dynamic which must push to the limit what it is possible to achieve in this respect. For the first time, none of the shots from no. to no. [no figures are given] must be filmed with a fixed camera. They must all be mobile

[abbreviated technical details follow]. Only the shots of Bonaparte will be still, with a fixed camera to cathedralise his psychology in this upheaval.'

35. The first draft specifies which churches – Notre Dame, Saint Germain l'Auxerrois, Saint Sulpice etc. – and that shots of these should be intercut with those of the bells, the crowd and a river in flood. He also specifies which cameras are to be used and the length of the shots – reducing from 80cm.

36. These are indications of the cameras and techniques to be used. Although similar abbreviations are used at other points in the manuscripts I have not been able to decipher them completely and have therefore left the initial letters of the French original (d.p.v. probably means 'dispositif de prises de vue' and m.t.r. 'mouvement très rapide'). The 'Sept' camera referred to a few lines above was a portable clockwork camera manufactured by Debrie. It was extensively used in *Napoleon* for the filming of rapid action sequences.

37. The *Rouge et le noir* text reads 'boudoir', already corrected in one of the handwritten revisions to 'bureau'.

38. The first line of a popular anti-monarchist song. Madame Veto is Marie-Antoinette.

39. Couthon's legs were paralysed.

40. Gance subsequently incorporated a short extract from this preface into two articles: 'Maladie et guérison du cinéma', *Pour vous*, 31 July 1930, and 'Images et écrits à propos de *La fin du monde*', *L'horizon* (Brussels), 17 January 1931.

41. Gance uses the same metaphor in a 1929 letter to Elie Faure. Patrick Vieuville suggests that it is a confusion between the Balm of Gilead (an aphrodisiac) and the biblical town of Galaad. ('Quand Abel Gance écrivait à Elie Faure', *Cahiers Elie Faure*, I, 1981, p. 84.)

42. This is followed by a deleted paragraph: 'There will be two directors in our enterprise: Mr Ivanoff for all that concerns the financial and commercial administration of our great work. I ask you to obey Mr Ivanoff blindly and absolutely. And myself for all that concerns the artistic production.'

43. Gance's title is 'Note primordiale'.

44. A marginal note reads: 'To grasp the spirit, the setting, the mood and the psychology of the Passion scenes in *La fin du monde*, I think it is useful to read at this point the following notes by Marie Noël on the Auxerre Passion play, taken from *Cahiers catholiques* no. 178.' Marie Noël's notes are inserted between the preface and the beginning of the screenplay.

45. De Murcie is, like Martial Novalic, an astronomer but an older and less prominent one, jealous of Novalic's prestige. His name indicates that he is a member of the aristocracy, but his first name Abraham suggests that he is also, like his villainous friend and ally Schomburg, a Jew.

46. Gance initially wanted Falconetti to play this part.

47. The words in brackets are scored out in the typescript. I include such deletions only when they seem necessary for the sense.

48. Carbon copy of typescript (CF). Noë Bloch, a Russian émigré, was head of Cinéfrance Films, a member of the production syndicate and Westi's agent in France. He and Edouard de Bersaucourt were executive producers of *Napoleon*.

49. See chapter 6, *Napoleon the exemplary*.

225

50. Where the Brienne sequences were filmed.

51. Difficulties with Westi, the principal backers of the film.

52. Gance eventually got his Cossacks and reshot some of the chase sequences.

53. Typescript original (CF/AG 37). Letterhead: Universum-Film-Aktiengesellschaft. Rudolf Becker, another Russian émigré, was Westi's executive director. After the company's collapse in the summer of 1925 he moved over to Ufa as commercial director.

54. Erich Pommer, Ufa's managing director. Gance had met Becker and Pommer in Paris in July 1925 and hoped for a while that Ufa might take over Westi's stake in the film. Negotiations continued until the autumn, with Ufa agreeing only to acquire the German distribution rights. All this correspondence is in CF/AG 37.

55. Typescript original (CNC). Hector de Béarn was the principal shareholder in the Société générale de films which took over the production of *Napoleon* after Westi's withdrawal. He acquired the rights to the film when the company went bankrupt and financed the 1935 sound version.

56. Dreyer's film had also been produced by the SGF.

57. Cf. Albert Banzhaf's letter to Gance, New York, 24 July 1924 (CF): 'Do not think it presumptuous on my part if I again presume to advise you to keep in mind the American market when you are producing in Germany and Austria, which means that you must not make your pictures too serious and convey them in as light a vain (*sic*) as possible, since the American theatregoing public, and I believe it will be universal in time, prefer to take their entertainment humorously rather than seriously.'

58. The problem was not a new one. Gance quotes Louis Nalpas, the director of Le film d'art, as saying to him in 1915: 'Go and make me an adventure film of 1,000m. Start the day after tomorrow and don't spend more than 6,000 francs. Above all, no psychology. A powerful drama with a good story and a happy ending.' (Interview with Roger Lion, *Filma*, 15 May 1920, p. 5.)

59. IDHEC collection and typescript copy, CNC. There are a number of letters on the reception of *Napoleon*. One from Léon Brézillac, Managing Director of the 'Family-Palaces' cinema chain, states: 'In all our establishments, *Napoleon* has justifiably been a great success.' The most interesting of them are unsolicited letters from individual spectators writing about the enthusiastic response to the 1928 release in rural cinemas.

60. See chapter 6. Gance took the distributors to court over this truncated version screened in March-April 1928. As a result Gaumont-Metro-Goldwyn agreed to restore a complete version, the one to which Bernard refers, released in the autumn of 1928.

5   Narrative and History

1. *Prisme*, p. 172.

2. See the note dated 9 September 1917 quoted by Roger Icart, chapter 4.

3. *Prisme*, p. 164.

4. In the letter dated 19 March 1921 published in *Scénario*, 1921, p. 749.

5. Soundtrack of *Bonaparte et la Révolution* (1971).

6. Paris is, in effect, the centre of the regenerated world.

7. CNC. Epic, Gance writes in the same note, is 'the sublime association of truth and poetry'.

8. *Abel Gance*, chapter 1.

9. *Cinémonde*, 3 November 1932 and unidentified article in the IDHEC collection.

10. *Prisme*, pp. 175–6.

11. On the contrary, he describes his film in a letter to Charles Pathé, Nice, 28 June 1920 (CF/AG 1) as 'a kind of modern *Oedipus Rex*, less morally elevated but just as powerful in its pathos'.

12. Notably *Cyrano et d'Artagnan* (1963).

13. There is an important dossier on this film in the CF archive (AG 33). Originally called *Au creux des sillons*, then *Terre maternelle*, it was directed by Robert Boudrioz at Nice in 1920–21 while Gance was making *La roue*. Produced by Les Films Abel Gance, it seems to have been financed, like *La roue*, by Charles Pathé. Other letters make it clear that Gance also supervised the filming.

14. 'La confession d'Abel Gance', *La revue hebdomadaire*, 25, 1923, reprinted in André Lang, *Déplacements et villégiatures littéraires*, Paris, La Renaissance du livre, 1924, pp. 137–46. The quotation is on p. 141.

15. *Prisme*, p. 176.

16. In films like *La fin du monde* and *La Vénus aveugle*, the heroes and heroines have no mothers. Jean's mother in the silent *J'accuse* is a loving but sickly presence, eventually effaced and absent in the remake. The heroines suffer in their motherhood, like Eve in *Mater dolorosa*, or are criminal mothers like Edith in the *J'accuse* remake.

17. *La fin du monde*, scénario arrangé par Joachim Renez, Paris, Tallandier, 1931.

18. In spite of what is often said, Gance does seem to have completed the filming himself, though he did rely on collaborators like Ruttmann and Epstein for some of the scenes. There are a number of letters in the CF files indicating that he was still working on the film in the early summer of 1930. When Gance ceded all his rights to Ivanoff except as artistic and literary director, he was still supposed to edit the film himself (Ivanoff to Gance, 30 May 1930 – CF).

19. CNC. It is worth noting that in a much earlier outline, probably written in 1918, there is only one Novalic, an idealistic scientist dedicated to the cause of humanity.

6 Politics and the Aesthetic

1. Abel Gance to Albert t'Serstevens, 30 June 1915.

2. *Prisme*, pp. 97–101. In an unpublished note dated Nice, 23 March 1920 – during the filming of *La roue* – Gance writes: 'There are in me both Nietzsche and Lenin. And that's not easy to reconcile. Yet these are the two psychological poles on which the axis of my personality turns.' (CF/AG 51)

3. *Journal d'un homme de quarante ans*, Paris, Grasset, 1934, p. 219.

4. Letter to Maurice Reclus, 27 June 1921. *Oeuvres complètes*, edited by Yves Lévy, Paris, Pauvert, 1964, III, pp. 1028–9.

5. *Méditations catastrophiques*, Paris, Flory, 1937, p. 10.

6. *La Mort de la pensée bourgeoise*, Paris, Grasset, 1929, pp. 143–8.

7. Notably in *L'homme qui vient. Philosophie de l'autorité*, Paris, Nouvelle librairie nationale, 1906, and reprinted many times through to the 1920s.

8. Letter to Jean-Richard Bloch, 7 December 1932. *Oeuvres complètes*, III, pp. 1104–5.

9. François Vinneuil, writing in *L'action française*, 30 January 1931.

10. Gance had approached Coty on 3 February 1924, presenting the project as 'a propaganda film, not political but French in the finest sense of the word'. Coty's categorical refusal is dated 6 February 1924. (CF)

11. *Le Figaro*, 23 September 1925. Coty's attack led to a series of articles, mostly in Gance's defence.

12. On Sorel's impact, see Georges Guy-Grand, *La philosophie syndicaliste*, Paris, Grasset, 1911, and Michael Curtis, *Three against the Third Republic*, Princeton University Press, 1959.

13. The most thorough study of the *Jeune Droite* is Jean-Louis Loubet del Bayle's *Les non-conformistes des années trente*, Paris, Le Seuil, 1969.

14. *Ni droite ni gauche. L'idéologie fasciste en France*, Paris, Le Seuil, 1983, pp. 291 and 311.

15. Gance had proposed a list of other projects including one or two that might be favoured by Mussolini (fragments of draft letter [CNC] and complete typescript copy [IDHEC]). But rather than alternatives to *Napoleon* these are possibly suggestions for a film that could be made while the epic was being prepared or in parallel with it.

16. Gance to Barattolo, 6 December 1923 (CNC). Gance's letters become quite agitated around this time because he has still not received any definite reply from Barattolo, and he writes again on 8 January 1924 requesting the return of the outline and all the documentation. The reply was eventually sent on 24 January 1924 (CNC) – the UCI did not wish to participate. This production company, financed by a syndicate of Italian banks and strongly supportive of fascism, was in fact in the process of going into liquidation.

17. Draft contract, May 1924 (CNC). For details, see Kevin Brownlow, *Napoleon*, pp. 44–5.

18. In spite of Gance's violent protests. There are many traces of these in his papers and echoes in the letter to Noë Bloch reproduced in chapter 4.

19. Correspondence in the CNC archive.

20. For details, see Kevin Brownlow, *Napoleon*, pp. 96–101.

21. Dated at the end of the manuscript and in the published version 3 December 1925.

22. The screenplay of *Vendémiaire*, dated October-November 1924 (CF), ends with Bonaparte's visit to the Convention chamber before his departure for Italy. Its climax is thus his promise, having restored order, to uphold the principles of the Revolution and the expression of his desire for a Universal Republic.

23. In the CF collection.

24. Gance's typescript is in the CNC archive.

25. Typescript outline, dated 15 September 1923, published with an intro-

duction by Norman King in *Cinématographe*, 83, 1982, pp. 4–7.

26. Typescript screenplay (CNC).

27. Notably in 'La porte entr'ouverte', *Paris-soir*, 17 March 1927.

28. See chapter 4.

29. The prologue was shown separately at the Madeleine and Gaumont-Palace cinemas.

30. Gaumont-Metro-Goldwyn to SGF, 9 July (CF/AG 56). Kevin Brownlow states that the Opéra version was 5,600m (255 minutes at 20fps, not 220 minutes as he suggests) but he does not take account of subsequent reductions. Roger Icart says it was 5,200m (i.e. 228 minutes). A contemporary review gives the running time as about 210 minutes – about 4,800m.

31. I.e. between 10,800 and 12,000m. Abel Gance to SGF administration (CF/AG 56).

32. 12,878m according to Kevin Brownlow using a much later note of Gance. This is probably a total metrage of the complete version, including the additional reels needed in the triptych sequences, although these were not used at the Apollo screenings.

33. Kevin Brownlow (*Napoleon*, p. 286) gives basic information about these versions. Other details are taken from cinema programmes and from correspondence in the CF collection. Gance claims (AG 56) that there were three 'Marivaux' versions of 3,700 to 4,000m but does not explain the differences between them. He repeats that the long version was 11,000m.

34. Gance orchestrated a campaign against this version and eventually took the distributor to court. It was as a result of this that G-M-G agreed to restore a complete version.

35. A version not noted by Kevin Brownlow. It was certainly publicised in the press as the complete version but no indications are given about its length.

36. Reduced in extreme cases to two 16mm spools, less fragmentary but no more comprehensible than the American release print of similar length.

37. Some of this material on the Fleuris is a reworking of my article 'Une épopée populiste', *Cinématographe*, 83, 1982, pp. 8–10. In my presentation of the 1923 outline in the same issue, I refer to a 1915 project entitled 'Le petit grognard' as a first working through of the subject in populist terms. I have since discovered the screenplay, misplaced by Gance in a file of screenplays by other writers (CF). Although less Napoleonic than I suggested (the setting is the Great War), it is in fact much closer than I had thought to a 'Fleuri' viewpoint. A child, like Marcellin a Napoleon enthusiast, follows his father to the Front and by casting shadows of tin soldiers representing the Emperor and his aides against the walls of a tent scares away the enemy and saves his father's life.

38. This summary is based on the most complete 'version' of the screenplay – a confrontation of manuscripts, published texts and contemporary accounts of the Apollo screenings.

39. Although he had pruned some of the Fleuri scenes in the shorter release prints, he wrote in a manuscript note to himself in September 1928 (CNC): 'The error of my *Napoleon* was the abusive utilisation of documentation. I lost popular appeal in my desire to be accurate and in the search for the authentic

detail. The power of *La roue* and *J'accuse* resides in the absence of the authenticated.'

40. Four if one counts the monarchy but, especially in the early versions of the screenplay, Louis XVI is rapidly dismissed as an irrelevance.

41. September 1923 outline.

42. *Bonaparte et la Révolution*, prologue.

43. And in the sonorised version for single screen.

44. Both letters dated 29 March 1928. Typescript copies, CF/AG 4.

45. Gance to François Coty, Paris, 20 June 1928 (CF/AG 4).

46. The rewrite completed in December 1925, less the scenes that had been cut later but not taking account of subsequent additions and modifications.

47. Gance's correspondence with Jean Arroy and with Robert Aron of the NRF provides details about the negotiations (CF/AG 4–7).

48. The reports are preserved in the CNC archive.

49. He announces that he has begun work on the project in a letter to Buraud, 15 January 1929 (CF/AG 6).

50. The draft statutes are in the CNC archive. A facsimile was published by Jacques Deslandes in *Revue internationale d'histoire du cinéma*, 2, 1975.

51. CF/AG 37.

52. *Pour vous*, 11 August 1932.

53. There are examples in CF/AG 37.

54. Indicated in an unidentified article on Gance written after the release of *La fin du monde*.

55. Principally sequences from *Napoleon* and *Cristallisation* shown at the Studio 28 in 1928.

56. CNC and CF/AG 9.

57. They apparently became the property of Hector de Béarn and were ceded to Gance for the sonorised remake but never returned (Kevin Brownlow, *Napoleon*, p. 176).

58. CNC.

59. Quotations are from the soundtrack of the film.

60. Quoted by Roger Icart, chapter 9.

61. Gance returned to the idea in February 1948, by which time Paul-Boncour had become President of the Republic (CF/AG 34).

62. He had also played Jean Diaz in the remake of *J'accuse*.

63. There is a copy of the letter in the CNC archive. For Renault-Decker's view of the project, see Rémy [Gilbert Renault-Decker], *Dans l'ombre du Maréchal*, Paris, Presses de la cité, 1971, pp. 15–30.

64. 'Je tournerai *Christophe Colomb* parce que le cinéma est une machine à ressusciter les héros', *Cinémonde*, 5 April 1939. A publicity leaflet (Rondel Collection, Bibliothèque de l'Arsenal) confirms this date and gives a list of collaborators, including Stève Passeur as scriptwriter and Henri Mahé as set designer.

65. Ibid.

66. Renault-Decker (*Dans l'ombre du Maréchal*, p. 30) mentions that in late 1939 he was to make the film in English for Kay Harrison but does not indicate how Gance came to be excluded. A letter in the CNC archive suggests that Renault-Decker suspected Gance had denounced him to Pétain.

67. The complete screenplay is in the CNC collection.

68. Châteauneuf, 12 December 1939 (CF/AG 14).

69. 'Abel Gance revient d'Espagne [...]', *Cinémonde*, 24 April 1940.

70. Together with *La fille du Rhin*, another propaganda project.

71. Filming began on 11 November 1940 (Jacques Siclier, *La France de Pétain et son cinéma*, Paris, Veyrier, 1981, p. 260). The date is also indicated by Roger Régent.

72. *Cinéma de France de 'La fille du puisatier' aux 'Enfants du paradis'*, Paris, 1948 (reprinted as *Cinéma de France sous l'Occupation* by Editions d'aujourd'hui, 1976), pp. 208–9.

73. Undated typescript (IDHEC 4).

74. Guy Haumet, 'Un grand bâtisseur: Abel Gance', *Filmagazine*, 1 October 1941, p. 11.

75. Admiral François Darlan (1881–1942) was Pétain's deputy.

76. CNC. The project was also announced in *Comoedia*, 27 September 1941.

77. Letters to M. Truelle, Madrid, 12 August 1944 and 18 March 1945 (handwritten drafts, CNC).

78. The committee also included Monsignor Sheen and Lady Ravensdale (CF/AG 48).

79. *Napoléon*, Paris, Crès, 1921, pp. 69 and 140.

80. Quoted by Jean-Claude Lovey, *Situation de Blaise Cendrars*, Neuchâtel, La Baconnière, 1965, p. 22.

81. *Fonction du cinéma*, Paris, Denoël-Gonthier, 1965, pp. 11–12.

82. *Mystique du cinéma*, *Oeuvres complètes*, III, p. 618 and *Fonction du cinéma*, pp. 51–2.

83. These points are taken up in chapter 7.

7 Image, Spectacle, Position

1. Notably in a short text published in *Le cinéopse*, 1 March 1926, and 'Qu'est-ce que le cinéma pur?', *Cinéa-Ciné pour tous*, 1 March 1927, pp. 9–10.

2. CNC. Quoted by Roger Icart, chapter 2.

3. Louis Feuillade (1874–1925) was one of the great pioneers in France of realist *mise en scène* and composition in depth. Gance had, at the beginning of his cinema career, written at least one screenplay for Feuillade and was clearly influenced by him in his plans to make popular serials.

4. Gance had already stressed the importance of off-screen space in a text published in *Le cinéopse*, December 1923, p. 46.

5. Kevin Brownlow, *Napoleon*, p. 143.

6. *On tourne lundi*, p. 126. Cf. 'Suppress as many close-ups as possible. Only leave them when they are really essential.' (undated early note, CNC).

7. It is only for want of a more adequate term that I use the word discursive here. Although Genette's appropriation of the story/discourse opposition was historically important for the analysis of narrative strategies, it has tended to disguise the fact that stories are themselves always discursive. 'Marks of enunciation' might sometimes be more appropriate, especially when the story is presented as if it existed independently of any mediating process. But what I specifically have in mind here and in what follows are explicit commentaries on the action or direct addresses to the spectator – what in

Genette's terminology would be called 'discours sur l'histoire'.

8.   Names have a similar function in *Napoleon*. When Bonaparte so frequently asks whom he is addressing, the response guides us through the narrative simply by telling us who all these people are, but they are also moments of recognition for the spectator, confirming the film's authenticity via the presence of characters whose names are already familiar. This practice recurs in *Cyrano et d'Artagnan* with the naming in a fictional story of Molière, Scarron, etc., and in *Austerlitz*.

9.   The frequently reproduced photograph showing Bonaparte and the Fleuris standing in a line, all joining in the singing of the 'Marseillaise', is a production still. In the film, Bonaparte remains an onlooker.

10.   What I mean here by spectacle is explained in the course of this section. Spectacle is explored in psychoanalytic terms in Steve Neale's important detailed study, '*Triumph of the Will*, notes on documentary and spectacle', *Screen*, 20, 1, 1979, pp. 63–86.

11.   This effect must have been even more marked in the triple-screen montage of this sequence that Gance initially planned to include in the Opéra version but decided to show separately as part of the polyvision programme at the Studio 28.

12.   *Qu'est-ce que le cinema?*, édition définitive, Paris, Le Cerf, 1975, pp. 64–5.

13.   The single-screen version in fact ends with the camera closing in on to Gance's autograph signature. Many of the later films are also 'signed' in this way.

14.   *L'écran*, 3, 1958, p. 65. This is in fact a text intended as a preface to the planned publication of the *Napoleon* triptychs. Faure's original manuscript is in the CNC archive, together with an accompanying note dated 11 March 1928.

15.   'La porte entr'ouverte', *Paris-soir*, 17 March 1927.

16.   Interview (1973), published in Steven Kramer and James Welsh, *Abel Gance*, Boston, Twayne, 1978, pp. 161–70.

Filmography

Abel Gance (Paris, 25 October 1889 – Paris, 10 November 1981)

After leaving the Collège Chaptal in 1904, Gance worked for a time as a lawyer's clerk but was more interested in literature and theatre than in a legal career. He was soon writing poems and plays, and after working for several years on an unfinished verse epic, *La dame du lac,* he completed his most important play, *La Victoire de Samothrace,* in 1913. He had begun acting in 1908 and continued until early 1914 to play a variety of roles in provincial repertory companies. His first experience of the cinema was also as an actor, notably in Léonce Perret's *Molière* (1909) and two Max Linder films (1910). By 1910 he was writing scenarios for Gaumont and Pathé, and in 1911 he and a group of friends founded a production company called Le film français so that he could direct his own screenplays. This collapsed after he had made four films and he was subsequently engaged as a director by Louis Nalpas (Le film d'art) and Charles Pathé. After the war Gance made various efforts to obtain a greater degree of financial independence and once again set up his own production company, Les films Abel Gance, which continued in existence until 1933. Most of his films, however, were funded by international syndicates or by small independent producers who rarely gave him the autonomy he desired. He returned briefly to the theatre in 1958 to direct Bertha Dominguez's *Cathédrale de cendres,* and worked occasionally for French television in the mid-1960s. But in his later years funding was a major difficulty and he made only three feature films for the cinema between 1943 and 1981.

Although this filmography concentrates on Gance's career as a director, it includes brief details of films he just scripted or produced. Information about the early screenplays and short films is often sparse and there are still uncertainties about precise dates and running-times. For the feature films, credits given in distribution prints and publicity material have where possible been used as a starting point. I have drawn extensively for further information on materials in the Gance archives, on Jean Mitry's *Filmographie universelle* (especially vol. 2 and the Gance section in vol. 25 – Paris, CNC, 1982, pp. 5–17) and on Raymond Chirat's *Catalogue des films de long métrage* (*Films sonores de fiction, 1929–1939,* new ed., Brussels, 1981 and *Films de fiction, 1940–1950,* Luxemburg, 1981). I have also referred to the filmographies by Jeanne and Ford (1963), Kramer and Welsh (1978) and Philippe d'Esnault (*Cahiers du cinéma,* 43, 1955, pp. 18–23), and I have incorporated additional details from Roger Icart's recent book on Gance.

Abbreviations

P.	Producer
D.	Director
Assoc. d.	Associate Director
Asst. d.	Assistant Director
Sup.	Supervision
Sc.	Screenplay

Dial.   Dialogues
Ph.   Cinematography
Sd.   Sound
Dec.   Decors
Cost.   Costumes
Ed.   Editor
M.   Music
Lyr.   Lyrics
Tech. Adv.   Technical Adviser
D. of P.   Director of Production
Lp.   Leading players

Lengths are given in metres and as far as possible are those of the original prints.

Le portrait de Mireille (1910)
P: Gaumont. D: Léonce Perret. Sc: Abel Gance.
Lp: Fabienne Fabrèges, Marc Mario.

La fille de Jephté (1910)
P: Gaumont. D: Léonce Perret. Sc: Abel Gance.
Lp: Renée Carl, Jeanne-Marie Laurent.

La fin de Paganini (1910)
P: Gaumont. D: Louis Feuillade. Sc: Abel Gance.
Lp: Renée Carl, Gaston Severin.

Le crime du grand-père (1910)
P: Gaumont. D: Léonce Perret, Jacques Roullet. Sc: Abel Gance.
Lp: Séverin-Mars, Suzanne Privat, Simone Vaudry, Suzanne Arduini.

La mort du duc d'Enghien (1910)
P: SCAGL (Pathé). D: Albert Capellani. Sc: Abel Gance.
Lp: Paul Capellani, René Leprince, Nelly Cormon, Henri Etiévant, Daniel Mendaille.

Un clair de lune sous Richelieu (1910)
P: SCAGL (Pathé). D: Albert Capellani. Sc: Abel Gance.
Lp: Jacques Grétillat, Paul Capellani, Claude Garry, Gabriel de Gravone, Jeanne Delvair.

Cyrano et d'Assoucy (1911)
P: SCAGL (Pathé). D: Albert Capellani. Sc: Abel Gance.
Lp: Henry Krauss, Paul Capellani, Jacques Grétillat.

234

Un tragique amour de Mona Lisa (La Joconde) (1911)
P: SCAGL (Pathé). D: Albert Capellani. Sc: Abel Gance.
Jacques Grétillat (*Leonardo da Vinci*), Aimée Raynal (*Mona Lisa*), Claude
Garry (*François I*), Mlle Barat (*La belle ferronnière*).

L'électrocuté (1911)
P: SCAGL (Pathé). D: Camille Morlhon. Sc: Abel Gance.

L'auberge rouge (1911)
P: SCAGL (Pathé). D: Camille Morlhon. Sc: Abel Gance.

La digue (Pour sauver la Hollande) (1912)
P: Le film français. D: Abel Gance. Sc: Abel Gance.
Lp: Pierre Renoir, Robert Lévy, Paulette Noizeux.

Il y a des pieds au plafond (1912)
P: Le film français. D: Abel Gance. Sc: Abel Gance.
Lp: Jean Toulout, Mathilde Thizeau.
(According to Gance, this film was not released.)

Le nègre blanc (1912)
P: Le film français. D: Abel Gance. Sc: Abel Gance.
Lp: Jean Toulout, Abel Gance, Mathilde Thizeau.

Le masque d'horreur (1912)
P: Le film français. D: Abel Gance. Sc: Abel Gance.
Lp: Edouard de Max, Mathilde Thizeau, Jean Toulout, Charles de
Rochefort, Mlle Rousseau.
Released February 1912.
367m. (tinted and toned)
New version released 24 May 1912.

L'infirmière (1915)
P: Le film d'art (Louis Nalpas). D: Henri Pouctal. Sc: Abel Gance. Dec:
Emile Bertin.
Lp: Yvonne Briey (*Simone Hubert*), Jeanne Brindeau (*Mme Delbet*), Jacques
Volnys (*Raleigh*), Lurville (*Hubert*).

Un drame au château d'Acre (1915)
P: Le film d'art. D: Abel Gance. Sc: Abel Gance. Ph: Léonce-Henry Burel.
Lp: Yvonne Briey, Henri Maillard, Aurèle Sydney, Jacques Volnys.

La folie du docteur Tube (1915)
P: Le film d'art. D: Abel Gance. Sc: Abel Gance. Ph: Léonce-Henry Burel.
Lp: Albert Dieudonné.
About 600m.

La fleur des ruines (1915)
P: Le film d'art. D: Abel Gance. Sc: Abel Gance. Ph: Léonce-Henry Burel.
Lp: Louise Colliney, Georges Raulin, Aurèle Sydney.

L'énigme de dix heures (1915)
P: Le film d'art. D: Abel Gance. Sc: Abel Gance. Ph: Léonce-Henry Burel.
Lp: Doriani, Emile Keppens, Henri Maillard, Paulette Noizeux, Aurèle Sydney.

L'héroïsme de Paddy (1915)
P: Le film d'art. D: Abel Gance. Sc: Abel Gance. Ph: Léonce-Henry Burel.
Lp: Louise Colliney, Albert Dieudonné, Georges Raulin.

Strass et Compagnie (1915)
P: Le film d'art. D: Abel Gance. Sc: Abel Gance. Ph: Léonce-Henry Burel.
Lp: Harry Baur, Emile Keppens, Gaston Michel, Jean Yonnel.

Fioritures (La source de beauté) (1915)
P: Le film d'art. D: Abel Gance. Sc: Abel Gance. Ph: Léonce-Henry Burel.
Jeanne Marken (*Anny Dorleville*), Léon Mathot (*Julien Darvoncourt*), Maud Richard (*Maud Dorleville*).

Le fou de la falaise (1915)
P: Le film d'art. D: Abel Gance. Sc: Abel Gance. Ph: Léonce-Henry Burel and Dubois.
Lp: Albert Dieudonné, Henri Maillard, Georges Raulin, Yvonne Sergyl.

Le périscope (1915)
P: Le film d'art. D: Abel Gance. Sc: Abel Gance. Ph: Léonce-Henry Burel.
Albert Dieudonné (*William Bell*), Henri Maillard (*Damorès*), Yvonne Sergyl (*Manoela Damorès*), Georges Raulin (*Geoffrey Bell*), Mlle Savigny (*Clélia Damorès*).

Ce que les flots racontent (1915)
P: Le film d'art. D: Abel Gance. Sc: Abel Gance. Ph: Léonce-Henry Burel.
Lp: Albert Dieudonné, Henri Maillard, Georges Raulin, Yvonne Sergyl.

Les gaz mortels (Le brouillard sur la ville) (1916)
P: Le film d'art. D: Abel Gance. Sc: Abel Gance. Ph: Léonce-Henry Burel and Dubois.
Lp: Doriani, Emile Keppens, Henri Maillard, Léon Mathot, Germaine Pelisse, Maud Richard, Jean Fleury.
Filmed Provence, January 1916.
Released 1 September 1916.
1,380m.

Barberousse (1916)
P: Le film d'art. D: Abel Gance. Sc: Abel Gance. Ph: Léonce-Henry Burel and Dubois.
Léon Mathot (*Trively*), Emile Keppens (*Gesmus*), Maud Richard (*Odette*), Germaine Pelisse (*Pauline*), Yvonne Briey, Henri Maillard, Doriani.
Filmed Provence, January 1916.
Released 13 April 1917.
1,600m.

236

Le droit à la vie (1916)
P: Le film d'art. D: Abel Gance. Sc: Abel Gance. Ph: Léonce-Henry Burel.
Paul Vermoyal (*Pierre Veryal*), Léon Mathot (*Jacques Alberty*), Andrée Brabant
(*Andrée Maël*), Georges Paulais (*Marc Toln*), Mme Bade (*Grandmother*), Lebrey
(*Magistrate*), Anthony Gildès.
Released 5 January 1917.
1,600m.

Mater dolorosa (1917)
P: Le film d'art. D: Abel Gance. Sc: Abel Gance. Ph: Léonce-Henry Burel.
Emmy Lynn (*Manon Berliac*), Firmin Gémier (*Emile Berliac*), Armand Tallier
(*François Rolland*), Anthony Gildès (*Jean*), Paul Vermoyal (*Jean Dormis*),
Gaston Modot, petit Carène.
Released 7 March 1917 (Pathé-Consortium-Cinéma)
1,510m.

La zone de la mort (1917)
P: Le film d'art. D: Abel Gance. Sc: Abel Gance. Ph: Léonce-Henry Burel.
Lp: Andrée Brabant, Clément, Anthony Gildès, Andrée Lionnel, Léon
Mathot, Gaston Modot, Georges Paulais, Paul Vermoyal.
Filmed winter 1917.
Privately screened April 1917. Released 12 October 1917 (Pathé-
Consortium-Cinéma).
4,000m, cut for distribution to 1,535m.

La dixième symphonie (1917)
P: Le film d'art. D: Abel Gance. Sc: Abel Gance. Ph: Léonce-Henry Burel.
Ed: Marguerite Beaugé. M: Michel-Maurice Lévy. Cost: Babani.
Séverin-Mars (*Enric Damor*), Jean Toulout (*Fred Rice*), Emmy Lynn (*Eve
Dinant*), Elizabeth Nizan (*Claire Damor*), André Lefaur (*Marquis de Groix
Saint-Blaise*), Ariane Hugon (*Dancer*).
Filmed, summer 1917.
Released 1 November 1918 (Pathé-Consortium-Cinema).
1,955m (shortened version 1,885m).

Ecce homo (Le soleil noir) (1918)
P: Le film d'art. D: Abel Gance. Sc: Abel Gance. Ph: Léonce-Henry Burel.
Albert t'Serstevens (*Jean Novalic*), Sylvio de Pedrelli, Berthe Bady, Dourga.
The first part of a planned trilogy: *Ecce homo, Les Atlantes, La fin du monde*.
Filming began at Nice in April 1918 but was abandoned before the com-
pletion of the first part.

J'accuse (1918–19)
P: Charles Pathé. D: Abel Gance. Asst. d: Blaise Cendrars. Sc: Abel Gance.
Ph: Léonce-Henry Burel, Marc Bujard, Maurice Forster. Ed: Andrée Danis,
Abel Gance.
Romuald Joubé (*Jean Diaz*), Séverin-Mars (*François Laurin*), Maryse Dauvray
(*Edith Laurin*), Maxime Desjardins (*Maria Lazare*), Angèle Guys (*Angèle*),
Mancini (*Jean's mother*), Elizabeth Nizan, Pierre Danis.

Released 25 April 1919.
5,250m (4 episodes), reduced to 4,350m (3 episodes) and re-edited in 1922 (3,200m).

La roue (1920–2)
P: Films Abel Gance/Charles Pathé. D: Abel Gance. Asst. d: Blaise Cendrars.
Sc: Abel Gance. Ph: Léonce-Henry Burel, Marc Bujard, Maurice Duverger.
Ed: Marguerite Beaugé, Abel Gance. Sd. effects: Paul Fosse.
Séverin-Mars (*Sisif*), Ivy Close (*Norma*), Gabriel de Gravone (*Elie*), Pierre
Magnier (*Hersan*), Georges Térof (*Machefer*), Max Maxudian, Gil Clary.
First screened December 1922. Released 17 February 1923 (Pathé-Consortium-Cinéma).
10,730m (prologue and 6 episodes). 9,200m (prologue and 4 episodes).
Reduced to 4,200m for re-release in February 1924. Re-edited 1928.

Autour de La roue (1920–1)
D: Blaise Cendrars (?).
A record of the filming of *La roue*.
300m(?).

L'âtre (1920)
P: Films Abel Gance. D: Robert Boudrioz. Sup: Abel Gance. Sc: Alexandre
Arnoux. Ph: Gaston Brun, Maurice Arnou.
Charles Vanel (*Bernard Larade*), Jacques de Feraudy (*Jean Larade*), Renée
Tandil (*Arlette*), Maurice Schutz (*Grandfather*), René Donnio (*Servant*).
Released December 1922.
1,840m.

Le petit poucet (1920)
P: Films Abel Gance. D: Robert Boudrioz.
Lp: Lily Fairlie, Christiana Delval, René Donnio, Charles Martinelli.
A sequence of *L'âtre*, removed from the film and screened separately.

Au secours (1923)
P: Films Abel Gance/Unione cinematografica Italiana. D: Abel Gance. Sc:
Abel Gance, Max Linder. Ph: Georges Specht.
Max Linder (*Max*), Jean Toulout (*Comte de Mornay*), Gina Palerme (*Renée*).
Filmed July 1923.
Released 17 June 1924.
900m, reduced to 500m.

Napoléon (1925–7)
P: Films Abel Gance/Société générale de films. D: Abel Gance. Asst. d: Henri
Andréani, Pierre Danis, Henry Krauss, Anatole Litvak, Mario Nalpas, Via-cheslav
Tourjansky, Alexandre Volkoff. Sc: Abel Gance. Ph: Jules Kruger.
Asst. Ph: Roger Hubert, Léonce-Henry Burel, Georges Lucas, Jean-Pierre
Mundviller, Emile Pierre. Ed: Marguerite Beaugé, Abel Gance. Art d: Alex-andre
Benois, Pierre Schildknecht, Jacouty, Meinhardt, Pimenoff. M: Arthur
Honegger. D of P: Louis Osmont, Noë Bloch, Edouard de Bersaucourt.

Albert Dieudonné (*Napoléon Bonaparte*), Wladimir Roudenko (*Bonaparte as a child*), Gina Manès (*Josephine de Beauharnais*), Nicolas Koline (*Tristan Fleuri*), Suzanne Charpentier [Annabella] (*Violine Fleuri*), Serge Freddy-Karl (*Marcellin Fleuri*), Edmond Van Daële (*Robespierre*), Alexandre Koubitzky (*Danton*), Antonin Artaud (*Marat*), Abel Gance (*Saint-Just*), Max Maxudian (*Barras*), Philippe Hériat (*Salicetti*), Acho Chakatouny (*Pozzo di Borgo*), Eugénie Buffet (*Laetizia Bonaparte*), Yvette Dieudonné (*Elisa Bonaparte*), Georges Lampin (*Joseph Bonaparte*), Sylvio Cavicchia (*Lucien Bonaparte*), Louis Sance (*Louis XVI*), Suzanne Bianchetti (*Marie-Antoinette*), Pierre Batcheff (*Hoche*), Philippe Rolla (*Masséna*), Alexandre Bernard (*Dugommier*), W. Percy Day (*Admiral Hood*), Génica Missirio (*Murat*), Raoul de Ansorena (*Desaix*), Harry-Krimer (*Rouget de l'Isle*), Marguerite Gance (*Charlotte Corday*), Roger Blum (*Talma*), Jean Henry (*Junot*), Maryse Damia (*La Marseillaise*), Henri Baudin (*Santo-Ricci*), Georges Hénin (*Eugène de Beauharnais*). (For a full cast and credits list, see Kevin Brownlow, '*Napoleon*', *Abel Gance's classic film*, pp. 258–63.)
Private screening, March 1927. Première, 7 April 1927 (Opéra). First screenings of complete version, 9–12 May 1927 (Apollo).
Released November 1927 (Gaumont-Metro-Goldwyn).
11,000m (Apollo). About 5,000m (Opéra), reduced to 3,700m.

Autour de Napoléon (1925–7)
P: Films Abel Gance/Société générale de films. D: Abel Gance.
A record of the filming of *Napoléon* made by the *Napoléon* crew.
Released 10 February 1928 (Studio 28).
1,605m, reduced to 1,200m.

Marine (1925–8)
P: Société générale de films. D: Abel Gance. Ph: as for *Napoléon*. Ed: Abel Gance, Marguerite Beaugé.
A triptych montage of seascapes shot during the filming of *Napoléon*. There was also a single-screen version.
Released 10 February 1928 (Studio 28).
About 300m (triple screen) and 600m (single screen).

Danses (1926–8)
P: Société générale de films. D: Abel Gance. Ph: as for *Napoléon*. Ed: Abel Gance, Marguerite Beaugé.
A triptych montage of the Bal des Victimes sequence in *Napoléon*.
Released 10 February 1928 (Studio 28).
About 300m.

Galops (1925–8)
P: Société générale de films. D: Abel Gance. Ph: as for *Napoléon*. Ed: Abel Gance, Marguerite Beaugé.
A triptych montage of Bonaparte's escape from Corsica.
Released 10 February 1928 (Studio 28).
About 300m.

Cristallisation (1928)
P: Société générale de films. D: Abel Gance. Ed: Abel Gance.
A triptych montage of *Kristallen* (P: Multifilm, Haarlem; D: S.L. Mol, 1925).
Released 20 April 1928 (Studio 28).

Napoleon auf St Helene (1928–9)
P: Peter Ostermayer. D: Lupu Pick. Sc: Willy Haas, Lupu Pick, adapted from
Abel Gance's screenplay *Sainte-Hélène*.
Werner Krauss (*Napoléon*), Albert Bassermann (*Hudson Lowe*), Philippe
Hériat (*Bertrand*), Lutz Altschul (*Montholon*), Paul Henckels (*Las Cases*), Suzy
Pierson (*Comtesse de Montholon*), Hermann Thimig (*Gourgaud*), Hanna Ralph
(*Mme Bertrand*).

La fin du monde (1930)
P: L'écran d'art (V. Ivanoff). D: Abel Gance. Asst. d: Jean Epstein, Walter
Ruttmann. Sc: Abel Gance (from a story by Camille Flammarion). Ph: Jules
Kruger, Roger Hubert, Georges Lucas, Nicolas Roudakoff. Sd: Robert
Baudouin, Walter Ruttmann. Sd. assts: Kahn, Wood, Yvonet. Special
effects: Nicolas Roudakoff. Dec: Lazare Meerson, W. Percy Day, Lacca,
Perrier, Pogedaieff. Ed: Marguerite Beaugé. M: Michel Levine, W. Zeder-
baum, R. Siohan. Advisers: Dimitri de Merejkowsky, René Delange, Georges
Buraud. D of P: G. Yablonski.
Abel Gance (*Jean Novalic*), Victor Francen (*Martial Novalic*), Colette Darfeuil
(*Geneviève de Murcie*), Samson Fainsilber (*Schomburg*), Jean d'Yd (*de Murcie*),
Sylvie Grenade (*Isabelle*), Georges Colin (*Werster*), Major Heitner (*Doctor*),
Wanda Gréville, Philippe Hersent, Albert Bras, Monique Rolland, Jeanne
Brindeau, Louis Laumon, Saint-Allier, A. Vertinsky.
Filmed January–May 1930.
Released 23 January 1931 (Olympic).
5,250m, reduced for release to 2,800m.

Autour de La fin du monde (1930)
P: L'écran d'art. D: Abel Gance.
A record of the filming of *La fin du monde*.

Mater dolorosa (1932)
P: Arci-Film. D: Abel Gance. Asst. d: Léopold Schlosberg. Sc: Abel Gance.
Ph: Roger Hubert, Georges Lucas. Sd: Bugnon. Dec: Robert Gys. Ed: Mar-
guerite Beaugé.
Line Noro (*Marthe Berliac*), Jean Galland (*Gilles Berliac*), Samson Fainsilber
(*Claude Berliac*), Gaston Dubosc (*Jean*), Antonin Artaud (*d'Hornis*), Gaby
Triquet (*Claudine Berliac*), Jean Gaudray, Alice Dufrène, Wanda Barcella.
Filmed July-August 1932 (Billancourt Studios).
Released 12 December 1932 (Cinédis).
3,200m.

Le maître de Forges (1933)
P: Directeurs français associés (Fernand Rivers). D: Fernand Rivers. Sup:
Abel Gance. Sc: Abel Gance, adapted from the novel by Georges Ohnet. Ph:

Harry Stradling, Georges Lucas. Dec: Henri Menessier. M: Henri Verdun.
Henri Rollan (*Philippe Derblay*), Gaby Morlay (*Claire de Beaulieu*), Paule
Andrale (*Marquise de Beaulieu*), Léon Bélières (*Moulinet*), Christiane Delyne
(*Athénaïs Moulinet*), Jacques Dumesnil (*Duc de Bligny*), Rivers cadet (*Baron de
Préfonds*), Guy Parzy (*Octave de Beaulieu*), Ghislaine Bru (*Suzanne Derblay*),
Irma Génin (*Baronne de Préfonds*), Jane Marken, Jean Dulac, Robert Ozanne,
René Maupré, Jacques Normand, Claude Bénédict, Pierre Mindaist, Eugène
Stuber, René Renoux, Maupi, Jean Kolb.
Filmed July-August 1933 (Paramount Studios).
2,680m.

Poliche (1934)
P: Films Criterium (Maurice Orienter). D: Abel Gance. Sc: Henri Decoin,
adapted from the play by Henri Bataille. Ph: Harry Stradling. Dec: Lazare
Meerson. M: Henri Verdun.
Constant Rémy (*Didier Méreuil/Poliche*), Marie Bell (*Rosine*), Edith Méra
(*Mme Laub*), Alexandre Darcy (*Saint-Wast*), Betty Daussmond, Catherine
Fonteney, Violaine Barry, Romain Bouquet, Marcel Delaître, Pierre Finaly,
Pierre Dac, Pierre Larquey, Claude Ivane, Josiane Lisbey.
Filmed February-March 1934.
2,450m.

La dame aux camélias (1934)
P: Films Fernand Rivers, Productions Maurice Lehmann. D: Fernand
Rivers. Sup: Abel Gance. Asst. d: Robert Bossis. Sc: Abel Gance, adapted
from the play by Alexandre Dumas fils. Ph: Harry Stradling, Aubourdier. Sd:
Albert Willmarth. Dec: René Renoux, Henri Menessier. Ed: André Versein.
M: Reynaldo Hahn, Fernand Masson. D of P: Edmond Pingrin.
Yvonne Printemps (*Marie Duplessis/Marguerite Gautier*), Pierre Fresnay
(*Armand Duval*), Lugné-Poë (*Armand's father*), Roland Armontel (*Gaston*),
Armand Lurville (*Saint-Gaudens*), André Dubosc (*The Duke*), Jane Marken
(*Prudence*), Irma Génin (*Nichette*), Andrée Lafayette (*Olympe*), Edy Debray
(*Varville*), Pierre Morin (*The doctor*), Renée Senac (*Nanine*), Noël Darzal,
Janine Berry, Marcelle Duval, Rivers cadet, Christiane Isola, Jérôme
Goulven, Anne-Marie Cérès, Claude Ivane.
Filmed August-September 1934.
3,250m.

Napoléon Bonaparte (1934–5)
P: Majestic films (Hector de Béarn). D: Abel Gance. Asst. d: Claude
Vermorel, Robert Bossis. Sc: Abel Gance. Ph: Roger Hubert. Sd: Paul
Duvergé. Dec: Henri Menessier, René Renoux. M: Henri Verdun. Ed:
Madeleine Crétolle, Abel Gance. Post-synch: Isy Pront.
The cast of the silent *Napoléon* plus José Squinquel (*Stendhal*), Pierre Morin
(*Béranger*), Georges Mauloy (*Crécy*), Cathelet (*Georgin*), Jane Marken
(*Anne-Marie*), Sylvie Gance (*Théroigne de Méricourt*), Georges Paulais
(*Vergniaud*), Marcel Delaître (*Capucine*), Pierre Mindaist (*Drapelin*), Gaby
Triquet, Armand Lurville, Claude Yvane, Edy Debray, Rivers cadet, with
voice-overs by Wladimir Sokoloff (*Tristan Fleuri*), Samson Fainsilber
(*Danton*), Jean Topart (*Narrator*).

Additional filming, Autumn 1934.
Released 11 May 1935 (Paramount).
3,850m.

Le roman d'un jeune homme pauvre (1935)

P: Maurice Lehmann. D: Abel Gance. Asst. d: Robert Bossis, F. Millaud. Sc: Claude Vermorel, adapted from the novel by Octave Feuillet. Dial: André Mouézy-Eon. Ph: Roger Hubert. Dec: Robert Gys. Sd: Marcel Courmes. Ed: Marguerite Beaugé, Madeleine Crétolle. M: Charles Cuvillier.

Pierre Fresnay (*Maxime Hauterive de Champcey*), Marie Bell (*Marguerite*), Pauline Carton (*Mlle Aubry*), Saturnin Fabre (*Bévallan*), Marthe Mellot (*Mlle de Porhoët*), Marcelle Praince (*Mme Laroque*), Gaston Dubosc (*Alain*), Jean Fleur (*Florimond*), Marcel Delaître (*Laroque*), Suzanne Laydeker (*Mlle Hélouin*), Mme Désir (*Concierge*), Josyane Lane (*Friend*), André Baugé (*Shepherd*), Robert Bossis, Made Siamé, André Marnay.
Filmed July-August 1935 (Billancourt Studios).
3,280m.

Jérôme Perreau, héros des barricades (1935)

P: Les productions parisiennes (Georges Milton). D: Abel Gance. Sc: Paul Fékété, adapted from the novel by Henri Dupuy-Mazuel. Ph: Roger Hubert, Jean Charpentier. Sd: Marcel Royné. Dec: Robert-Jules Garnier, Armand Bonamy. M: Maurice Yvain. Lyr: Lucien Boyer. Tech. d: Baudouin. D of P: Max Dorigny.

Georges Milton (*Jérôme Perreau*), Samson Fainsilber (*Conti*), Robert Le Vigan (*Mazarin*), Tania Fédor (*Anne of Austria*), Valentine Tessier (*Mme de Chevreuse*), Irène Brillant (*Marie Perreau*), Jane Lamy (*Princesse Conti*), Janine Borelli (*Jeanne Broussel*), Fernand Fabre (*Beaufort*), Jean Bara (*Louis XIV*), Serge Grave (*Louis Perreau*), Claire Saint-Hilaire (*Mme de Longueville*), Made Siamé (*Mme de Villèle*), Abel Tarride (*Broussel*), Georges Mauloy (*Laporte*), Bernard Lancret (*Barzanges*), Saint-Allier (*Comminges*), Emile Mylos (*Guitaut*), Robert Sellier (*Molé*), Julien Clément (*Monk*), Irène Jeanning, Denise Jovelet, Gabriel Farquette, Jean Buquet, Yves Gladine.
Filmed August-September 1935 (Gaumont-France-Film-Aubert Studios).
Released 22 November 1935 (Rex).
3,140m.

Lucrèce Borgia (1935)

P: Henri Ullmann. D: Abel Gance. Sc: Léopold Marchand, Henri Vendresse. Ph: Roger Hubert, Boris Kaufman. Dec: Henri Menessier, René Renoux. Cost: Granier, Bétout. Ed: Roger Spiri-Mercanton. M: Marcel Lattès.
Edwige Feuillère (*Lucrezia Borgia*), Roger Karl (*Pope Alexander VI*), Gabriel Gabrio (*Cesare Borgia*), Josette Day (*Sancia*), Maurice Escande (*Giovanni, Duke of Gandia*), Jacques Dumesnil (*Sforza*), Aimé Clariond (*Machiavelli*), Philippe Hériat (*Filippo*), Daniel Mendaille (*Micheletto*), Gaston Modot (*Fracassa*), Antonin Artaud (*Savonarola*), Max Michel (*Alfonso of Aragon*), Louis Eymond (*Mario*), René Bergeron (*Pietro*), Mona Dol (*La Vespa*), Yvonne Drinès (*Fiametta*), Jean Fay (*Tybald*), Georges Prieur (*Baron de Villeneuve*), Jeannine Fromentin (*La Malatesta*), Chabrier (*Savonarola's envoy*),

Nita Raya, Louis Perdoux, Annie Farrer, Myriam Saint-Paul, Georges Serrano, Jacques Cossin.
Filmed October-November 1935.
Released 21 December 1935 (Aubert-Palace).
2,610m.

Un grand amour de Beethoven (1936)
P: Général Production. D: Abel Gance. Asst. d: Jean Arroy. Sc: Abel Gance. Dial: Abel Gance, Stève Passeur. Ph: Robert Le Febvre, Marc Fossard. Sd: Georges Leblond. Dec: Jacques Colombier. Ed: Marguerite Beaugé, André Galitzine. M: Beethoven, arr. Louis Masson. D of P: Christian Stengel, Marc Le Pelletier.
Harry Baur (*Beethoven*), Jany Holt (*Giulietta Guicciardi*), Annie Ducaux (*Therese Brunswick*), Paul Pauley (*Zchuppanzigh*), Jane Marken (*Esther*), Sylvie Gance (*Mother of dead child*), André Nox (*Humphoiz*), Georges Saillard (*Breuning*), Lucas Gridoux (*Smeskall*), Roger Blin (*de Ries*), Jean Debucourt (*Gallenberg*), Jean-Louis Barrault (*Karl*), Lucien Rozenberg (*Guicciardi*), Marcel Dalio (*Steiner*), Yolande Laffon (*Countess Guicciardi*), Rika Radifé (*Frau Johann van Beethoven*), Gaston Dubosc (*Anton Schindler*), Georges Paulais (*Doctor*), André Bertic (*Johann van Beethoven*), Dalméras (*Schubert*), André Moreau (*Karl van Beethoven*), Jean Paqui (*Pierrot*), Gisèle Préville, Nadine Vogel, Nadine Picard, Philippe Richard, Enrico Glori, René Stern, Henry Richard, Maurice Devienne.
Filmed July-August 1936 (Gaumont Studios).
Released 16 January 1937 (Agriculteurs, Bonaparte, César).
6,515m, reduced for distribution to 3,800m.

J'accuse (1937)
P: FRD/Star Films (Gilbert Renault-Decker). D: Abel Gance. Asst. d: Jacques Saint-Léonard. Sc: Abel Gance. Dial: Abel Gance, Stève Passeur. Ph: Roger Hubert. Dec: Henri Mahé. Ed: Madeleine Crétolle. M: Henri Verdun. D of P: Jean Rossi.
Victor Francen (*Jean Diaz*), Line Noro (*Edith Laurin*), Marcel Delaître (*François Laurin*), Jean Max (*Henri Chimay*), Renée Devillers (*Hélène*), Sylvie Gance (*Flo*), Paul Amiot (*Captain*), André Nox, Georges Saillard, Georges Paulais, Georges Rollin, Georges Cahuzac, Lucien Callamand, Rivers cadet, Lucien Walter, Sylvain Itkine, Félix Clément, Jean-Pierre Thisse, André Siméon.
Filmed May-August 1937.
Released 21 January 1938 (Ermitage).
4,500m reduced to 3,300m for distribution and to 2,750m for re-release in 1947.

Le voleur de femmes (1937)
P: Films Union. D: Abel Gance. Sc: Abel Gance, adapted from the novel by Pierre Frondaie. Dial: Julien Fave. Ph: Roger Hubert, Jean Charpentier. Dec: Jacques Colombier. M: Henri Verdun.
Jules Berry (*Sadoc Torner*), Saturnin Fabre (*Academician*), Annie Ducaux (*Anita*), Suzanne Desprès (*Mme Torner*), Gilbert Gil (*Pierrot*), Sylvie Gance (*Pivoine*), Jean Max (*Barchevin*), Bianchette Brunoy (*Madeleine*), Lisa Matrey,

Princess Khandou, Jaque Catelain, Robert Ozanne.
Filmed January 1937 and September–October 1937.
Released March 1938.
2,450m.

Louise (1938)

P: Société parisienne de production de films (Weyler and Goldinberg). D:
Abel Gance. Asst. d: Jacques Saint-Léonard. Sc: Roland Dorgelès, Abel
Gance, adapted from the operetta by Gustave Charpentier. Dial: Stève
Passeur. Ph: Curt Courant, André Bac. Sd: Paul Duvergé. Dec: Henri Mahé,
Georges Wakhévitch. Cost: Georges Annenkov, Marcelle Dormoy. Ed:
Léonide Azar. M: Gustave Charpentier, arr. Louis Beydt. D of P: Jean Erard.
Grace Moore (*Louise*), Georges Thill (*Julien*), André Pernet (*Louise's father*),
Suzanne Desprès (*Louise's mother*), Ginette Leclerc (*Lucienne*), Robert Le
Vigan (*Gaston*), Jacqueline Gauthier (*Alphonsine*), Pauline Carton (*Supervisor*),
Jacqueline Prévôt (*Seamstress*), Rivers cadet (*Singer*), Marcel Pérès (*Sculptor*),
Edmond Beauchamp (*Philosopher*), Félix Clément, Claude Bénédict, Roger
Blin, Philippe Janvier, Hélène Ray, Simone Gautier, Lucie Vallot, Carmen
Laporte, Roger Lécuyer, Georges Douking.
Filmed October-November 1938.
Released December 1938.
2,350m.

Le paradis perdu (1939)

P: Taris Film (Joseph Than). D: Abel Gance. Asst. d: Robert Bossis. Sc:
Joseph Than. Dial: Stève Passeur. Ph: Christian Matras, Robert Juillard,
Maurice Pecqueux, Ernest Bourreaud. Sd: René Louge, Louis Perrin. Dec:
Henri Mahé. Cost: Marcelle Dormoy, Rosevienne, Karinsky. Ed: Léonide
Azar. M: Hans May. Lyr: Roger Fernay. D of P: F. Brun.
Fernand Gravey (*Pierre Leblanc*), Micheline Presle (*Janine/Jeannette*), Monique
Rolland (*Laurence*), Robert Le Vigan (*Edouard Bordenave*), André Alerme
(*Calou*), Robert Pizani (*Lesage*), Jane Marken (*Concierge*), Gérard Landry
(*Gérard*), Elvire Popesco (*Sonia Vorochine*), Anne Byron, Gaby Andreu, Dora
Doll, Myno Burney, Marcel Delaître, Edmond Beauchamp, Jean Marconi,
Marcel Pérès, Jean Brochard, Roger Monteaux, Sylvain, Rivers cadet,
Raymonde Devarennes, Noël Darzal, Nila Cara, Liliane Lesaffre, Carine
Nelson, Nicolas Amato, The Bluebell Girls.
Filmed April-May 1939 (Buttes-Chaumont Studios).
Released 13 December 1940 (Marivaux).
2,820m.

La Vénus aveugle (1940–1)

P: France Nouvelle (J. Mecatti). D: Abel Gance. Asst. d: Edmond Gréville.
Sc: Abel Gance, Stève Passeur. Ph: Léonce-Henry Burel, Henri Alekan. Sd:
Lecoq. Dec: Henri Mahé, Paul Bertrand. Ed: Andrée Danis. M: Raoul
Moretti, Abel Gance. D of P: Pierre Danis.
Viviane Romance (*Clarisse*), Georges Flament (*Madère*), Sylvie Gance
(*Mireille*), Lucienne Lemarchand (*Giselle*), Henri Guisol (*Ulysse*), Jean
Aquistapace (*Indigo*), Gérard Landry (*Gazul*), Marcel Millet (*Goutare*),

Renée Reney (*Singer*), Toni Rocca (*Singer*), Jean-Jacques Mecatti (*Admirer*), Marion Malville (*Marceline*), Micheline Promeyrat, Roland Pégurier, Philippe Grey, Gérard Lecomte, Roquefort, Georges Térof, Adrien Caillard, Marc Raymondun, Charlot, Porto, Jean-François Martial, Pierre Javenet.
Filmed Autumn-Winter 1940–1.
Première, 14 September 1941 (Vichy).
Released 1 October 1943 (Lord Byron).
3,800m, reduced for distribution in the Occupied Zone to 2,740m.

Le capitaine Fracasse (1942–3)
P: Lux/Zénith. D: Abel Gance. Sc: Abel Gance, Claude Vermorel, adapted from the novel by Théophile Gautier. Dial: Stève Passeur. Ph: Nicolas Hayer. Sd: Jean Putel. Dec: Henri Mahé. Cost: Beytout. Ed: Lucienne Déméocq. M: Arthur Honegger. Lyr: André de Badet. D of P: Marc Le Pelletier.
Fernand Gravey (*Baron de Sigognac*), Assia Noris (*Isabelle*), Vina Bovy (*Séraphine*), Alice Tissot (*Mme Léonarde*), Jean Weber (*Duc de Vallombreuse*), Maurice Escande (*Marquis des Bruyères*), Mona Goya (*Marquise des Bruyères*), Roland Toutain (*Scapin*), Lucien Nat (*Agostin*), Paul Oettly (*Matamore*), Josette France (*Zerbine*), Sylvie Gance (*Yolande de Foix*), Nino Costantini (*Léandre*), Philippe Rolla (*Malartic*), Jacques François (*Vidalinc*), Pierre Labry (*Hérode*), Jean Fleur (*Blazius*), Roger Blin (*Fagotin*), Paul Mondollot (*Pierre*), Jacques Roussel (*Provost*), Jacqueline Florence (*Chiquita*), Andrée Guize, Ritou Lancyle, Albert Bovy, Max Fontal, Guy-Henry.
Filmed August 1942-February 1943 (Studios Saint-Maurice).
Released 19 June 1943.
3,200m, reduced to 2,950m.

Manolete (1944)
P: J. A. Montesinos. D: Abel Gance. Sc: Abel Gance. Dial: Eduardo Marquina. Ph: Enrique Guerner, André Costey.
Lp: Manolete, Isabel de Pomès, Sylvie Gance, José Garcia Nieto, Felix de Pomès, Juan Calvo, Manuel Requena, Luciano Diaz.
Filmed December 1944 (Madrid). Unfinished.
Surviving footage screened at the 1963 San Sebastian Festival.

14 juillet 1953 (1953)
P: Georges Rosetti/Gaumont/Debrie. D: Abel Gance. Asst. d: Jacques Chastel.
A polyvision documentary on the 14 July celebrations in Paris.
Demonstration screening at the Gaumont cinema, 19 August 1953.
Released 16 July 1954.
About 600m.

La reine Margot (1953)
P: Lux-Films/Films Vendôme. D: Jean Dréville. Sc: Abel Gance, Jacques Companeez, adapted from the novel by Alexandre Dumas. Dial: Paul Andréota. Ph: Henri Alekan, Roger Hubert. M: Paul Misraki.
Jeanne Moreau (*La reine Margot*), Françoise Rosay (*Catherine de Médicis*),

Armando Franciolini (*La Mole*), André Versini (*Henri de Navarre*), Robert Porte (*Charles IX*), Henri Genes (*Coconas*).

Lumière (1954)
D: Paul Paviot. Sc: Abel Gance. Ph: Ghislain Cloquet. M: Joseph Kosma. 880m.

La Tour de Nesle (1954)
P: Fernand Rivers/Costellazione (Rome). D: Abel Gance. Asst. d: Michel Boisrond, Yvan Jouannet. Sc: Abel Gance, adapted from the play by Alexandre Dumas and Frédéric Gaillardet. Dial: Abel Gance, Etienne Fuzelier. Ph: André Thomas. Dec: René Bouladoux. M: Henri Verdun.
Pierre Brasseur (*Buridan*), Sylvana Pampanini (*Marguerite de Bourgogne*), Lia di Leo, Christina Grado (*Marguerite's sisters*), Marcel Raine (*Orsini*), Constant Rémy (*Landry*), Paul Guers, Michel Bouquet, Jacques Toja, Jacques Meyran, Rivers cadet, Paul Demange, Michel Etchevery, André Gabriello, Maffioly, Claude Sylvain, Rellys, Nelly Kaplan.
Filmed Summer 1954 (Epinay Studios).
Released October 1954.

Magirama (1956)
P: Abel Gance. D: Abel Gance, Nelly Kaplan. Sc: Abel Gance, Nelly Kaplan. M: Henri Verdun, Michel Magne, Debussy. Commentary spoken by Abel Gance, René Vatier.
A programme of short polyvision films consisting of:
Two extracts from the 1937 *J'accuse* re-edited for triple screen.
An extract from the triple-screen finale of the 1927 *Napoléon*.
An extract from *Begone dull care* by Norman McLaren, re-edited for triple screen by Abel Gance and Nelly Kaplan.
Auprès de ma blonde. (Lp: Michel Bouquet)
Châteaux de nuages.
Une fête foraine.
Released 19 December 1956 (Studio 28).

Austerlitz (1959–60)
P: Alexandre and Michel Salkind/Compagnie française de production internationale/Galatea (Rome)/Doubrova Film (Zagreb). D: Abel Gance. Assoc. d: Roger Richebé. Asst. d: Louis Pascal, Pierre Lary, Nelly Kaplan, Bata Stojanovic. Sc: Abel Gance. Ph: R. Picon-Borel, Robert Foucard, Milan Babic. Sd: Pierre Calvet. Dec: Jean Douarinou, Jean Taillandier, M. Desages, G. Brugaillerie. Ed: Léonide Azar, Yvonne Martin. M: Jean Ledrut. D of P: Dominique Drouin, Georges Chaillot. Tech. adv: André Smagghe.
Pierre Mondy (*Napoléon*), Martine Carol (*Joséphine*), Claudia Cardinale (*Pauline Bonaparte*), Elvire Popesco (*Laetizia Bonaparte*), Jean Mercure (*Talleyrand*), Leslie Caron (*Mme de Vaudrey*), Vittorio De Sica (*Pope Pius VII*), Orson Welles (*Fulton*), Rossano Brazzi (*Lucien Bonaparte*), Jean Marais (*Carnot*), Polycarpe Pavlov (*Kutusov*), Michel Simon (*The Grognard*), Georges Marchal (*Lannes*), Nelly Kaplan (*Mme Récamier*), J. L. Horbette (*Benjamin*

Constant), Ettore Menni, Jack Palance, Jacques Castelot, Jean-Louis Trintignant, André Certes, J.-M. Bory, Lucien Raimbourg, Anna Moffo, Janez Vrhovec, Daniel Gelin, Anthony Stuart, Louis Eymond, Marcel Randall, Maurice Teynac, Gianni Esposito, Ivan Desny, Anne-Marie Ferrero, Daniella Rocca.
Filmed in Yugoslavia, Rome and Paris, October 1959–January 1960.
Released 16 June 1960 (Gaumont-Palace).
4,580m reduced for distribution to about 4,000m.

Cyrano et d'Artagnan (1963)
P: Circe Productions (Paris)/Champion (Rome)/Agata Film (Madrid). D: Abel Gance. Asst. d: Nelly Kaplan, Maurizio Lucci, Louis Pascal. Sc: Abel Gance. Ph: Arturo Zavattini, Otello Martelli. Sd: Ivo Benedetti. Dec: Jean Douarinou. Cost: Dario Cecchi. Ed: Eraldo da Roma. M: Michel Magne. D of P: Luigi Ceccarelli, Armand Becué.
José Ferrer (*Cyrano de Bergerac*), Jean-Pierre Cassel (*d'Artagnan*), Sylva Koscina (*Ninon de l'Enclos*), Dahlia Lavi (*Marion Delorme*), Michel Simon (*Duc de Mauvières*), Philippe Noiret (*Louis XIII*), Laura Valenzuela (*Anne*), Rafael Rivelles (*Richelieu*), Ivo Garrani (*Laubardemont*), Mario Passante, Polidor, Guy Henry, Bob Morel, Vanni Lisenti, Barco Bari, David Montemuri, Henry Crémieux, Diégo Michelotti, Carlo Dori, Nando Angelini, André Lauriault, Vincent Parca, Gabrielle d'Orziat, Fernando Caiati, Massimo Pietrobon, Josette Laroche.
4,000m reduced for distribution to about 3,750m.

Marie Tudor (1965–6)
P: ORTF. D: Abel Gance. Sc: Abel Gance, adapted from the play by Victor Hugo. Ph: Nicolas Hayer. Dec: Raymond Nègre. Cost: Christiane Coste.
Françoise Christophe (*Mary Tudor*), Pierre Massimi (*Fabiani*), Marc Cassot (*Gilbert*), Lucien Raimbourg (*Joshua*), Colette Bergé (*Jane*), Michel de Ré (*Simon Renard and Henry VIII*), Bernard Dheran (*Dudley*), Gabriel Jabbour (*Jewish Beggar*), Jacques Maire (*Holbein*), Francomme (*Osley*), Robert Porte (*Norfolk*), Jean Ozenne (*Cranmer*), Caty Fraysse (*Mary as a child*), Jean-Louis Durer (*Montagu*), Jean-Claude Houdinière (*Brown*), Samson Fainsilber (*Clinton*), Pierre Stephen (*Chandos*), Michel Thomas (*Boatman*), Pierre Duncan (*Dermik*), Jean-Claude Abadie (*Peter*), Roc Hongar (*Butta*).
Broadcast on French television 23 and 30 April 1966, repeated 10 and 17 November 1973 and 5 and 12 October 1980.
200 mins.

Valmy (1967)
P: ORTF. D: Abel Gance. Sc: Abel Gance. Ed: Jean Mauduit, Huguette Meunier. Georges Chamarat (*Dr Guillotin*), Pierre Bertin (*Dr Louis*), Maria Laborit (*Princesse de Lamballe*), Colette Castel (*Mme Roland*), Jean-Pierre Dougnac (*Camille Desmoulins*), Bernard Dheran (*Robespierre*), William Sabatier (*Danton*), Marc Eyraud (*Jean-Jacques Rousseau*), Aram Stéphan (*Louis XVI*), Julien Bertheaux (*Dumouriez*), Henri Virjoleux (*Marat*).
The first of three programmes on Valmy broadcast on French television 27 March 1967.
70 mins.

Bonaparte et la Révolution (1969–71)
P: Abel Gance/Les Films 13. D: Abel Gance. Sc: Abel Gance. Ph: Jean Collomb, Dany Lévy. Sd: Jean Duguet (post-synchronisation: Claude Pessis). Ed: Abel Gance, Janine Boublil, Henry Rust, Max Seldinger. D of P: Pierre Pardon.
A re-edit of the 1927 and 1935 versions of *Napoléon* with some new footage and a preface by Abel Gance.
Released September 1971 (Kinopanorama).
7,254m (shortened version 6,956m).

Bibliography

This bibliography is a highly selective one. Section 2 lists only screenplays which have been published or adapted as *ciné-romans*. Most of the remainder, including scripts for unrealised projects, can be consulted in one or other of the archive collections referred to in section 1. Some extracts published in periodicals and compilations are included since these often contain additional technical information. Section 3 lists Gance's principal writings plus a selection of interviews relevant to the issues discussed in this book. And in sections 5 to 7, I list only some of the books, articles and compilations which have seemed particularly useful in providing a context for the study of Gance's films. Inclusion or exclusion of particular items does not imply approval or disapproval: there is a great deal more writing on Gance than I have attempted to indicate here. Most of the references to articles and reviews quoted in text and notes are not repeated in the bibliography.

1 Archive material

Centre national de la cinématographie (Claude Lafaye), Paris
Cinémathèque française, Paris
Bibliothèque de l'Institut des hautes études cinématographiques, Paris.
(The CNC archive is extensively quoted by Roger Icart and, for material on *Napoleon*, by Kevin Brownlow. The other two collections, ceded by Gance to the Cinémathèque française and to IDHEC at various times during the 1950s and 60s, are to my knowledge used here for the first time. These three collections contain the great bulk of Gance's papers. They include screenplays, working notes, projects, production files, literary manuscripts and personal papers. There are a few Gance items at Bois d'Arcy and in the Bibliothèque de l'Arsenal. The remainder is in various private collections.)

2 Screenplays

La digue (1911)
'Scénario dramatique' in *L'écran*, 3, 1958, pp. 33–4.

Le masque d'horreur (1912)
Facsimile of manuscript in *Revue internationale d'histoire du cinéma*, 2, 1975 (microfiche).

Mater dolorosa (1917)
Mater dolorosa. Adaptation romanesque illustrée par des photographies du film d'Abel Gance, Paris, Gauthier Villars, 1927.

J'accuse (1917–19)
L[éon] M[oussinac], *J'accuse d'après le film d'Abel Gance*, Paris, La lampe merveilleuse, 1922.

249

Extracts of the original screenplay in *Filma*, 15 May 1920, pp. 9–16; summary in *La cinématographie française*, 17, April 1919, pp. 37–52.

La roue (1920–2)
Ricciotto Canudo, *La roue, roman d'après le film d'Abel Gance*, Paris, Ferenczi, 1923.
La roue, scénario original arrangé par Jean Arroy, Paris, Tallandier, 1930.
Extracts of the original screenplay in Charles Ford, *On tourne lundi*; René Jeanne and Charles Ford, *Abel Gance* (same extract); Abel Gance, 'Comment on fait un film'. (See above, ch. 4, notes 1–2 for details.)

Napoleon (1925–7)
Napoléon vu par Abel Gance. Epopée cinégraphique en cinq époques. Première époque: Bonaparte, Paris, Plon, 1927.
'Le premier *Napoléon*' (1923 outline), *Cinématographe*, 83, 1982, pp 5–7.
Extracts of original screenplay in *Photo-ciné*, 1927, pp. 58–61 (the Cordeliers sequence); *Cinéa-ciné pour tous*, 15 August 1927, pp. 13–16 (the enlistment of 1792); *La revue française*, 17 April 1927 (Toulon); *Le rouge et le noir*, July 1928, pp. 7–17 (the Tenth of August 1792); *L'écran*, 3, 1958, pp. 50–63 (triptychs).

Sainte-Hélène (1928)
Extract of original screenplay (facsimile) in *Revue internationale d'histoire du cinéma*, 2, 1975 (microfiche).

La fin du monde (1930)
Joachim Renez, *La fin du monde, d'après le scénario d'Abel Gance*, Paris, Tallandier, 1931.
Extracts of original screenplay in Charles Ford, *On tourne lundi*, Paris, Vigneau, 1947, pp. 160–7; *L'écran*, 3, 1958, pp. 41–7 (final sequence).

Mater dolorosa (1932)
Mater dolorosa, scénario original arrangé par Joachim Renez, Paris, Tallandier, 1932.

Lucrèce Borgia (1935)
Abel Gance, *Lucrèce Borgia, Roman illustré de nombreuses photographies*, Paris, 1936.

Un grand amour de Beethoven (1936)
L'avant-scène Cinéma, 213, 1978 (*découpage* of an incomplete distribution print).
Extract of outline scenario in Charles Ford, *On tourne lundi*, Paris, Vigneau, 1947, pp. 101–6.

Le royaume de la terre (unrealised project, mid-1950s, in collaboration with Nelly Kaplan).
Extracts of screenplay in *Le surréalisme même*, 2, 1957, pp. 115–42; *Film culture*, 14, 1957, pp. 10–13, and 16, 1958, pp. 14–16; *L'écran*, 3, 1958, pp. 69–75.

3 Gance's writings and interviews

'Qu'est-ce que le cinématographe? Un sixième art!', *Ciné-journal*, 9 March 1912 (reprinted in Marcel L'Herbier, *L'intelligence du cinématographe*, Paris, Corréa, 1946, pp. 91–2).

La Victoire de Samothrace (1913). Extract in *L'écran*, 3, 1958, pp. 35–40.

Roger Lion, 'Un grand artiste français: Abel Gance', *Filma*, 15 May 1920, pp. 5–8.

'Abel Gance . . . ses idées . . . sa formule', *Scénario*, 1921, p. 749.

André Lang, 'La confession d'Abel Gance', *La revue hebdomadaire*, 23 June 1923 (reprinted in *Déplacements et villégiatures littéraires*, Paris, La renaissance du livre, 1924, pp. 137–46).

V. Remay, 'Abel Gance nous parle de *La roue* et de ses projets', *Mon ciné*, 12 April 1923, pp. 10–11.

'Le cinéma, c'est la musique de la lumière', *Cinéa-ciné pour tous*, 15 December 1923, p. 11.

Jean Mitry, 'Abel Gance nous parle de *La roue*', *Cinéa-ciné pour tous*, 15 December 1923, p. 8.

Jean Mitry, 'Le présent et l'avenir du film: Abel Gance', *Le théâtre et Comoedia illustré*, 1 May 1924.

Jean Listel 'Au sujet de Napoléon' *Cinémagazine*, 3 October 1924.

Jean Arroy, 'Quelques minutes avec Abel Gance', *Cinéa-ciné pour tous*, 15 August 1925, pp. 7–8.

'La beauté à travers le cinéma', *Cinémagazine*, 10–12, 1926, pp. 485–6, 524–6, 588–90 (also published in *Bulletin de l'Institut général de psychologie*, 26, 1926).

'La porte entr'ouverte', *Paris soir*, 17 March 1927.

'Le temps de l'image est venu!', in Léon Pierre-Quint, Germaine Dulac, Lionel Landry and Abel Gance, *L'art cinématographique II*, Paris, Alcan, 1927, pp. 83–102.

'Comment j'ai vu Napoléon', programme of the Opéra première of *Napoleon*, 7 April 1927 (reprinted in *Cinémagazine*, 25 November 1927, pp. 341–2 and other cinema programmes, translated in programmes for the reconstructed versions of the film).

'Au spectateurs de *Napoléon*', programme for the screenings of *Napoleon* at the Marivaux cinema, Paris, November 1927 (reprinted in various programmes for provincial screenings, translated in Kevin Brownlow, *'Napoleon', Abel Gance's classic film*, London, Cape, 1983, pp. 163–6).

'Le sens moderne – comment on fait un film', *Conférencia*, 16, 1928, pp. 197–209.

'Autour du moi et du monde: le cinéma de demain', *Conférencia*, 23, 1929, pp. 277–91.

Jean Arroy, 'Abel Gance face à l'océan', *Cinémagazine*, 8 February 1929, pp. 239–42.

Pierre Heuzé, 'Abel Gance nous dit sa foi dans le film parlant', *Cinémonde*, 18 July 1929, p. 667.

Prisme, Paris, Gallimard, 1930 (reprinted by Editions Vrac, Paris, 1983).

'Maladie et guérison du cinéma', *Pour vous*, 89, 31 July 1930, p. 3.

Jean Beaux, 'Entretien avec Abel Gance qui se rend à Moscou pour y tourner *La Campagne de Russie*', *Pour vous*, 30 July 1931, p. 3.

Jean Vidal, 'Les projets et les conceptions de M. Abel Gance', *Pour vous*, 11 August 1932, pp. 6 and 14.

Lucie Derain, 'Abel Gance nous parle de *Mater dolorosa*, du *Vaisseau fantôme* et de l'avenir du cinéma européen', *Cinémonde*, 3 November 1932, pp. 885–6.

Roger Régent, '*Napoléon* d'Abel Gance ressuscité, enrichi de la perspective sonore', *Pour vous*, 2 May 1935.

'Je tournerai *Christophe Colomb* parce que le cinéma est une machine à ressusciter les héros, *Cinémonde*, 5 April 1939, p. 5.

Yvonne Moustiers, 'Abel Gance veut énergiquement servir la France avec cette arme puissante: le cinéma', *Cinémonde*, 15 November 1939.

Claude Vermorel, 'Où en sommes-nous?', *Pour vous*, 29 November 1939, p. 3.

G.V., 'Abel Gance rentre d'Espagne où il a perdu *Christophe Colomb*', *Cinémonde*, 24 April 1940.

'A propos de *La Vénus aveugle*', *Cinéma-spectacles*, December 1941.

'Progrès techniques du cinéma', *La technique cinématographique*, 33, December 1946.

'La divine tragédie', *Revue internationale du cinéma*, 2, 1949, pp. 33–4.

'Pourquoi je veux tourner *La divine tragédie*', *Ecclésia*, 10, January 1950.

Francis Koval, 'France's greatest director', *Films in Review*, 3, 1952, pp. 436–42 and 462.

'Jean Epstein, cinéaste-philosophe', *La technique cinématographique*, 132, 1953, pp. 149–50 (extracts from a speech delivered at Cannes in May 1953; followed – pp. 150–2 – by an article on Gance by I. Landau).

'Les nouveaux chapitres de notre syntaxe', *Cahiers du cinéma*, 27, 1953, pp. 25–33.

'Le Protérama', *La technique cinématographique*, 136, 1953, pp. 231–3.

'Un mort parle à un vivant', *Combat*, 13 January 1954, p. 2 (on Louis Lumière).

'Départ vers la polyvision', *Cahiers du cinéma*, 41, 1954, pp. 4–9.

Jacques Rivette and François Truffaut, 'Entretien avec Abel Gance', *Cahiers du cinéma*, 43, 1955, pp. 6–17.

'Eviter le naufrage du cinéma', *Lettres françaises*, 10–17 March 1955, p. 1.

'Ma contribution au progrès du cinéma sonore', *Arts et techniques sonores*, April, 1955.

'Mon ami Epstein', *Cahiers du cinéma*, 50, 1955, pp. 57–9 (further extracts from the 1953 Cannes speech).

'Le temps de l'image éclatée', in Sophie Daria, *Abel Gance hier et demain*, Paris-Geneva, La palatine, 1959, pp. 167–75.

Preface for Michel Humbert, *Les mains vides*, Paris, 1962.

Michel Guibert, 'Abel Gance parle du cinéma d'aujourd'hui, de la Longue Marche et des Soldats de l'An II, de la Chine et de de Gaulle', *Notre République*, 5 February 1965.

'[Surréalisme et cinéma]', *Etudes cinématographiques*, 38–39, 1965, pp. 36–40.

Jacques Deslandes, 'Gance avant *Napoléon*', *Cinéma 71*, 152, January 1971, pp. 57–63.

'Gance on Gance: film as incantation', in Steven Kramer and James Welsh, *Abel Gance*, Boston, Twayne, 1978 (reprinted from *Film Comment*, 2, 1974, pp. 19–22).

4 Books on Abel Gance

Jean Arroy, *En tournant 'Napoléon' avec Abel Gance. Souvenirs et impressions d'un Sans-culotte*, Paris, La renaissance du livre, 1927.

Kevin Brownlow, *'Napoleon', Abel Gance's classic film*, London, Cape, 1983.

Sophie Daria, *Abel Gance hier et demain*, Paris-Geneva, La palatine, 1959.

Roger Icart, *Abel Gance*, Toulouse, Institut pédagogique national, 1960.

Roger Icart, *Abel Gance*, Lausanne, L'âge d'homme, 1984.

René Jeanne, *Napoléon vu par Abel Gance*, Paris, Tallandier, 1927 (a brief account of the film).

René Jeanne and Charles Ford, *Abel Gance*, Paris, Seghers, 1963.

Nelly Kaplan, *Manifeste d'un art nouveau: la polyvision*, Paris, Caractères, 1955 (a defence of the triple screen with a preface by Philippe Soupault).

Nelly Kaplan, *Le sunlight d'Austerlitz*, Paris, Plon, 1960 (an account of the filming of *Austerlitz*).

Steven Kramer and James Welsh, *Abel Gance*, Boston, Twayne, 1978.

5 Articles and sections of books on Abel Gance

Richard Abel, 'Abel Gance's other neglected masterwork: *La roue* (1922–1923)', *Cinema Journal*, 22, 2, 1983, pp. 26–41.

Richard Abel, 'Charge and countercharge: coherence and incoherence in Abel Gance's *Napoleon*', *Film Quarterly*, 35, 1982, pp. 2–12.

Jean Arroy, 'Abel Gance, sa vie, son oeuvre', *Cinéa-ciné pour tous*, 15 December 1923, pp. 5–7.

Robert de Beauplan, 'Un effort de régénération du cinéma français, *La roue*', *L'illustration*, 17 December 1921, pp. 598–600.

Kevin Brownlow, *The parade's gone by*, London, Secker and Warburg, 1968, pp. 521–64.

Léonce-Henry Burel, *Souvenirs (Revue internationale d'histoire du cinéma*, 3, 1975 – microfiche).

Ricciotto Canudo, *L'usine aux images*, Geneva, Office central d'édition, 1927, pp. 126–9 (on *La roue*).

Jean-Philippe Domecq, 'Napoléon vu par Abel Gance: une épopée?', *Positif*, 256, 1982, pp. 2–8.

Bernard Eisenschitz, 'Abel Gance', in *Cinema, a critical dictionary*, ed. Richard Roud, London, Secker and Warburg, 1980, I, pp. 404–15.

Bernard Eisenschitz, 'The music of time: from *Napoleon* to *New Babylon*', *Afterimage*, 10, 1981, pp. 49–55.

Elie Faure, 'Triptyque', *L'écran*, 3, 1958, p. 65 (written in 1928 as a preface to the projected publication of the triptych sequences of *Napoleon*).

Henri Fescourt, *La foi et les montagnes*, Paris, Montel, 1959, pp. 148–73 and 242–52 (remarks on Gance's early career by a contemporary film-maker).

Louis Herbeumont, 'A la suite de *Napoléon* d'Abel Gance', *Le cinéopse*, May-September 1926, pp. 393–4, 479–82, 557–60, 641–4, 719–22 (a record of the filming of *Napoleon*).

Roger Icart, 'Abel Gance ou le défi épique', *Lumière du cinéma*, 5, 1977, pp. 48–55.

Roger Icart, 'A la découverte de *La roue*', *Cahiers de la cinémathèque*, 33–34, 1981, pp. 185–92.

Roger Icart, 'La représentation de Napoléon Bonaparte dans l'oeuvre d'Abel Gance', *Cahiers de la cinémathèque*, 35–36, 1983.

René Jeanne, 'Les metteurs en scène français: Abel Gance', *Ciné-miroir*, 15 March 1923, p. 86 (preceded by a summary of *La roue*).

René Jeanne and Charles Ford, *Histoire encyclopédique du cinéma*, I, *Le cinéma français*, 1895–1927, Paris, Laffont, 1947, pp. 321–43 (a well documented study of Gance's silent films).

Norman King, 'Poètes de l'action: les *Napoléon* d'Elie Faure et d'Abel Gance', *Cahiers Elie Faure*, 1, 1981, pp. 52–71.

Norman King, 'Une épopée populiste', *Cinématographe*, 83, 1982, pp. 8–10.

Robert Lachenay, 'Abel Gance, désordre et génie', *Cahiers du cinéma*, 47, 1955, pp. 44–6.

André Lang, *'La fin du monde*, violente et pathétique, vue et entendue par Abel Gance', *Pour vous*, 15 January 1931, pp. 8–9.

Marcel Lapierre, *Les cent visages du cinéma*, Paris, Grasset, 1948, pp. 150–2.

Standish D. Lawler, *The Cubist cinema*, New York, New York University Press, 1975, pp. 79–98 (on Gance and Cendrars).

Pierre Leprohon, 'Abel Gance désordre et génie', *Ciné-france*, 26 February 1937 (on *Un grand amour de Beethoven*).

Pierre Leprohon, *Présences contemporaines: cinéma*, Paris, Debresse, 1957, pp. 9–27.

Marcel Martin, 'Identification d'un cinéaste', *La revue du cinéma*, 363, 1983, pp. 46–50.

Claude Nerguy, 'L'empereur des sensations', *Avant-scène-cinéma*, 213, 1978, pp. 4–5.

Peter Pappas, 'The superimposition of vision: *Napoleon* and the meaning of fascist art', *Cineaste*, 11, 2, 1981, pp. 4–13.

Richard Philpott, 'Whose *Napoleon?*', *Framework*, 20, 1983, pp. 8–12.

Fernand Rivers, *Cinquante ans chez les fous*, Paris, Girard, 1945 (includes a brief account of Gance's collaboration with Rivers).

Pierre Scize, 'On "tourne" au pays de Napoléon', *Lectures pour tous*, August 1925, pp. 1459–68 (on the filming of the Corsica sequences of *Napoleon*).

Philippe Soupault, 'Des primitifs italiens au cinéma de l'avenir', *L'écran*, 3, 1958, pp. 76–8 (on polyvision).

François Vanoye, 'Cendrars et Gance à La roue', *Blaise Cendrars vingt ans après*, *Colloque de Nanterre 12–13 juin 1981*, ed. Claude Leroy, Paris, Klincksieck, 1983, pp. 189–92.

'Abel Gance vu par Alexandre Volkoff', *Photo-ciné*, April 1928.

6 Films, television and radio programmes on Abel Gance

Louis Mollion and Albert Riera, *Le bureau des rêves perdus*, radio programme, 13 November 1956 (transcript in *L'écran*, 3, 1958, pp. 16–26).

Abel Gance hier et demain, film directed by Nelly Kaplan, 1963, 28 mins.

Janine Bazin and André Labarthe, *Cinéastes de notre temps*, ORTF, 1964 (the series included a programme on Gance).

The charm of dynamite, film directed by Kevin Brownlow, 1968, 56 mins.

Jacques Chancel, *Radioscopie*, 28 February 1971 (radio interview available on cassette).

Armand Panigel, *Un soleil dans chaque image* (interview for French television, 25 October 1973).

Armand Panigel, *Histoire du cinéma français par ceux qui l'ont fait*, 1974–5 (an ambitious series of 13 TV programmes only partially broadcast in 1974–5 but in its entirety in August 1981 on channel 1).

Jean-Pierre Chartier and Maurice Bessy, *Les grandes heures d'Abel Gance*, 1976 (four TV programmes on Gance broadcast on French television – FR 3 – in February–March 1976).

Claude-Jean Philippe, *Encyclopédie du cinéma français*, 1978–9, repeated on FR 3, summer 1982.

7 Film theory and politics

André Bazin, *Qu'est-ce que le cinéma?*, édition définitive, Paris, Le cerf, 1975.

Ernst Bloch and others, *Aesthetics and politics*, London, New Left Books, 1977.

David Bordwell, *French Impressionist cinema: film culture, film theory and film style*, Ph.D. thesis, University of Iowa, 1974.

Michel Décaudin (editor), *Canudo* (Quaderni del Novecento francese 3), Rome-Paris, Bulzoni/Nizet, 1976.

Ian Christie, 'French avant-garde film in the twenties: from "specificity" to surrealism', *Film as film. Formal experiment in film, 1910–1975*, London, ACGB, 1979, pp. 37–45.

René Clair, *Cinéma d'hier, cinéma d'aujourd'hui*, Paris, Gallimard, 1970.

Jean-Louis Comolli, 'Technique et idéologie: caméra, perspective, profondeur de champ', *Cahiers du cinéma*, 229–241, 1971–2.

Germaine Dulac, 'Les esthétiques, les entraves, la cinégraphie intégrale', *L'art cinématographique II*, Paris, Alcan, 1927, pp. 29–50.

Germaine Dulac, 'Films visuels et anti-visuels', *Le rouge et le noir*, July 1928, pp. 31–41.

Jean Epstein, *Ecrits sur le cinéma*, Paris, Seghers, 1974 (2 vols.).

Elie Faure, *Fonction du cinéma*, Paris, Editions d'histoire et d'art, 1953 (reprinted by Gonthier, 1963).

Elie Faure, *Napoléon*, Paris, Crès, 1921 (reprinted with a preface by Norman King, Denoël-Gonthier, 1983).

Elie Faure, *Oeuvres complètes*, edited by Yves Lévy, Paris, Pauvert, 1964 (3 vols.).

Jean-Pierre Faye, *Langages totalitaires*, Paris, Hermann, 1972 (and doctoral thesis, Paris, 1971).

Charles Harpole, *Gradients of depth in the cinematic image*, Ph.D. thesis New York University, 1977.

Image et magie du cinéma français, Paris, 1980 (catalogue of exhibition at the Conservatoire national des arts et métiers).

Walter Laqueur, *Fascism, a reader's guide*, London, Wildwood House, 1976 (reprinted by Penguin Books, 1979).

Henri Langlois, 'L'avant-garde française', *Cahiers du cinéma*, 202, 1968, pp. 8–18.

Paul Léglise, *Histoire de la politique du cinéma français*, Paris, Lherminier, 1977.

Marcel L'Herbier, *Intelligence du cinématographe*, Paris, Corréa, 1946 (reprinted by Editions d'aujourd'hui, 1977).

Pierre Lherminier, *L'art du cinéma*, Paris, Seghers, 1960.

Maria-A. Macciocchi, *Eléments pour une analyse du fascisme*, Paris, UGE, 1976 (2 vols.).

Jean Mitry, *Le cinéma expérimental, histoire et perspectives*, Paris, Seghers, 1974.

Léon Moussinac, *L'âge ingrat du cinéma*, Paris, Editeurs français réunis, 1967.

Steve Neale, *'Triumph of the will*: notes on documentary and spectacle', *Screen*, 20, 1, 1979, pp. 63–86.

Steve Neale, 'Art cinema as institution', *Screen*, 22, 1, 1981, pp. 11–39.

Roger Régent, *Cinéma de France, de 'La fille du puisatier' aux 'Enfants du paradis'*, Paris, Bellefaye, 1948 (reprinted as *Cinéma de France sous l'Occupation*, Editions d'aujourd'hui, 1976).

René Rémond, *La droite en France de 1815 à nos jours*, Paris, Aubier, 1954.

Jacques Siclier, *La France de Pétain et son cinéma*, Paris, Veyrier, 1981.

P. Adams Sitney, *The avant-garde film. A reader of theory and criticism*, New York, New York University Press, 1978.

Zeev Sternhell, *Ni droite ni gauche. L'idéologie fasciste en France*, Paris, Le Seuil, 1983.

Alain Weber, *Idéologies du montage ou l'art de la manipulation (CinémAction*, 23, 1983).

Index

Age d'or, L', 50
Annonciation, L', 18, 164
Anouilh, Jean, 170
Arcole, 14, 146, 147, 148, 164, 219
Argent, L', 52
Aron, Robert, 230
Arroy, Jean, 12, 18–20, 21, 123, 219, 220, 230
Astruc, Alexandre, 219
Atre, L', 129, 227, 238
Auberge rouge, L', 238
Au secours, 188, 238
Austerlitz, 5, 146, 147, 150, 159, 232, 246–7
Autour de La fin du monde, 240
Autour de La roue, 238
Autour de Napoléon, 239

Balzac, Honoré de, 174
Banzhaf, Albert, 226
Barattolo, Giuseppe, 146, 169, 228
Barberousse, 236
Barbusse, Henri, 144
Barrès, Maurice, 140
Bataille, Henri, 126
Battleship Potemkin, 32, 38
Bazin, André, 139, 185, 202, 217
Béarn, Hector de, 117, 121, 166, 226, 230
Becker, Jacques, 5
Becker, Rudolf, 117, 118, 119–20, 226
Bergson, Henri, 177
Berl, Emmanuel, 144
Bernard, Paul, 117, 122, 226
Bernstein, Henri, 126
Bersaucourt, Edouard de, 225
Bertrand, Paul, 170
Birth of a Nation, 125
Bleu, blanc, rouge, 169, 170
Bloch, Jean-Richard, 228
Bloch, Noë, 117–9, 120, 225, 228
Bonaparte, Napoleon, 1, 2, 7, 17, 31, 32, 33, 34–49, 71, 87, 90, 92, 94–6, 97–105, 124, 125, 144, 146–63, 165, 166–8, 174, 176, 177, 190, 191–6, 197, 198, 205–11, 213, 219, 221, 223–5, 228–30, 231, 232
Bonaparte et la Révolution, 1, 5, 125, 166, 213, 227, 230, 247
Boudrioz, Robert, 227
Boussinot, Roger, 6, 219
Breton, André, 51
Brézillac, Léon, 226

Brienne, 147–8
Brownlow, Kevin, 1, 149, 220, 222, 223, 228, 229, 230, 231
Buñuel, Luis, 49–50, 144, 221
Buraud, Georges, 12, 13–18, 21, 55, 123, 124, 164, 220, 230
Burel, Léonce-Henry, 123, 170, 223

Campagne de Russie, La, (1812), 146, 165
Canudo, Ricciotto, 21, 78
Capitaine Fracasse, Le, 175, 245
Carlyle, Thomas, 159, 218
Céline, Louis-Ferdinand, 3, 174, 177, 218
Cendrars, Blaise, 13, 123, 141, 177, 231
Ce que les flots racontent, 236
Chancel, Jacques, 222
Chang, 64
Charpentier, Gustave, 169
Charpentier, Suzanne, 148
Chirat, Raymond, 233
Christophe Colomb, 125, 169, 175, 230
Clair, René, 21, 23–4, 50, 52, 83, 124, 130, 144, 188–9
Clair de lune sous Richelieu, Un, 234
Cocteau, Jean, 30, 80
Cogniet, Léon, 93, 224
Cooper, Merian, 64, 222
Coppola, Francis Ford, 149
Coty, François, 144, 164, 228, 230
Crime du grand-père, Le, 234
Cripps, Sir Stafford, 176
Cristallisation, 230, 240
Curtis, Michael, 228
Cyrano et d'Artagnan, 5, 6, 82, 126, 132, 213, 222, 226, 232, 247
Cyrano et d'Assoucy, 234

Dame aux camélias, La, 241
Dame du lac, La, 233
D'Annunzio, Gabriele, 20, 140, 163, 220
Danses, 239
Danseuse de Pampelune, La, 177
Darlan, Admiral François, 171, 175, 231
Debrie, André, 209, 225
Delluc, Louis, 30
Deslandes, Jacques, 230
Diaz le briseur de fortunes, 141
Dieudonné, Albert, 77, 190
Digue, La, 235
Divine tragédie, La, 5, 82, 125, 175, 220

18 brumaire, 146
Dixième symphonie, La, 13, 128, 176, 177, 181–2, 189, 191, 208, 237
Domarchi, Jean, 219
Domecq, Jean-Philippe, 220
Dominguez, Bertha, 233
Douin, Jean-Luc, 1
Drame au château d'Acre, Un, 235
Dreyer, Carl, 121, 226
Drieu la Rochelle, Pierre, 145
Droit à la vie, Le, 129, 131, 237
Duhamel, Georges, 54
Dulac, Germaine, 21, 23, 26–8, 57, 220
Dumas, Alexandre, 44, 221
Dumur, Guy, 219

Ecce homo, 20, 220, 237
Eisenstein, Sergei, 3, 32, 38, 202, 212, 218
Electrocuté, L', 235
Emerson, Ralph Waldo, 159
Enigme de dix heures, L', 236
Epstein, Jean, 4, 13, 21, 23, 28–30, 57, 124, 189, 219, 227
Esnault, Philippe d', 233
Esparbès, Georges d', 42, 44, 221, 223

Fainsilber, Samson, 52
Fairbanks, Douglas, 33, 45, 47
Falconetti, 225
Fantômas, 141
Faure, Elie, 17, 31, 57, 140, 142, 144, 145, 163, 177, 209, 220, 225
Feuillade, Louis, 180, 231
Feuillet, Octave, 214
Fiametta, La, 177
Fille de Jephté, La, 234
Fille du Rhin, La, 231
Fin de Paganini, La, 234
Fin du monde, La, 4, 10, 12, 50–4, 79, 105–16, 125, 126, 129, 131, 135, 136, 137, 141, 144, 157, 162, 164–5, 166, 169, 175, 183, 191, 198–201, 202, 212, 220, 221, 225, 227, 230, 240
Fioritures, 236
Flaherty, Robert, 63, 222
Flammarion, Camille, 52, 221
Flammarion, Gabrielle, 221
Fleur des ruines, La, 235
Folie du docteur Tube, La, 3, 23, 181, 235
Ford, Charles, 6, 83, 188, 223, 233
Fou de la falaise, Le, 236
Francen, Victor, 169
Franco, General Francisco, 8, 145, 169, 176
Frau im Mond, Die, 51
Frondaie, Pierre, 168

Gain, André, 32, 33
Galops, 239
Gaulle, General Charles de, 175
Gaumont, Léon, 233
Gautier, Théophile, 175
Gaz mortels, Les, 236
Genette, Gérard, 231–2
Grand amour de Beethoven, Un, 4, 6, 7, 51, 126, 168, 173, 176, 191, 243
Grande illusion, La, 168
Grands initiés, Les, 127, 164, 165, 175
Gravone, Gabriel de, 123
Grémillon, Jean, 171
Griffith, D. W., 57, 83, 125, 218
Guéhenno, Jean, 141
Guy-Grand, Georges, 228

Haas, Willy, 220
Halifax, Earl of, 175
Harris, Robert, 149
Harrison, Kay, 230
Haumet, Guy, 231
Héroïsme de Paddy, L', 236
Herriot, Edouard, 78, 222
Honegger, Arthur, 40
Hoover, Herbert, 175

Icart, Roger, 7, 9, 83, 126, 226, 229, 230, 231, 233
Il était un petit navire, 166
Il y a des pieds au plafond, 235
Infirmière, L', 235
Ingenue, The, 49
Ivanoff, V., 225, 227

J'accuse (1919), 3, 7, 9, 30, 122, 125, 126, 130, 132–4, 135, 137, 141–2, 143, 150, 158, 162, 164, 179, 214, 227, 230, 237–8
J'accuse (1937), 9, 51, 137, 166, 168, 169, 214, 227, 230, 243
Jaurès, Jean, 169
Jeancolas, Jean-Pierre, 7, 8, 175
Jeanne, René, 6, 83, 148, 223, 233
Jérôme Perreau, 7–8, 168, 242
Joan of Arc, 121

Kael, Pauline, 2, 6
Kaplan, Nelly, 147
Keller-Dorian process, 74
King of Kings, 45
Koubitsky, Alexandre, 42
Kramer, Steven, 8, 165, 232, 233
Kuleshov, Lev, 202

Lang, André, 50–1, 130, 227

Lang, Fritz, 51
Le Gallo, Emile, 33
Léger, Fernand, 21, 22, 123, 220
Letter from an Unknown Woman, 191
Lévy, Yves, 228
Linder, Max, 233
Lion, Roger, 222, 226
Louise, 169, 244
Lovey, Jean-Claude, 231
Luchaire, Julien, 33
Lucrèce Borgia, 168, 243–4
Lumière, Louis, 63, 76
Lumière, 246
Lumière d'été, 171

McLaren, Norman, 80
Maeterlinck, Maurice, 67, 222
Magirama, 79, 221, 246
Mahé, Henri, 170, 230
Maître de Forges, Le, 240–1
Malle, Louis, 219
Malraux, André, 213, 220
Manolete, 245
Marcorelles, Louis, 219
Marey, Etienne-Jules, 76
Marie Tudor, 247
Marine, 239
Marion, Denis, 50, 239
Maritain, Jacques, 145
Marseillaise, La, 168
Masque d'horreur, Le, 235
Masson, Frédéric, 45, 221
Mater dolorosa (1917), 3, 9, 126, 134–5, 137, 162, 173, 182–3, 188, 189–90, 191, 214, 227, 237
Mater dolorosa (1932), 4, 9, 126, 134–5, 166, 176, 182–8, 189, 191, 214, 240
Melodie der Welt, 52
Méric, Victor, 33
Mérimée, Prosper, 150
Millaud, Fernand, 174
Milton, Georges, 8
Mitry, Jean, 222, 233
Moana, 63
Molière, 233
Mort du duc d'Enghien, La, 234
Mounier, Emmanuel, 145
Moussinac, Léon, 10, 13, 30–1, 32, 33, 34–40, 87, 124, 144, 148, 157, 163, 220
Mussolini, Benito, 8, 32, 163–4, 176, 214, 228

Nalpas, Louis, 3, 219, 226, 233
Nanook of the North, 63
Napoleon, 1, 2, 3, 4, 5, 7, 8, 9, 10, 12, 13, 17,
19, 20, 21, 23, 31, 32, 33, 34–49, 50, 51, 69–73, 77, 79, 87–105, 117–22, 124, 125, 126, 131, 137, 140, 144, 146–63, 164, 165, 166, 177, 178, 179, 180, 185, 188, 189, 191–6, 197, 198–9, 205–11, 212, 214, 217, 219, 220–1, 222, 223–6, 228–30, 232, 238–9
Napoleon auf St Helene, 240
Napoleon Bonaparte, 4, 5, 8, 9, 121, 146, 166–8, 175, 176, 226, 241–2
Neale, Steve, 232
Nègre blanc, Le, 235
Nietzsche, Friedrich, 16, 17, 72, 80, 140, 177, 227
Noël, Marie, 225
Novalis, 16

Ophuls, Max, 191, 197

Pappas, Peter, 8, 9, 128, 165
Paradis perdu, Le, 6, 169, 197, 244
Paris qui dort, 52
Passeur, Stève, 230
Pathé, Charles, 3, 185, 226, 233
Patrie en danger, La, 170
Paul-Boncour, 169, 230
Périscope, Le, 236
Perret, Léonce, 233
Pétain, Marshal Philippe, 7, 8, 146, 168, 169, 170, 171, 174, 175, 176, 230
Petit grognard, Le, 229
Petit poucet, Le, 238
Philpott, Richard, 219
Pick, Lupu, 14, 147, 164, 220
Poliche, 241
Pommer, Erich, 119, 226
Portrait de Mireille, Le, 234
Prisme, 14, 16, 17, 55, 164, 222, 226, 227

Quatorze Juillet 1953, 79, 245

Ravensdale, Lady, 231
Reclus, Maurice, 228
Régent, Roger, 170, 231
Reine Margot, La, 245–6
Rémond, Alain, 2, 219
Renault-Decker, Gilbert, 169, 230
Renoir, Jean, 128, 168
Reynaud, Paul, 170
Riefenstahl, Leni, 3
Rivette, Jacques, 219
Rohmer, Eric, 219
Roman d'un jeune homme pauvre, Le, 168, 214, 242
Rostand, Edmond, 42, 44, 127, 221

Roue, La, 3, 4, 5, 7, 10, 13, 16, 17, 21–30, 31, 32, 34, 66, 68, 71, 83–7, 122, 124, 127, 128–30, 131, 135, 137, 140, 143, 162, 164, 173, 176, 179, 180, 185, 201–4, 219, 220, 222, 223, 226, 230, 238
Royaume de la terre, Le, 20, 220
Rude, 90, 189, 224
Ruttmann, Walter, 50, 52, 227

Sadoul, Georges, 30
Sainte-Hélène, 14, 147, 153, 164, 174, 219
Sardou, Victorien, 44, 221
Schoedsack, Ernest, 64, 222
Sheen, Monsignor, 231
Siclier, Jacques, 231
Sorel, Georges, 145, 177, 228
Soupault, Philippe, 49, 50, 51, 52–4, 124, 200, 221
Spengler, Oswald, 145
Sternberg, Josef von, 221
Sternhell, Zeev, 145
Strass et Compagnie, 236
Thomas, Albert, 164
Tour de Nesle, La, 5, 6, 246
Tragique amour de Mona Lisa, Un, 235
Truelle, M., 231
Truffaut, François, 5, 6, 51, 219

t'Serstevens, Albert, 123, 227

Vaillant-Couturier, Paul, 30
Vaisseau fantôme, Le, 165
Valéry, Paul, 140
Valmy, 247
Valois, Georges, 144
Vendémiaire, 147, 148, 223, 228
Vénus aveugle, La, 7, 8, 131, 132, 139, 146, 166, 168, 170–6, 191, 202, 227, 244–5
Verdun, Henri, 166
Victoire de Samothrace, La, 14, 55, 164, 233
Vidor, King, 221
Vieuville, Patrick, 225
Vinneuil, François, 228
Virmaux, Odette and Alain, 221
Voleur de femmes, Le, 168, 243–4
Volkoff, Alexandre, 123
Voyage au bout de la nuit, 174
Vuillermoz, Emile, 10, 13, 30, 31–2, 33, 42–9, 87, 124, 163, 209, 214, 220

Waterloo, 110
Wéber, Alain, 219
Welsh, James, 232, 233

Zone de la mort, La, 129, 237